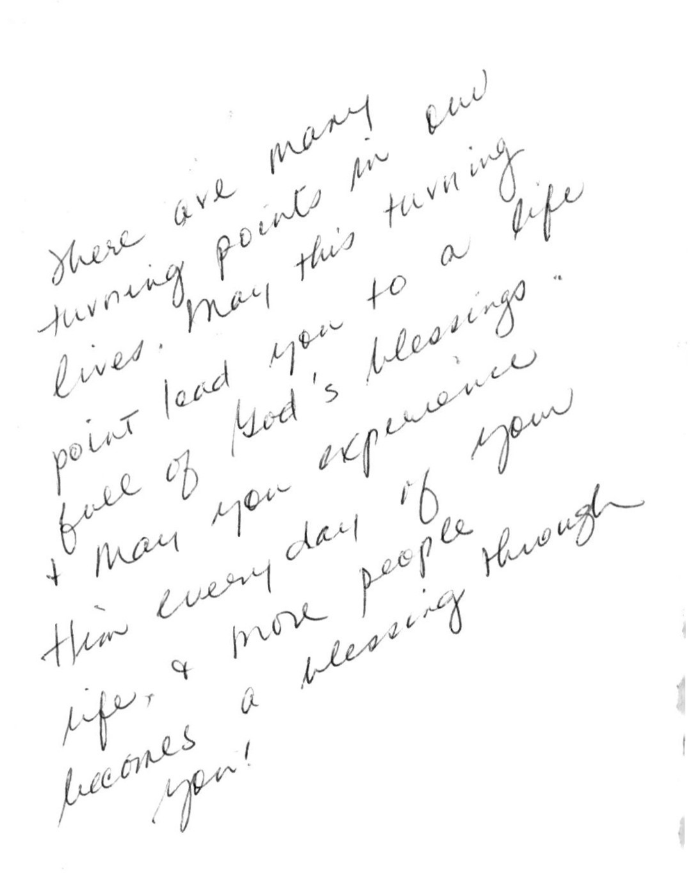
There are many turning points in our lives. May this turning point lead you to a life full of God's blessings. + May you experience them every day of your life, & more people becomes a blessing through you!

PRESENTED TO:

Ivy

FROM:

Jeanne

12/20/08

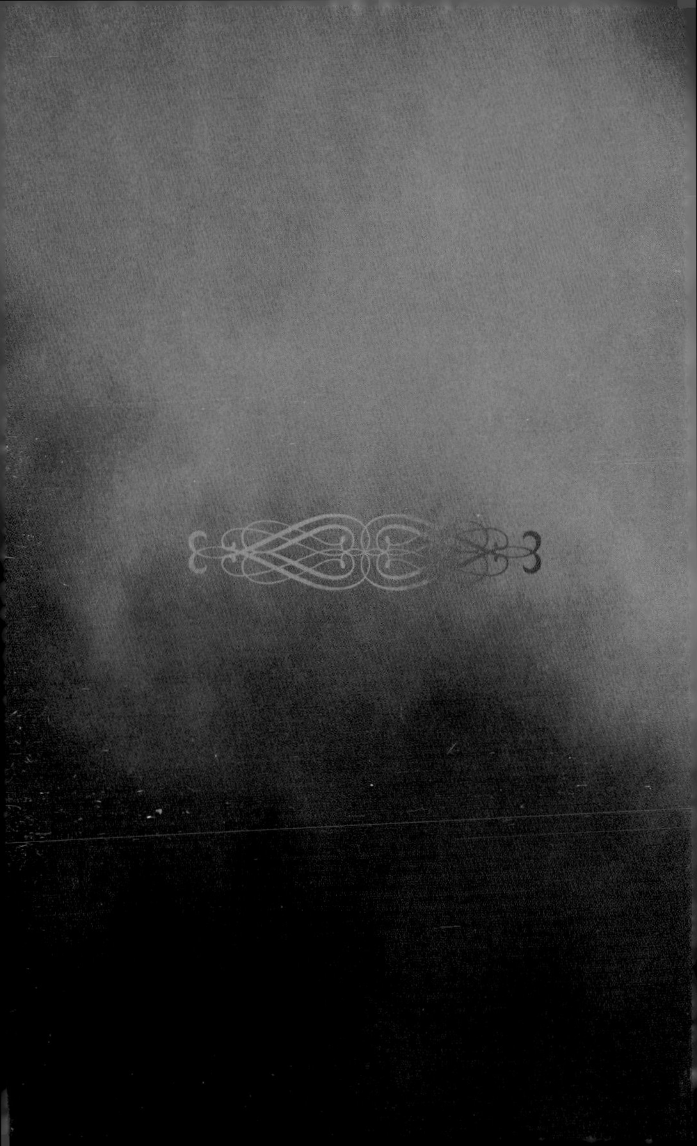

DEVOTIONS *for* EVERY DAY *of the* YEAR

TURNING POINTS

FINDING MOMENTS *of* REFUGE *in the* PRESENCE *of* GOD

DAVID JEREMIAH

TURNING POINTS

Published by Integrity Publishers, a division of Integrity Media, Inc., 5250 Virginia Way, Suite 110, Brentwood, TN 37027

HELPING PEOPLE WORLDWIDE EXPERIENCE
the MANIFEST PRESENCE *of* GOD.

Published in association with Yates & Yates, LLP, Attorneys and Literary Agents, Orange, California.

Cover and Interior Design: Brand Navigation, LLC — Bill Chiaravalle,
Russ McIntosh, www.brandnavigation.com

Cover Photo: Stone, Doug Armand

Library of Congress Cataloging-in-Publication Data

Jeremiah, David.

Turning points / by David Jeremiah.

p. cm.

Summary: "Topically arranged book of devotions regarding biblical truths to the reality of everyday living"—Provided by publisher.

ISBN 1-59145-067-5 (hardcover)

1. Devotional literature. 2. Christian life--Meditations. I. Title.

BV4832.3.J47 2005

242'.2—dc22

2005012161

Printed in China

05 06 07 08 09 RRD 10 9 8 7 6 5 4 3 2 1

Introduction

Your word is a lamp to my feet and a light to my path.

Psalm 119:105

Think of the watershed events that history now recognizes: Gutenberg's printing press in 1455, the Industrial Revolution in the eighteenth century, the Normandy invasion on D-Day in 1944, the invention of the Internet in the late twentieth century. Each of these events changed the world forever. The time was right, choices were made, and a turning point was realized.

Individuals experience turning points just as nations and cultures do. Sometimes these events are obvious—a crisis will demand a choice that changes our lives in a matter of days or hours. Other turning points may not be recognized until after the fact. Looking back, we realize we are no longer walking in the same direction. We see that our path turned without our being aware of it.

The greatest turning point in life is when one comes to know the true and living God through His Son, Jesus Christ. There is no greater turning point than the day we move from darkness to light, from

death to life, from fear to faith.

But there are countless other potential turning points in life—potential because they happen only if we make the right choices and only if we are armed daily with the truth, which allows us to turn when and where we should. We need God's truth, God's perspective, God's wisdom.

Turning Points is a collection of daily meditations from God's Word that will equip you to live with God's perspective. Only by thinking His thoughts will you know how to choose when you arrive at your next turning point.

Your next personal turning point may not change the whole world, but it will definitely change yours. Thinking God's thoughts after Him will cause you to change in His direction.

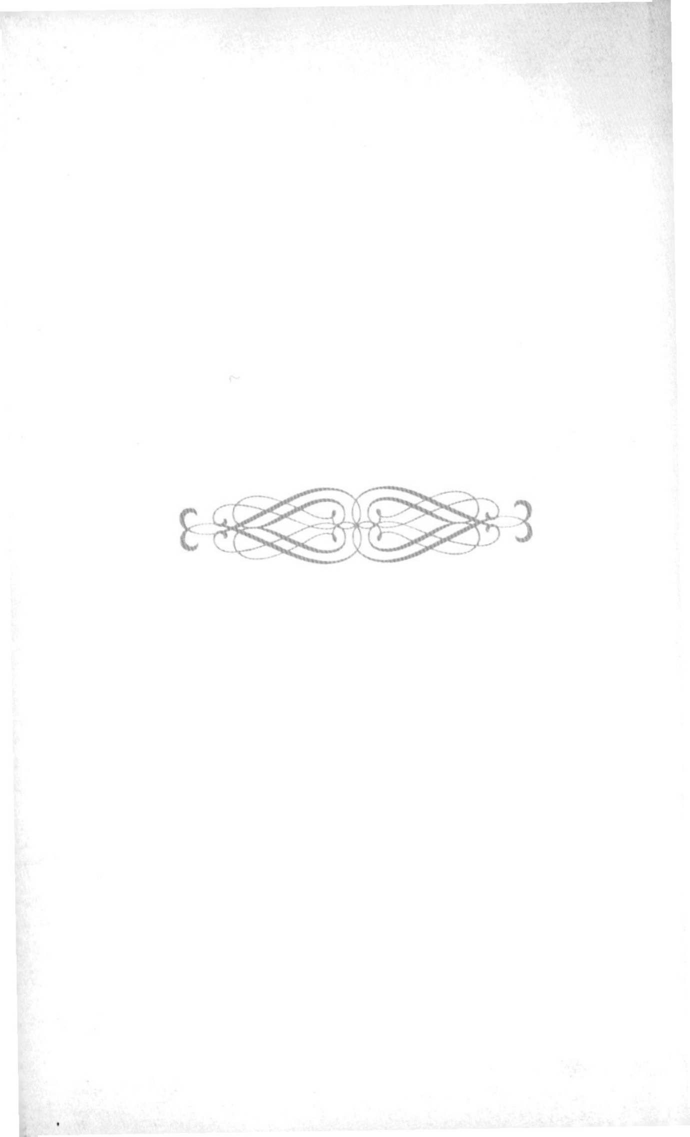

January

REALISTIC RESOLUTIONS

Therefore, my beloved brethren, be steadfast, immovable, always abounding in the work of the Lord.

1 CORINTHIANS 15:58

In December 2001, the American Society of Plastic Surgeons issued a report suggesting that many Americans are making plastic surgery one of their New Year's resolutions. If you haven't been able to keep all those other resolutions from years past—like lose weight, protect yourself with sunscreen, and exercise more—a nip here and a tuck there can take care of the damage. It's the American way—have your cake and lose it too.

New Year's resolutions are a traditional part of life, but it takes more than a "1" on the January calendar to bring about real change. Instead of trying to start something brand-new this year, consider taking something you're already doing to the next level: living with passion for God.

Christians have God-given passion already at some level; you couldn't have said yes to Christ without it. But how deep is it? Are you more passionate about God than about anything else in life? When your family and friends think of you, do they know that you love Jesus more than anything?

Make a realistic resolution this year—to go further on the road you're already traveling with Christ.

A CLEAN HEART

Create in me a clean heart, O God.
PSALM 51:10

D. L. Moody did not want any sin to disrupt his intimacy with God. Because of this, Moody kept short accounts with God, immediately confessing any known sin. Each night, he also allowed the Lord to shine an interrogating spotlight on all the events of the day. Before retiring for the evening, Moody would review his day with the Lord, asking God to reveal anything that displeased Him.

D. L. Moody exemplifies the kind of heart preparation needed before coming to God in worship. When we worship God, we must make sure we come with a clean heart, confessing any known sin in our lives. It is also good to prayerfully ask God to examine our actions, thoughts, motives, and words. Because God is perfectly holy, He cannot tolerate sin or commune with unrighteousness. Light has no fellowship with darkness (1 John 1:5–7).

In the Psalms, David offered up a prayer, very similar to D. L. Moody's. He, too, desired to come to God with a clean heart. Today, take a moment to make the following prayer your own: "Search me, O God, and know my heart . . . and see if there is any wicked way in me" (Psalm 139:23–24).

PRAISE THE LORD

Let everything that has breath praise the LORD.
PSALM 150:6

Many Christians have sung Charles Wesley's famous hymn "O for a Thousand Tongues to Sing." But did you know there is an earlier German hymn entitled "O That I Had a Thousand Voices"? It was written by Pastor Johann Mentzer, who labored in the seventeenth century in the little village of Kemnitz in eastern Germany.

Pastor Mentzer was known for his attitude of praise and thanksgiving, and he encouraged his flock to praise the Lord whatever the circumstances. One night as he returned home from a nearby village, Mentzer saw flames shooting into the sky. Hastening to the scene, he found his home—the church parsonage—engulfed. Later, as he inspected the smoldering ruins, someone tapped him on the shoulder. "So, Pastor," said the man, "are you still in the mood for praise and thanksgiving?"

Pastor Mentzer was still in the mood for praise and thanksgiving, and out of that experience he wrote his hymn wishing for a thousand voices with which to praise the Lord.

We praise the Lord because it's a great therapy for the soul, but we praise Him most of all because He is worthy of praise. Let everything that has breath praise the Lord!

CHAOS UNDER CONTROL

He who is the blessed and only Potentate,
the King of kings and Lord of lords.
1 TIMOTHY 6:15

In the 1960s, meteorologist Edward Lorenz proved that accurate long-range weather forecasting is impossible. This seemingly common-sense "discovery" was an outgrowth of what scientists call "chaos theory," which states that systems behave unpredictably due to the conditions in which they started. In other words, the slightest influences in the beginning can result in completely unpredictable results as systems develop. These are called "chaotic systems."

Many people, without understanding the science, subscribe to the "chaos theory." They believe the world is totally out of control and is careening through the universe on a collision course with some accidental destiny.

It is not wrong to think of this world as a "system." Indeed, the Greek word *kosmos* (translated "world") means an ordered arrangement. But it is completely wrong to view this world in terms of modern chaos theory. While the earth was at one time chaotic—"without form, and void" (Genesis 1:2)—it is now being carried in the hands of "Him who works all things according to the counsel of His will" (Ephesians 1:11).

Every headline that surprises us should be a reminder that there is no news in heaven.

DEFINED BY CONTENTMENT

Not that I speak in regard to need, for I have learned in whatever state I am, to be content.
PHILIPPIANS 4:11

Two teardrops were floating down the river of life. One teardrop asked the other, "Who are you?" The second teardrop replied, "I am a teardrop from a girl who loved a man and lost him. But who are you?" The first teardrop replied, "I am a teardrop from the girl who got him."

That's the way life goes, isn't it? We cry over what we don't have, not realizing we might have cried twice as hard had we gotten it. One of the reasons the apostle Paul lived a life characterized by such joy and gratitude was because he had learned the secret of being content. He was thankful for what he had and not sorry about what he didn't have (Philippians 4:12).

Paul passed on that secret to his new converts. While living in the end of the age, he told the Corinthians to be content where they were. He urged them not to be envious and try to gain what they didn't have, because "the time is short" (1 Corinthians 7:29). We live two thousand years later, so the time is shorter. Learn to be content where you are and with what—and who—you have.

People who are content live with a flexible cup; it expands or contracts to fit what God has supplied.

CHICKEN SOUP

Faith without works is dead.
JAMES 2:20

I believe some chicken soup will help Johnny get over his cold," said Grandma as she put a chicken in the pot, peeled some vegetables, and prepared the tonic. Later that afternoon, she said, "I believe those flowers need some water." She filled her watering can and gave them a good dousing. "I believe I need a good night's sleep," she said that evening and headed toward bed.

Grandma's "I believes" were all followed by activities, illustrating a vital point: we behave according to our beliefs. As James put it, "I will show you my faith by my works" (2:18). Faith leads to action, and faith in God leads to obedience. He hasn't asked us to put our trust in warm, fuzzy feelings about Him. He tells us to put our trust in the revelation He has already given—His Word. When we obey, we are exercising faith. If you want an accurate measurement of your faith, see if you're obeying God's commands.

George MacDonald once said, "You can begin at once to be a disciple of the Living One—by obeying Him in the first thing you can think of in which you are not obeying Him. We must learn to obey Him in everything, and so must begin somewhere. Let it be at once, and in the very next thing that lies at the door of our conscience."

THE TWELVE SPIES

Caleb quieted the people before Moses, and said, "Let us go up at once and take possession, for we are well able to overcome it."
NUMBERS 13:30

During Operation Iraqi Freedom, U.S. Army Special Forces operated inside Iraq well in advance of the war, and American spy agencies had operatives in place long before the first missile was fired. In impending war, "human assets" are critical, and that's why Moses sent twelve men to spy out Canaan in advance of the anticipated invasion by the children of Israel.

In this case, however, the human assets became liabilities. Ten spies returned with daunting tales of giants, walled cities, and overwhelming foes. Only two—Joshua and Caleb—had a faith-based perspective. The ten compared themselves with the giants; the two compared the giants with God. Rather than aiding the victory, the ten spies discouraged the people.

Are you facing challenges today? Do you have some giant problems? Don't be discouraged. Don't compare yourself with the giants; compare the giants with God. He has promised victory in advance. Though the future appears daunting, you have a divine Commander in Chief who does all things well. Trust Him, for with Him you are well able to overcome.

BEING BEFORE DOING

As the branch cannot bear fruit of itself, unless it abides in the vine, neither can you, unless you abide in Me.
JOHN 15:4

Harriet Beecher Stowe once wrote a wonderful book titled *How to Live on Christ*, in which she said, "How does the branch bear fruit? Not by incessant effort for sunshine and air; not by vain struggles. . . . It simply abides in the vine, in silent and undisturbed union, and blossoms and fruit appear as of spontaneous growth." We often forget that our walk with the Lord is more important than our work for the Lord. Abiding in Christ comes before abounding in labor.

Before the Bible records the mighty miracles of Moses, it describes the eighty years God spent preparing him for his mission. Before we read of Joseph's exploits in Egypt, we read chapter after chapter describing his preparation—before the palace came the pit and the prison. Even our Lord spent thirty years in Nazareth before devoting three years to public ministry.

If you feel that your life isn't making an impact, that your ministry is fruitless, give that over to God. Focus instead on abiding in Him. Spend much time in secret, in the Word and in prayer. We're often enamored by what a person does, but God is more concerned with who we are. Being always comes before doing in His eyes.

A Choice to Make

Choose for yourselves this day whom you will serve. . . . But as for me and my house, we will serve the LORD.
Joshua 24:15

The American poet Robert Frost wrote simple yet powerful poems about life and nature. "The Road Not Taken" is about the different choices we make: "Two roads diverged in a wood, and I—I took the one less traveled by, and that has made all the difference."

Frost's road "less traveled by" reminds the reader of Jesus' "narrow" gate and "difficult" way (Matthew 7:14). Many are called to discover that less-traveled-by way, but few ultimately find it (Matthew 22:14).

Abraham was one who did find the way. We sometimes want to excuse those who don't find Christ or who make destructive choices in life. Given the times, we say, it's almost inevitable that we cannot escape corruption. But some do; and because some do, it means that all may. The difference is in choice: whom do we choose, this day, to serve? Abraham chose to serve the living God, while others chose to serve the gods of this life. If you are contemplating choices in your life today, make the ones that lead to life, now and forever.

A wise choice delayed is a wise choice not made. Choose life for you and yours today.

HOW TO SAVE A MARRIAGE

Be kindly affectionate to one another with brotherly love, in honor giving preference to one another.
ROMANS 12:10

Randy and Victoria got engaged in February 1994. A short time later, Randy's doctor informed him that the diabetes he had suffered with since age twelve had ruined his kidneys. He would need a transplant to live. Victoria volunteered to be tested, and their immune systems matched perfectly. A month after their marriage, they underwent surgery to share equally Victoria's two healthy kidneys.

Randy had originally taken Victoria to the doctor's appointment so she could be sure she wanted to go through with being married to someone who might die. Little did he know that she was not only willing to marry him but to sacrifice part of herself to save his life. What a powerful example of everything that makes a marriage work: voluntary submission, willing sacrifice, generous sharing, and humble gratitude. While most biblical exhortations regarding love in marriage are given to the husband, love is a mutual responsibility. If your spouse has a need, do what you can to meet it. Sharing generously is a prescription for marital health.

Proof of possession is realized only in the giving away of possessions to benefit another.

Keep Reading

Your word is truth.
John 17:17

Do you find the Bible confusing? It's one book with two great sections—the Old and New Testaments. These are divided into sixty-six books, 1,189 chapters, and 31,102 verses, written by forty-plus authors. Even the newest parts of the Bible are nearly two millennia old. So is the Bible outdated? Incomprehensible? Untrustworthy? Irrelevant?

Not at all. The Bible is timeless. It reveals the mind of an eternal God who is the same yesterday, today, and forever. He was, is, and is to come. He is "I Am," the self-existent one who knows tomorrow's headlines before they're printed.

The Bible is timely, giving us daily encouragement and guidance. Missionary Amy Carmichael said, "Whatever need or trouble you are in, there is always something to help you in your Bible, if only you go on reading 'til you come to the word God specially has for you."

The Bible is knowable. It can be both taught and learned. It may seem puzzling to you now, but if you'll prayerfully keep on reading, hearing, and studying it, you'll increasingly understand its themes, discover its truths, claim its promises, echo its prayers—and share its message.

Don't get discouraged. Bible study is a lifelong habit. Keep reading!

STRUGGLES TO STRENGTH

Recall the former days in which . . . you endured a great struggle with sufferings.
HEBREWS 10:32

The cocoon of the emperor moth is flask-like in shape. To develop into a perfect insect, the moth must force its way through the neck of its cocoon with hours of intense struggle. Entomologists explain that this pressure is nature's way of forcing a life-giving substance into its wings.

Wanting to lessen the seemingly needless trials and struggles of the moth, an observer said, "I'll lessen the pain and struggles of this helpless creature!" With small scissors, he snipped the restraining threads to make the moth's emergence painless and effortless. But the creature never developed wings. For a brief time before its death, it simply crawled, instead of flying through the air on rainbow-colored wings! If only the moth had been allowed to finish struggling, its life had been transformed into beauty. Similarly, sorrow, suffering, trials, and tribulations are wisely designed to grow us into being like Christ.

Today's temptation can become tomorrow's strength; today's trial, tomorrow's triumph; today's crisis, tomorrow's crown. Christians suffer from spiritual atrophy when they are not strengthened through struggles. The refining and developing processes are oftentimes slow; but through grace, we emerge triumphant.

GUESS WHO MOVED?

For the perverse person is an abomination to the LORD, but His secret counsel is with the upright.
PROVERBS 3:32

A couple was driving home from their twenty-fifth wedding anniversary dinner, she in the passenger seat and he behind the wheel. Dreamily, the wife said, "Honey, remember when we used to sit right next to each other in the car?" The husband answered, "Well, sweetheart, I haven't moved. I've been right here all the time."

Sometimes Christians remember the early days of their walk with God. They have memories of a more intimate relationship with God. Over time, that relationship became formal and distant. But God never wanted it that way; He desires intimate relationships with all His children.

Abraham, the friend of God, found out just how close God wants to be. Before destroying Sodom, God said, "Shall I hide from Abraham what I am doing?" (Genesis 18:17). God shared His plans with His friend and gave Abraham the chance to respond—which he did! Christianity is a relationship, not a religion; and relationships demand time together if they are to grow. If God wanted to tell you a secret, would you be available?

If God doesn't seem as close as He used to, guess who moved?

Thanking God for Health

Beloved, I pray that you may prosper in all things and be in health, just as your soul prospers.
3 John 1:2

Following World War II, Field Marshall Montgomery was sitting in a session of the English House of Lords when he turned to the man next to him and said, "Excuse me, but I'm having a coronary thrombosis." He then quietly left the chamber to seek medical help.

Granted, heart attacks and other illnesses aren't always preceded by such clear warning signs. But if the signs were there, would we recognize them? To paraphrase old Timex watch commercials, it's amazing how much of a licking our bodies can take and still keep on ticking. Stress, too little sleep and exercise, too many empty calories—we take our good health for granted. The body's ability to stay healthy is truly a gift from God.

None of us enjoys now the perfect health we look forward to in heaven. But until then, we can express our gratitude to God for the health we have by being good stewards of these miraculous "earth suits" in which we work, serve, and play each day. Giving thanks for health (whether good or bad) is evidence that we understand this truth: our bodies are not our own (1 Corinthians 6:19).

What Keeps Us Going

Then Jonathan, Saul's son, arose and went to David in the woods and strengthened his hand in God.
1 Samuel 23:16

Army historian Brigadier General S. L. A. Marshall, after extensive interviews with soldiers returning from combat, concluded that the primary motivation for a soldier to fight is a sense of unity with his immediate combat unit. "I hold it to be one of the simplest truths of war," he said, "that the thing which enables an infantry soldier to keep going ... is the near presence or presumed presence of a comrade."

Paul didn't go to the mission field alone; he always had partners. Jesus sent His evangelists two by two. The three Hebrews in Daniel 3 proved that "a threefold cord is not quickly broken" (Ecclesiastes 4:12). What would David have done without Jonathan's support in the wilderness? Even our Lord Jesus wanted His closest friends near Him in Gethsemane. Our faith is strengthened when godly peers stand with us in difficulty.

But the question isn't, "do I have a close friend on whom I can lean?" It's, "how can I be such a friend?" Look around today for someone needing encouragement. Spend extra time praying for one in need. Be cheerful at work or school. Speak to the custodian. Share a verse with a neighbor. Brighten the corner where you are!

The Best Medicine

Love never fails.
1 Corinthians 13:8

"Love, true love," wrote psychiatrist Karl Menninger, "is the medicine for our sick old world. If people can learn to give and receive love, they will usually recover from their physical and mental illnesses." He's right; but when the Bible talks about love, it isn't talking about the glossy, romantic, starry-eyed passion portrayed in songs or movies. It's talking about a reasoning, redeeming, choosing type of sacrificial love. It is the power that moves us to respond to someone's needs with no expectation of reward.

That kind of love is preeminent; it never fails.

An evangelist wrote about a wise physician who told a young doctor, "I've been practicing medicine for a long time. I've prescribed many things. But in the long run, I've learned that the best medicine is love."

"What if it doesn't work?" asked the young man.

"Double the dose," replied the doctor.

If things are tense at home, if you're having trouble with a loved one, if someone has insulted or hurt you, love that person anyway. And if that doesn't work, double the dose.

Isaac's Blessings

Bless me—me also, O my father!
Genesis 27:34

Every child needs his parents' blessing. Isaac longed for his father's blessing, love, and approval. Ross Campbell, in *How to Really Love Your Child*, suggests that most parents really do love their children, but they don't always convey that love to their children in a way that really makes the kids feel secure. A child doesn't just need to be loved; he needs to feel loved. He needs to experience his parents' blessings.

There are several excellent ways to bless our children with love. We can, of course, tell them we love them. But we can also convey our love through our eye contact, by the amount of time we spend with them, and by appropriate physical interaction with our youngsters—touching, holding, hugging, roughhousing, and kissing.

We also bless our children by pointing out their strengths. Motivational expert Zig Ziglar said, "Children who are raised in a spirit of praise and approval are going to be happier, more productive, and more obedient than the ones who are constantly criticized."

After all, our heavenly Father liberally dispenses His blessings on us. He expects us to do the same to others, especially to our children.

BETTER DAYS AHEAD

. . . a living hope through the resurrection of Jesus Christ.
1 PETER 1:3

The best is yet to be," said poet Robert Browning. For the Christian, that isn't just a nice sentiment about growing older; it's a reality based on the resurrection of Christ. Our futures are just as bright as the flash of glory that burst from the tomb on the first Easter morning. Our tomorrows are just as promising as the first words of the risen Christ to the astonished disciples: "Peace be with you" (John 20:19).

You may have a heavy load to bear just now. Perhaps you've received bad news from the doctor. Maybe you've been rejected by the school to which you applied. Perhaps the bank turned down your loan request. Maybe you're worried about a child. Or maybe you've been struck by depression.

Jesus' friends were depressed the day before Easter. It was a Saturday filled with disappointment, discouragement, depression, and despair. They were whipped. But what a difference a day made!

Among other things, the resurrection of Christ validates all His other claims and promises. Because He rose again, He proved that He is who He said He was, and He can do what He promised to do. Because He lives, we can rest in His promises, knowing that the best is yet to come.

Our Glorious Hope

Our citizenship is in heaven, from which we also eagerly wait for the Savior . . . who will transform our lowly body that it may be conformed to His glorious body.
Philippians 3:20–21

Scottish Presbyterian Robert Baillie learned in 1684 that he would be hanged for his faith, then drawn and quartered with his head and hands nailed to a local bridge. Referring to Philippians 3:20–21, Baillie replied, "They may hack and hew my body as they please, but I know assuredly nothing will be lost, but that all these my members shall be wonderfully gathered and made like Christ's glorious body."

At the resurrection, the bodies of Christians will be raised and reconstituted to resemble the risen body of our Lord. When Jesus rose on Easter, He had a body that was the prototype of the ones we'll have throughout eternity.

Some things about Jesus' glorified body were similar to the one He had before He died. He resembled Himself; He could eat and drink; He could be touched. Yet He could pass through walls, and He appeared in various places without traveling by recognized means. His transformed body no longer aged, nor was it subject to sickness and death.

If you're battling aches and pains or if you're afflicted with illness or disease, take comfort. One day you'll have a body like His.

Trusting God for Work

And let the beauty of the LORD our God be upon us, and establish the work of our hands for us; yes, establish the work of our hands.

Psalm 90:17

One story goes that a company's employees found this note on the office bulletin board: "It has come to management's attention that workers dying on the job are failing to fall down. This practice must stop, as it makes it impossible to distinguish the dead employees from those still working. Any employee found dead in an upright position will be immediately dropped from the payroll."

Many Christians have to be reminded that work is a sacred calling. The sacred or secular mentality infects many: anything related to "the spiritual life" is sacred, while work is secular. Nothing could be more unbiblical! Man was created for a lifetime of service to God, making all of life a sacred endeavor. While work became more difficult after sin entered the world, it did not change the fundamental value of work. It is meaningful and required of all who bear God's image. Whether you work for money or as a volunteer, in the home or the community, work is a gift and calling from God.

Do you know a person who is discouraged with his or her work? Your encouragement may help that person's toil become work that reflects the beauty of the Lord.

THE JOY OF WORSHIP

Let the hearts of those rejoice who seek the LORD!
PSALM 105:3

Charles Spurgeon once said, "My happiest moments are when I am worshipping God, really adoring the Lord Jesus Christ, and having fellowship with the ever-blessed Spirit. In that worship I forget the cares of the church and everything else. To me it is the nearest approach to what it will be in heaven."

Worship has a way of refreshing our hearts and rejuvenating our spirits. As we reflect on God's attributes—His power and sovereignty—we view our circumstances through a different lens—God's lens. In the light of His power, giant-sized problems become mouse-like. Although we may enter into His presence with a heavy heart, we leave with a new sense of hope and joy. Through worship we are reminded of the following truth—God Almighty is in control of our lives, and He is fully capable of managing our concerns. The psalmist sums it up precisely with these words: "Why are you cast down, O my soul? . . . Hope in God" (42:5).

Rejoice, believer! God has given you "the garment of praise for the spirit of heaviness" (Isaiah 61:3). When you worship Him, darkness and despair are dispelled.

THE CURRENCY OF COMMUNICATORS

These are the things you shall do: Speak each man the truth to his neighbor.
ZECHARIAH 8:16

On May 13, 2003, the United States Bureau of Engraving and Printing introduced a new twenty-dollar bill into circulation. The new bill incorporates advanced security features in an attempt to stay one step ahead of currency counterfeiters: a thin security thread imbedded in the bill, ink that changes color in changing light, watermarks that can be seen on both sides of the bill, and a redesigned portrait of Andrew Jackson.

Official Federal Reserve notes (dollar bills) are the currency of our country—they're how we do business. If someone uses a counterfeit bill, the transaction is invalidated because no real money changed hands.

There is a currency for communicators as well—especially marriage partners who want to communicate successfully. The currency of communicators is truth. The truth is what enables spouses to accomplish the "business" of marriage. If couples don't communicate honestly, then trust is destroyed. And as trust goes, so goes the marriage. Don't be a communication counterfeiter in your marriage. When you speak, speak the truth—in love.

False words create a foundation of fantasies on which no house can permanently stand.

HOME BEFORE DARK

Teach me, O LORD, the way of your statutes, and I shall keep it to the end.
PSALM 119:33

It'd be nice if the power of temptation lessened as we grew older, but there's no security in age. King David was fifty when he fell into sin with Bathsheba; and in that culture fifty was older than it is now, for life expectancy was much shorter. The hot blood of youth was no longer flowing through David's veins, but he fell into sin anyway.

Midlife and old age have their own sets of temptations, and we must never let down our guard. It's true that we should grow wiser and stronger as we grow older. We should grow in grace. But don't think you'll ever be immune from temptation in this life, whatever your age.

J. Oswald Sanders writes, "Nothing is easier for the aging person who is growing increasingly infirm and experiencing some depression as a result than to turn inward and become self-occupied. That attitude of mind only exacerbates the problem. It is when with firm purpose we turn away from our own grief, aches, and ailments, and busy ourselves to relieve those of others, that we will obtain relief from our own."

REWARDS FOR HOLDING ON

For I consider that the sufferings of this present time are not worthy to be compared with the glory which shall be revealed in us.
ROMANS 8:18

In 1946, Akio Morita invented the world's first transistor radio in Tokyo. An American company offered to buy him out at a generous price, but Morita wanted his company's name on the product. He declined and struggled to stay in business. But his perseverance paid off as his company, Sony, became a world leader in electronics.

Far too often our focus is on today's suffering instead of tomorrow's reward. Morita could have sold out early and relieved his cash-strapped condition. But he was convinced that if he held on, greater rewards would come his way. And he was right!

The Christian life is like that. We frequently experience significant, unexplained, even undeserved suffering in this life. But the apostle Paul tells us to hold on—don't sell out! The suffering of this life—or the temporary relief we might enjoy by giving up our faith—cannot compare with the glory and rewards that await us in heaven.

Has the devil made you an offer you can't refuse? Don't sell out! What you'll lose in heaven is far more valuable than what you'll gain on earth.

A LESSON IN HUMILITY

When pride comes, then comes shame; but with the humble is wisdom.
PROVERBS 11:2

Booker T. Washington, the renowned black educator, was an outstanding example of this truth. One day he was walking in an exclusive section of town when a wealthy white woman stopped him. Not recognizing him, she asked if he would like to earn a few dollars by chopping wood for her. Professor Washington smiled, rolled up his sleeves, and proceeded to do the humble chore she had requested.

The next morning, the embarrassed woman went to see Mr. Washington and apologized profusely when she learned who he was. "It's perfectly all right, madam," he replied. "Occasionally I enjoy a little manual labor. Besides, it's always a delight to do something for a friend." Not long afterward, the woman showed her admiration by persuading some wealthy acquaintances to join her in donating thousands of dollars to the Tuskegee Institute.

Human nature desires attention and credit for good deeds done, but God calls us to be humble and to offer the praise to Him. Just as Christ humbled Himself and gave His life for the world, we are called to let go of arrogance and pride and to be servants.

Are you concerned with impressing people, or are you concerned with having a humble spirit? A truly humble man is hard to find, yet God delights to honor such selfless people.

God's Heart, My Heart

I have found David the son of Jesse, a man after My own heart, who will do all My will.
Acts 13:22

Ruth Bell Graham writes of an encounter she had with a young Indian student named Pashi. She spoke with Pashi about Christ, to which he replied, "I would like to believe in Christ, and many in India would like to believe, but we have never seen a Christian who was like Christ."

A friend of Mrs. Graham told her to tell Pashi, "I'm not offering you Christians. I am offering you Christ." Good point. No one will ever be excused for not believing in Christ on the basis of Christians' lack of faithfulness. On the other hand, we should ask ourselves the question, "What does a person look like who says he's a follower of Christ? Should Christians be like Jesus Christ?"

Perhaps the most well-known answer to that question is the description given of David: a man after God's own heart, committed to doing all of God's will. Perhaps, then, that's what a Christian should be—a person committed to doing all of God's will. If a government order were issued to arrest everyone who appears to be a Christian, would you be incarcerated?

The person after God's heart is the person whose own heart seeks first the kingdom of God.

Grand People

When I call to remembrance the genuine faith that is in you, which dwelt first in your grandmother . . .
2 Timothy 1:5

Do you enjoy Fanny Crosby's great hymns, like "Blessed Assurance," "To God Be the Glory," "All the Way My Savior Leads Me," and "He Hideth My Soul"? They would not have been written but for a grandmother's love.

Fanny was blinded at six weeks of age by a spurious doctor, but her grandmother Eunice was determined that Fanny would never grow up feeling disabled or disadvantaged. Eunice spent years training Fanny in all sorts of things—teaching her the Bible, helping her explore nature, and enabling her to develop remarkable powers of memory. With her grandmother's encouragement, Fanny memorized large portions of the Bible. From that vast storehouse of memorized scripture, she later produced her hymns. "My grandmother was more to me than I can ever express by word or pen," Fanny wrote long afterward.

Don't underestimate the influence you can have as a grandparent. As you pour yourself into your grandchild, you will be molding a mighty servant of the Lord. Grandparents have the joyous responsibility of showing God's strength and power to the generations that follow.

GROCERY SHOPPING

Fathers, do not exasperate your children; instead, bring them up in the training and instruction of the Lord.
EPHESIANS 6:4 NIV

A man in the supermarket was pushing a cart that contained, among other things, a screaming baby. As the man proceeded along the aisles, he kept repeating softly, "Keep calm, George. Don't get excited, George. Don't get upset, George. Don't yell, George."

A lady watching with admiration said to the man, "You are certainly to be commended for your patience in trying to quiet little George."

"Lady," he declared, "I'm George."

Every parent can relate to George. Doesn't it sometimes seem like Ephesians 6:4 should read: "Children, don't annoy your fathers while in the supermarket"? But it doesn't. Perhaps the reason is that parents are to be the example of God's love, and children learn the best from observation. Even shopping at the grocery store is an opportunity to show your children the proper way to behave.

There is no greater role model for children than a parent. Colossians 3:21 says, "Fathers, do not provoke your children, lest they become discouraged." Be an example of patience and love to your children. From potty-training to driver's education—parents are set in place by God to be a tool that transforms the precepts of the Bible into a living testimony to their children.

REDEEMED OR RELIGIOUS?

For there is one God and one Mediator between God and men, the Man Christ Jesus, who gave Himself a ransom for all.
1 TIMOTHY 2:5–6

Don't think of Christianity as a religion, a ritual, a routine, or a set of rules. It may have elements of all those things, but it is primarily and essentially a relationship with the living God through Christ our Redeemer.

As quarterback for the Oakland Raiders, Rich Gannon has enjoyed his share of fame and fortune. But the high point of his life came while playing backup quarterback with the Minnesota Vikings. "I went to chapel, and I heard a speaker give his testimony. I felt so guilty inside," he said. "I was a young, strapping athlete who had basically everything. But I felt I wanted something he had. I knew what he had was that inner joy and peace that a relationship with Jesus brings."

It's a relationship with Jesus that brings joy to our lives. Someone said that religion is man seeking God; Christianity is God seeking man. Becoming a Christian isn't primarily a matter of doing good works, but of coming to Christ in simple faith and asking forgiveness for sin. When you receive His forgiveness, gained through His shed blood, your sin is washed away and His righteousness takes its place.

If you've never done that, why not today? Why not now?

RSVPING TO GOD

Come to Me, all you who labor . . . and I will give you rest.
MATTHEW 11:28

Many of the practices of Western etiquette came from the French court of King Louis XIV in the late seventeenth and early eighteenth centuries. At his palace, Versailles, Louis XIV had the rules for court behavior written on "tickets," or etiquette. It's also why our familiar RSVP means *Répondez, s'il vous plaît*—Respond, if you please.

Jesus told a parable about how the Jewish nation politely RSVPed to God—but with the wrong reply. When God sent Jesus to the Jews as their Messiah, they should have interpreted His invitation to "come to Me" (Matthew 11:28–30) as an invitation to enter God's eternal kingdom. But they made up excuses to reject God's invitation. In the parable, the recipients of the invitation to a great banquet replied that, sorry, they were too busy. So the host reissued the invitation to the forgotten of society, the inhabitants of the highways and byways, and brought them in. Those to whom the invitation was originally sent missed out on that chance to enter the kingdom.

If you've RSVPed to God with a "Sorry; too busy," you might want to reconsider—and accept! When an invitation comes from God, failing to respond is the same as saying no.

Little Foxes

The little foxes that spoil the vines . . .
Song of Solomon 2:15

According to *Psychology Today*, 70 percent of high school students and nearly half of college students confess to cheating. *USA Today* reported that 91 percent of Americans lie routinely.

Our culture says, "If you want to get ahead, you have to break a few rules." But the Bible warns that "little sins" can be just as damaging as the big ones—or more so. Commentator Matthew Henry writes, "Adam's eating forbidden fruit seemed but a little sin, but it opened the door to the greatest."

Are you being tempted to compromise your integrity? Tempted to cheat at school? Pressured to be dishonest at work? Drawn into an "innocent little relationship"? We must live by biblical principles, faithful to the standards of a holy God. As evangelist Charles Finney put it, "A person who is dishonest in little things isn't really honest in anything." On the other hand, Jesus rewards those who are "faithful over a little" (Matthew 25:21 ESV).

Make sure the little, hidden areas of your life are governed by your convictions, not corrupted by your compromises.

FEBRUARY

SELF-JUDGING

If we would judge ourselves, we would not be judged.
1 CORINTHIANS 11:31

Jonathan knew he shouldn't use the company computer to access personal Web sites, but he did it anyway. As a result, his boss appeared in his office one day, asked for Jonathan's keys and files, and summarily marched him outside the building, firing him. Jonathan was humiliated, but he had no one to blame but himself. If he had evaluated and corrected his behavior, others would not have done so. If he had judged himself, he would not have been judged.

To judge our sins means to see them as God sees them. It means to hate those sins and to know that God wants to put them out of our lives. It means to honestly acknowledge moral failures in our lives and to deal with them through genuine, lasting confession and repentance.

King David did this in Psalm 32:3–5: "When I kept silent, my bones grew old through my groaning all the day long. For day and night Your hand was heavy upon me; my vitality was turned into the drought of summer. I acknowledged my sin to You, and my iniquity I have not hidden. I said, 'I will confess my transgressions to the LORD,' and You forgave the iniquity of my sin."

Does anything in your life need to be evaluated and corrected today?

LOTS OF LOTS

. . . for you are still carnal.
1 CORINTHIANS 3:3

Not long ago, a man in Louisville, Kentucky, stole a credit card from a woman at church who, noticing her purse open, called the police. Authorities soon caught the man. He was using the card at a Christian bookstore to buy ten copies of a Bible study called *Moving Beyond Your Past.*

We don't know the thief's spiritual condition, but we do know that many Christians never move far beyond their past. They come to Christ, but the evidence of maturity and spiritual growth is sparse. Paul called such people "carnal."

The carnal man is saved and Spirit indwelled, but he is controlled and dominated by his own life. The Holy Spirit is a resident, but He is not president. Lot is a good biblical example. He was enamored with the world, pitching his tent toward Sodom. Soon he was in Sodom, sitting at the gate, all wrapped up in materialism and with the world.

You have to read all the way through the Bible until you come to 2 Peter 2:7 before you find out that Lot was a believer. There are lots of Lots today. If you had to indict them for Christianity, you couldn't get enough evidence for a conviction.

Are you a "carnal" Christian? Renew your wholehearted commitment to Christ, and let Him be President, Lord, Boss, and King of your life.

FERVENT PRAYERS

When you have shut your door, pray to your Father who is in the secret place.
MATTHEW 6:6

Bishop Joseph Hall, an ardent seventeenth-century Anglican once imprisoned in the Tower of London for his faith, spent his final years on a farm in the countryside writing devotional classics. Here's what he said about prayer:

> An arrow, if it be drawn up but a little way, goes not far; but if it be pulled up to the head, flies swiftly and pierces deep. Prayer, if it be only dribbled forth from careless lips, falls at our feet. It is the strength of [discharge] and strong desire that sends it to heaven, and makes it pierce the clouds. It is not the arithmetic of our prayers, how many they are; not the rhetoric of our prayers, how eloquent they be; nor the geometry of our prayers, how long they be; nor the music of our prayers, how sweet our voice may be; nor the logic of our prayers, how argumentative they may be; nor the method of our prayers, how orderly they may be; nor even the divinity of our prayers, how good the doctrine may be—which God cares for. Fervency of spirit is that which availeth much.

The Lord uses men and women who pray earnestly. Were you going to rush through your prayers today? Why not pause and talk to your Father awhile?

Lost and Found

Have mercy upon me, O God, according to Your lovingkindness; according to the multitude of Your tender mercies, blot out my transgressions.
Psalm 51:1

John Vassar was an agent for the American Tract Society in the 1850s. He left a Bible in the home of a Christian woman whose husband was an infidel. When the husband discovered the Bible, he chopped it in two. Later, in an hour of despair, he began reading Luke 15, the story of the prodigal son, in his half of the Bible. Desperate to read the conclusion, he begged his wife for her half, read the story over and over, and was saved.

It's easy to tell when the grace of God has opened the spiritual eyes of a sinner—he comes to a clear conclusion that he is a sinner! And it's also easy to tell when personal sin is not clear to an individual—he sees sin in everyone but himself. The parable Jesus told of the two brothers (Luke 15:11–32) has an example of each. The younger, prodigal brother recognized his sin and repented before his father. The older brother, however, was indignant that his younger sibling had been forgiven. He couldn't extend grace to others probably because he may not have experienced it himself.

Which "brother" would you have been in Jesus' parable? Being forgiven by God only makes sense to those who know they've sinned.

The Sympathizing Jesus

He gently leads those that have young.
Isaiah 40:11 NIV

Though brilliant and well liked, young Aurelius Augustine (354–430) lived in utter immorality. For more than three decades, his mother, Monica, prayed for him, following him to Carthage, to Rome, and on to Milan, weeping, pleading, and assaulting heaven with perpetual missiles of prayer. The Lord finally answered in wondrous ways, for Monica's wild and wayward son became one of the most influential figures in the history of Christianity.

There was never a distraught parent in the Gospels who came to Jesus on behalf of a troubled child and found Him unresponsive. Notice how sympathetically He dealt with the distressed father in John 4:46–54.

But God's miracles come in many packages, and He deals with us all differently. As we see in the Gospels, for example, Jesus did not always heal in the same way. Sometimes He touched, sometimes He spoke, sometimes He healed in stages, and sometimes He made mud from spittle, smeared it on a blind person's eyes, and told him to wash it off.

He custom-designs His aid to fit our circumstances, to develop our souls, and to meet our needs. If you're troubled about a loved one today, trust Jesus and await His special miracle for you.

WORSHIPING GOD ALONE

And when He had sent the multitudes away, He went up on the mountain by Himself to pray.
MATTHEW 14:23

Jesus Christ was unique in that He was both human and divine. Because we tend to think of Him as the Son of God more than the Son of Man, we often overlook what we can learn from His human experience.

When Jesus miraculously fed five thousand people near the Sea of Galilee, His divine power and prerogatives were clear (Matthew 14:13–21). Yet after this event, we see the humanity of Jesus in ways we should be able to easily identify with. After dismissing the crowd and sending His disciples away, Jesus withdrew to a solitary spot on the mountainside to be alone with God.

How is it that the Son of God needed to be alone with God? While that mystery may remain, one thing is clear: the stark contrast between the crush of a huge crowd and the solitude of being completely alone. Most Christians today only experience the former. Note that Jesus created His solitude by sending the others away. When was the last time you created time for the express purpose of worshiping God by yourself?

People are necessary for many things, but worshiping God alone is not one of them.

JOHN, THE LOYAL DISCIPLE

Now there was leaning on Jesus' bosom one of His disciples, whom Jesus loved.
JOHN 13:23

The Greek word *agape* is one of the most important words in the New Testament. It means unconditional love—the no-strings-attached love with which God loves us. *Agape's* Hebrew parallel in the Old Testament, *hesed*, is less familiar but no less important. It means loyal love and describes God's everlasting love for His people, Israel (and Israel's spiritual descendants, the church).

Loyalty is almost a lost value in today's world. Everything seems to be for sale, including friendship, affection, and devotion—the things that make up loyalty. Even Jesus' disciples found themselves lacking in loyalty on the day Jesus was crucified—all the disciples except one, that is. The disciple named John seems to have had a devotion to Jesus that the others lacked prior to His resurrection. John was the only one of the original band of disciples who stood at the foot of the cross in Jesus' final hours. John was loyal to the very end. Every Christian should ask himself, "Would I have been there with John? Will I be loyal to Jesus regardless of the price?"

The deeper our understanding of God's *agape*, the deeper the manifestation of our *hesed*.

WARNING: GOD AT WORK!

For it is God who works in you both to will and to do for His good pleasure.
PHILIPPIANS 2:13

Before the apostle Paul encountered Christ on the Damascus road, his entire life had been dedicated to the study of the Old Testament. When he became a follower of Christ, it is likely he thought all his years of meticulous study as a Pharisee were wasted. Yet God had providentially prepared Paul to show how Christ was the fulfillment of the Old Testament scriptures he knew so well.

It's easy to fall into the trap of thinking that God doesn't begin working in our lives until the day we come to know Christ. But Scripture says He "foreknew" us, meaning He chose us and prepared us long before we ever met Him (Romans 8:29–30). David says that God wrote out all the days of his life before they ever came to pass (Psalm 139:16), and we can assume He has done the same for us.

God is at work in our lives in ways we know nothing about. When the road gets bumpy and the fog rolls in, don't project your confusion onto God. Even when you can't see His hand at work, He is always active in you to bring about His good pleasure.

Faith changes the question "Is God at work?" into a declarative statement of faith: "God is at work!"

A GOOD AND FAITHFUL SERVANT

Well done . . . you were faithful over a few things, I will make you ruler over many things.
MATTHEW 25:21

Several years before slaves were legally set free by Lincoln's Emancipation Proclamation, a Virginia slave agreed to purchase his freedom from his master. He was released to find work where he could. When Lincoln freed all slaves, this man still owed his master three hundred dollars. In spite of his legal freedom, the slave walked from his home in Ohio to his master's home in Virginia to pay his final debt. His reason? He had given his word, and he would not be able to enjoy his freedom without fulfilling his promise.

Daniel the prophet had been made a slave of the Babylonian and, later, Persian empires in Mesopotamia. Separated from Jerusalem and his own spiritual culture, he nonetheless continued to worship God faithfully. At the time of the evening offering in Jerusalem (3:00 p.m.), Daniel was found to be faithfully in prayer in Persia—and this after being separated from Jewish practices for nearly seventy years (Daniel 9:21). Without the support structure of your friends and local church, would you remain faithful to God as Daniel did?

Faithful servants are those who live obediently even when they don't have to—and they are rewarded by God accordingly.

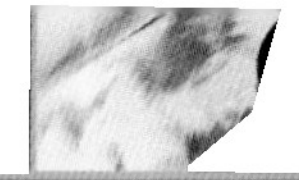

SHADRACH, MESHACH, AND ABED-NEGO

Our God whom we serve is able to deliver us . . . and He will deliver us. . . . But if not . . . we [will not] worship the gold image which you have set up.
DANIEL 3:17–18

In 1555, in Oxford, England, Hugh Latimer and Nicholas Ridley were burned at the stake for their biblical views that failed to conform to the ruling (Catholic) church. As the flames consumed them, Latimer called out, "Be of good comfort, Master Ridley, and play the man. We shall this day light such a candle by God's grace in England as I trust shall never be put out!"

God didn't deliver Latimer and Ridley from the flames on earth, but He did deliver them from the flames of eternal judgment by their faith in Christ. These two martyrs were imitating the faith of three who came before them in the Old Testament—Shadrach, Meshach, and Abed-Nego. They were thrown into a fiery furnace for refusing to worship a golden image; but God delivered them, though they didn't know that was His plan. Their faith had prepared them to die or be delivered—the choice was God's, and they were fine with that. Has your faith prepared you to be fine with the choices God is making in your life today?

Faith sees no difference between kinds of deliverance, as long as the deliverance is from God.

ABIDING

Abide in Me, and I in you.
JOHN 15:4

When the great missionary J. Hudson Taylor was badly overworked and worried, he read a letter from a friend who had discovered the secret of abiding in Christ. The letter deeply moved Taylor, and he realized that his oneness with Christ should produce joy and fulfillment, not worry and stress.

Soon thereafter, Taylor wrote his sister, saying, "As to work, mine was never so plentiful or so difficult; but the weight and strain are now gone. The last month has been perhaps the happiest in my life; and I long to tell you a little of what the Lord has done for my soul. . . . I looked to Jesus and saw that He had said, 'I will never leave you.' Ah, there is rest. For has He not promised to abide with me? As I thought of the Vine and the branches, what light the blessed Spirit poured into my soul!"

Are you abiding in Christ? You are if you have come to Him in simple faith, taking Him at His word, trusting in His promises of forgiveness and blessing, and seeking to live a life of daily obedience. "Abide in Me," said Jesus, "and I in you. As the branch cannot bear fruit of itself . . . neither can you, unless you abide in Me."

THE FREEDOM OF SLAVERY

Likewise he who is called while free is Christ's slave.
1 CORINTHIANS 7:22

In a speech to a regiment of Union soldiers during the Civil War, Abraham Lincoln said, "Whenever I hear anyone arguing for slavery, I feel a strong impulse to see it tried on him personally." He was referring, of course, to the coercive form of slavery. But many people have personally, and permanently, made themselves slaves of a different kind.

Some of the most unusual language of the New Testament comes from the pens of the apostles Paul, Peter, James, and Jude. Each of these church leaders, along with other coworkers, referred to themselves as slaves. Modern Bible translations soften the Greek word *doulos* to "servant" instead of "slave." But in the first century, a *doulos* was a person who voluntarily submitted himself to a master to be a permanent slave. A *doulos* willingly laid everything he had at the feet of his master then picked it up again to accomplish his master's will.

The apostles were free to live or free to die because of their obedience to their Master. Have you considered living your life as a voluntary *doulos* of the Lord Jesus Christ?

If perfect freedom is found in perfect obedience, how would you measure your own freedom?

TOO THANKFUL TO BE ANYTHING ELSE

My brethren, count it all joy when you fall into various trials.
JAMES 1:2

When Mike McAdams's wife, Cheryl, was in the intensive care unit in a Nashville hospital, she was barely able to respond. When a friend asked how she was doing, Mike replied, "It's touch and go. We held hands, prayed, and remembered James 1:2: 'Count it all joy.' You know, it's impossible to be thankful and anxious at the same time."

It's hard to be thankful and negative at the same time. When was the last time you felt thankful and resentful? Thankful and lonely? Thankful and angry? Thankfulness seems to take the edge off our negative or self-centered thoughts and actions. Why? It's because our focus is taken off ourselves and turned toward God. Fifteen times in the Old Testament we find the phrase, "Give thanks to the Lord." It's a little hard to imagine saying, "Thank You, Lord" and "Lord, I'm so lonely (or mad, or depressed)" at the same time. After all, if God provided the circumstances that we find to our liking, isn't He also in control of the circumstances that don't suit us? Yes—and genuine thankfulness will acknowledge Him in both cases.

A thankful life is not an escape from reality but an evidence of true spirituality.

THE LOCKET OF YOUR HEART

Teach me your way, O LORD; and I will walk in your truth; give me an undivided heart, that I may fear your name.
PSALM 86:11 NIV

A young woman in England always wore a golden locket that she would not allow anyone to open or look into. Everyone thought there must be some romance connected with the locket, and within the locket must be a picture of the one she loved. After the woman died, someone opened the locket and found a little slip of paper with these words written upon it: "Whom having not seen, I love." Her Lord Jesus was the only lover she knew and the only lover she longed for.

This woman was wholeheartedly devoted to Christ. She exemplifies the kind of devotion God desires from each of us in worship. He wants us to worship Him with our whole heart, with our minds focused solely on Him. In a world that aggressively competes for our affections, we must make a deliberate effort to keep God first.

If someone were to open the locket of your heart, what or who would they find there? Has your devotion to God been replaced by other affections? By money? Sports? Success? A relationship? Today, take time to pray and ask God to give you an undivided heart.

FAITHFUL IS HE

If we are faithless, He remains faithful; He cannot deny Himself.
2 TIMOTHY 2:13

In 1947, Dr. Chandrasekhar, professor of astrophysics at the University of Chicago, was scheduled to teach an advanced seminar. He lived in Wisconsin at the time, but he planned to drive in the dead of winter twice a week to the class. When only two students signed up for the class, everyone expected him to cancel. But all winter, twice a week, he made the 100-mile trip—for two students, each of whom later won the Nobel Prize.

Dr. Chandrasekhar, a Nobel Prize winner himself, displayed one of God's characteristics: faithfulness. The response or commitment of the students did not dictate his actions. He had promised to teach the class, and that is what he did—and that is how God relates to us. God is faithful regardless of our attitudes or actions. Even when we are faithless—when we have no faith—He is faithful. God's faithfulness is based in His character and revealed in His promises. For instance, when we sin, "He is faithful and just to forgive us" (1 John 1:9).

Faithfulness is acting like God regardless of how others act toward us.

Better Safe Than Sorry

Therefore, whether you eat or drink, or whatever you do, do all to the glory of God.
1 Corinthians 10:31

In the early years of his Christian faith, General Thomas "Stonewall" Jackson, the great battlefield leader of the Civil War, purposed to glorify God in all things. He tithed his income and gave up all activities that might distract his thoughts from holy things. If he was asked about the good or evil of a particular activity, he would smile and reply, "Well, I know it is not wrong not to do it, so I'm going to be on the safe side."

Many Christians today flirt with sin, hoping to stop themselves just before they cross the line. Technically, they don't sin. But General Jackson's attitude is the biblical one: move toward God in all things, and sin will lose its strength. In other words, better to be safe than sorry.

How about you? How much of your life is given to the pursuit of the glory of God? Even in times of sickness, of testing, of suffering, of doubt—are you still committed to staying close to God and allowing Him to be glorified by being your strength? Paul said even his difficulties could "cause thanksgiving to abound to the glory of God" (2 Corinthians 4:15).

Bringing glory to God in all things is the only way to stay safe and avoid sorrow.

The Church's One Foundation

For no other foundation can anyone lay than that which is laid, which is Jesus Christ.
1 Corinthians 3:11

In 1972, Dean Kelley wrote a book that has become a classic in the study of church growth: *Why Conservative Churches Are Growing*. He chronicled the decline of mainstream, liberal churches and the growth of conservative, Bible-teaching churches. There was a direct correlation between churches' acknowledgement of the authority of the Bible and whether or not they grew.

While we can be thankful for Kelley's historical analysis, we might have looked no further than the Book of Acts for an earlier example of his thesis. The greatest numerical growth in the history of the church took place when Jesus was preached in the power of the Spirit by the apostles in Jerusalem. No gimmicks—just the message about Jesus. And people responded by the thousands (Acts 2:41, 47). Just as no building can be erected without a firm foundation, so the church cannot be raised except on the foundation of Jesus Christ her Lord.

Whatever your role is in your church, are you making sure nothing replaces Jesus Christ and His Word as the foundation?

WORK ON THAT RELATIONSHIP

Work hard and cheerfully at whatever you do.
COLOSSIANS 3:23 NLT

For hundreds of years, inventors have been working on various versions of perpetual motion machines, trying to invent a device that will keep going without any input of energy. No one has yet succeeded.

Many people think love, marriage, and friendship are perpetual motion machines that will keep going without our energy and effort. They aren't. We have to work at spending time together, being patient with each other, and listening to what the other is saying. We have to work at serving the other person without complaint.

Whether with our spouse, kids, or friends, a good partnership takes work; otherwise, at some point, the relationship will lose steam.

Contrary to popular opinion, love is not having a trouble-free relationship. It's caring deeply about the needs of the other person even if and when there is stress in the relationship. Love means putting up with the faults, flaws, and failures of the other. This kind of love isn't of the earth, but from above. It flows into imperfect hearts and heals imperfect circumstances, for it comes from an infinite and infallible God who loves us.

Do you need to work a little harder on that troubled relationship? Why not start today?

Connecting the Dots

I am the Alpha and the Omega, the Beginning and the End… who is and who was and who is to come, the Almighty.
Revelation 1:8

One of the most popular documentary series ever shown on public television was titled *Connections*. It was based on the work of the British scientific historian and author James Burke. In each segment of the series, Burke explored the development of scientific advancements and showed how seemingly unconnected discoveries were in fact related—like fast food and black holes in space, and corn flakes and Einstein's theory of relativity.

It takes a scientist or historian to tediously follow the chain of events that lead from one discovery to another, to connect history's seemingly random dots. What about God's plan of redemption? Who would have thought that God's calling of a Mesopotamian pagan worshiper named Abram would result in spiritual blessing for the whole world (Genesis 12:1–3)? Every seemingly mundane event in world history has taken place as part of God's plan. And He knows everything about your life as well—the beginning, the middle, and the end. His plan is perfect and will be fulfilled.

When the parts of your life seem disjointed, remember: God has all the dots connected.

Refiner's Fire

Every branch in Me that does not bear fruit He takes away; and every branch that bears fruit He prunes, that it may bear more fruit.
John 15:2

As evidenced by the devastation in California in 2003, wildfires have an out-of-control nature. Each year, more than one hundred thousand wildfires occur in the United States. Did you know that these fires are a natural way of clearing old growth in order to make room for new growth? In fact, some trees cannot survive without periodic blazes—and most animals escape and even benefit from wildfires. They simply find a new place to live. Thus the forest's cycle of life starts over—lasting decades or centuries, until the forest grows back and the departed animals return.

Sometimes there is no way to stop the out-of-control flames but to pray and wait for the flames to fall silent.

How do we handle the fires that rage through our lives—divorce, unemployment, or disappointments? Remember that God is with you in the midst of those trials. He has plans for new growth in your heart. His reasons are not always known, but the benefits of trusting God through hard times are eternal.

Meditate on these lyrics from Brian Doerksen's worship song "Refiner's Fire": "Refiner's fire, my heart's one desire is to be holy, set apart for You, Lord. I choose to be holy, set apart for You, my master, ready to do Your will."

Streams in the Desert

. . . and that Rock was Christ.
1 Corinthians 10:4

Have you experienced deserts in your life? Ever felt you were wandering in a wilderness, surrounded by problems, hemmed in by distress? Charles Weigle was an itinerant evangelist who enjoyed traveling and preaching, despite the rigors of the road. His wife, however, grew disillusioned with her frequently absent husband. One day, Charles returned home to find this note: "Charlie, I've been a fool. I've done without a lot of things. . . . From here on out, I'm getting all I can of what the world owes me. I know you'll continue to be a fool for Jesus, but for me it's good-bye!"

Charles was stunned, and depression swept over him like a tidal wave. One day, sitting on the porch of a cottage in Florida, he contemplated suicide. *Your work is finished*, said an inner voice. *No one cares* . . . But another voice pierced his gloom: *Charlie, I haven't forgotten you* . . . I care for you. Instantly, Charles was on his knees, rededicating himself to Christ.

Sometime later, he wrote the words to the well-known gospel song: "No one ever cared for me like Jesus; there's no other friend so kind as He. No one else could take the sin and darkness from me; O how much He cared for me."

He cares for you too—even in the desert.

ENJOY WHAT YOU HAVE

Better is the sight of the eyes than the wandering of desire. This also is vanity and grasping for the wind.
ECCLESIASTES 6:9

In his book *Racing to Win*, NFL coach and racecar owner Joe Gibbs recounts some of his financial failures. As a young coach seeking to make more money, he invested in three different ventures, all of which failed—the last taking nearly five years of frugal living to pay off. It was only after he started seeking God instead of wealth that he became successful.

When Benjamin Franklin wrote that "a bird in the hand is worth two in the bush," he might have been paraphrasing King Solomon, who wrote that "a living dog is better than a dead lion" (Ecclesiastes 9:4). In other words, God's provision is far more secure than something that exists only in our dreams and fantasies. Solomon also said that "the hand of the diligent makes rich" (Proverbs 10:4). Get-rich-quick schemes are a dime a dozen, and they usually confirm the old saying, "If it sounds too good to be true, it usually is." Focus today on your work and enjoying the fruits of your labor. Both are gifts from God.

Truth is better than time, talent, and treasure. The truth of abundant life is about enjoying what we have been given, not lusting after what we have not.

TRUSTING GOD FOR FAMILY

Train up a child in the way he should go, and when he is old he will not depart from it.
PROVERBS 22:6

The line of kings of Judah from Rehoboam to Jehoram represented five generations of fathers and sons: Rehoboam (bad), Abijah (bad), Asa (good), Jehoshaphat (good), and Joram (bad). Bad fathers produced both bad and good sons, and good fathers produced both good and bad sons. Where is the predictability?

There are no guarantees when it comes to family. True, Proverbs 22:6 says to invest in our children so they become wise adults. But the Book of Proverbs contains guidelines, not promises. Sometimes, good parents (like King David) produce bad sons (like Absalom) who bring shame to their fathers. David might have wondered if the line of promise was going to fizzle out with his sons, given their character. But the grace of God was at work in David's son, Solomon; and the Messiah appeared right on schedule (Matthew 1:1–16; Luke 3:23–38). Salvation came to the earth through human families just like yours. Even our familial flaws can't keep God's purposes from being accomplished!

Take a moment to thank God that His purposes don't depend on your perfection as a parent or child, but on His faithfulness.

REDEEMING THE TIME

Teach us to number our days, that we may gain a heart of wisdom.
PSALM 90:12

Alarm to the Unconverted is a little book written by Joseph Alleine (1634–1668). Though not as recognized as it once was, it has left its mark in Christian history as a Puritan classic.

Alleine was a serious young man who felt that his commitment to Christ required the wise use of his time. He wanted to use every moment, in one way or another, for the Lord. As a student, he often neglected his friends for his studies. "It's better they should wonder at my rudeness," he explained, "than that I should lose time; for only a few will notice the rudeness, but many will feel my loss of time."

As a minister, Joseph habitually rose at four in the morning, praying and studying his Bible until eight. His afternoons were spent calling on the unconverted. At the beginning of the week, he would remark, "Another week is now before us; let us spend this week for God." Each morning, he would say, "Now let us live this one day well!"

Though he died at age thirty-four, Joseph Alleine did more for Christ than many twice his age. Are you being a good steward of your time? Are you using your moments wisely for Christ?

JUST TRY IT

And try Me now in this.
MALACHI 3:10

Before his death, Pastor Harvey Hill of Winter Haven, Florida, wrote out his life's story. He said that when he and his wife, Sylvia, were married, they didn't have a penny. It was during the Depression, and not many people had a car. They walked to church, to work, and to visit with friends; and they lived hand to mouth. One day the pastor of their church asked them if they tithed—that is, if they were in the habit of giving at least 10 percent of their income to the Lord.

"No," said Harvey. "We can't afford it."

"Just try it," the pastor replied, "and see if God doesn't bless you."

Struck by the challenge, Harvey and Sylvia agreed to try. From that day until their deaths within a few weeks of each other seventy years later, they never failed to bring God their tithes and offerings. And He never failed to meet their needs.

Malachi 3:10 says, "'Bring all the tithes into the storehouse, that there may be food in My house, and try Me now in this,' says the LORD of hosts, 'if I will not open for you the windows of heaven and pour out for you such blessing that there will not be room enough to receive it.'"

Are you tithing? You should just try it, and see if God doesn't bless you.

Problem Children

Please go and see if it is well with your brothers.
Genesis 37:14

Jacob was worried about his boys. They were strong-willed, immature "problem kids." Even when they were absent, he was concerned. Sometimes they acted like a band of thugs. Their shenanigans caused Jacob endless heartache. In Genesis 37, they were shepherding their flocks in Shechem, and Jacob, perhaps sensing trouble, sent Joseph to find out if all was well. The brothers saw Joseph coming, seized him, stripped him, threw him into a pit, and sold him to a passing caravan as a slave.

The situation seemed hopeless. But fast-forward to the end of Genesis: Joseph is prime minister of Egypt, he and his brothers are reconciled, Jacob is happy and honored, and his twelve sons become the patriarchs of the Jewish nation.

Don't give up on your children, even when they worry you, even when circumstances seem impossible. God can devise implausible solutions and do impossible things. Luke 18:27 says, "The things which are impossible with men are possible with God."

Maybe it's not your child—maybe it's your spouse, your sibling, your neighbor, or your best friend. We can't change another's heart, but God can. Do your best and then let Him do the rest.

For Want of a Wall

Whoever has no rule over his own spirit is like a city broken down, without walls.
Proverbs 25:28

The Great Wall of China was erected in the third century BC as a defense against raids by nomadic peoples from the north. Throughout succeeding centuries, especially during the Ming dynasty (1368–1644), the Great Wall was repaired and extended in length, finally stretching for forty-five hundred miles.

Centuries before the Great Wall was begun, biblical cultures used walls to protect themselves from marauders as well as to draw boundaries around themselves for purposes of identity. To be effective, walls had to be maintained. The slightest foothold in a fortress wall could give the enemy a fateful advantage (Ephesians 4:27 NIV).

Modern armaments have made walls obsolete as defensive structures. But there is one wall that is the Christian's primary defense against personal destruction: the wall of self-control. Failure to maintain self-control is like opening the city gates to the enemy, like issuing an invitation to the devil and his legions. Make a defensive assessment today, and fix what has fallen into disrepair.

Kingdoms have been lost for want of a strong wall. Don't let a lack of self-control be the ruin of yours.

GREAT EXPECTATIONS

And they were greatly amazed in themselves beyond measure, and marveled.
MARK 6:51

Canada has suffered its share of natural disasters in recent years, prompting the Canadian Red Cross to begin a preparedness program to help schoolchildren deal with sudden crises. The slogan is "Expect the Unexpected."

In the Gospels, the disciples were often left slack-jawed and wide-eyed at Jesus' behavior, His words, and His miracles. When He healed the paralytic in Mark 2, for example, "all were amazed and glorified God, saying, 'We never saw anything like this!'" (v. 12). They learned to expect the unexpected when they were with Him.

If you're a disciple, you're learning to expect the unexpected, for we never know what Christ is going to do next for us, in us, around us, or through us. It's an exciting, adventuresome way to live. Discipleship is an experience that dispels boredom and keeps the Christian looking up in amazement.

Expect Him to answer your prayers and to overrule the problems of your life and cause all things to work together for good. Expect Him to open doors, create opportunities, meet your needs, and bless your efforts. Say with the psalmist: "My soul, wait silently for God alone, for my expectation is from Him" (Psalm 62:5).

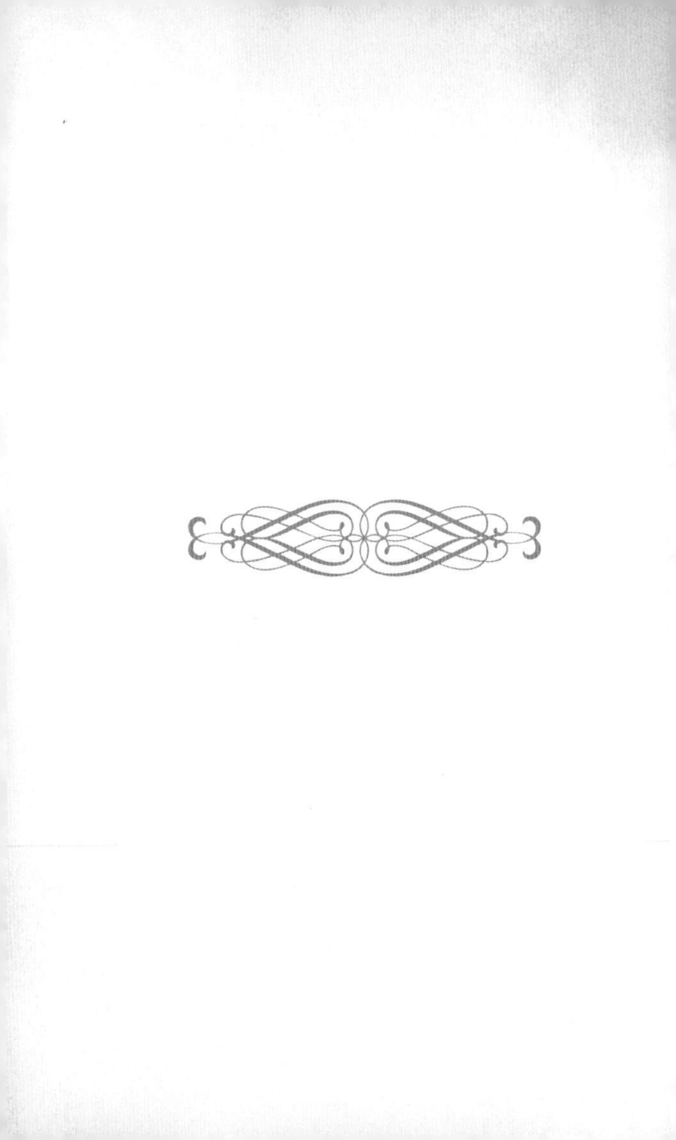

March

REMEMBER TO FORGET

For I will forgive their iniquity, and their sin I will remember no more.
JEREMIAH 31:34

Diane Sollee of the Coalition for Marriage and Family reports a powerful fact concerning conflict in marriage: couples who are happy and stay married have the same number of disagreements and conflicts as couples who are unhappy and get divorced. So it is not the absence of conflict that preserves marriages, but the ability to manage conflict when it happens.

What does it mean to "manage conflict"? It certainly means practicing the kind of self-control that keeps conflicts from mushrooming into hurtful and divisive standoffs. But it also means knowing what to do with hurt feelings, anger, disappointment, and dashed expectations. It means, in other words, knowing how to forgive and forget. But what does that mean?

Emotional hurt and tension is almost impossible to forget; the harder we try, the more we remember. Therefore, couples have to remember to forget. They have to act like God, who chooses not to hold against us what He knows about us. If you are holding something against your spouse, why not choose to forget it?

You may never forget how you've been hurt, but you can choose to forget about it.

TIGHTEN YOUR RESOLVE

Resolve this, not to put a stumbling block or a cause to fall in our brother's way.
ROMANS 14:13

J. Wilbur Chapman, a powerful evangelist of an earlier era, formulated what he called "my rule for Christian living." He said, "The rule that governs my life is this: Anything that dims my vision of Christ, or takes away my taste for Bible study, or cramps my prayer life, or makes Christian work difficult, is wrong for me, and I must, as a Christian, turn away from it."

We can also add: "Anything that hurts my testimony or stunts the growth of another Christian is likewise wrong."

There are many issues, habits, and convictions that differ among Christians. The apostle Paul deals with these "gray areas" in Romans 14 and 1 Corinthians 10, and he warns us against allowing our Christian liberty to become a stumbling block to ourselves or to others. If we practice our Christian liberty in such a way as to tempt others to violate their consciences or to engage in activities that may for them be doubtful, we are not exercising our freedom in a wise or loving way.

Is there an area in your life that needs to be tightened? Is there an activity that needs changing?

Dad, I'm Sorry

Blessed is he whose transgression is forgiven.
Psalm 32:1

Dad, I'm really sorry." Jeremy could barely get the words out. Having borrowed his dad's credit card for groceries, he had used it to purchase beer for his buddies. His dad might never have known about it, but for that little device inside the human heart called a conscience. "I shouldn't have bought the beer, I shouldn't have lied about my age, and I shouldn't have used your credit card to do it. You trusted me, and I let you down. I'm sorry. I will never do it again."

That's confession. That's what we must do in our prayers.

In the New Testament, the Greek word translated "confession" means to agree with God concerning His opinion about a matter. It means to admit our guilt. When we confess our sins, we are agreeing with God concerning the sin in our lives as revealed through His Word and by the Holy Spirit. When we confess, we verbalize our spiritual shortcomings and admit our sin.

Confession is painful, but it keeps our relationship with our heavenly Father clear, open, and close. Hiding our sin builds a barrier between us and God.

Do you have a sin to confess? "If we confess our sins, He is faithful and just to forgive us our sins and to cleanse us from all unrighteousness" (1 John 1:9).

WHEN JEALOUSY IS A GOOD THING

For you shall worship no other god, for the LORD, whose name is Jealous, is a jealous God.
EXODUS 34:14

In the late sixth century, Pope Gregory the Great codified various lists of major sins circulating in the church, settling on seven deadly ones (listed by him in the decreasing order of their offense against love): pride, envy, anger, sadness, avarice (greed), gluttony, and lust. In the seventeenth century, sadness was replaced by sloth. Interestingly, jealousy isn't one of the seven deadly sins.

Jealousy doesn't appear probably because it has both a positive and a negative dimension (see if you can find a positive aspect of any of the seven above). Jealousy can be focused on self ("I am jealous of someone or something because of what I can't have"), or on others ("I am jealous for you because of what I want you to have"). The former is self-centered; the latter is others-centered.

God's jealousy for His children is others-centered, for our benefit. He is jealous for us that we might remain pure and holy. God moves aggressively against idolatry not because He is threatened (jealous), but because He cares for (is jealous for) us.

The proper response to God's jealousy is to have no other gods before Him.

FOLLOWING YOUR WAY TO FELLOWSHIP

If we say that we have fellowship with Him, and walk in darkness, we lie and do not practice the truth.
1 JOHN 1:6

Think of the last time you experienced tension in a relationship—perhaps with a family member or someone at work. Conversation is superficial, and you're more comfortable apart than together. When something happens between people who are normally close, the first thing to vanish is the evidence of fellowship.

It's the same way with the Lord. We think we can stop following Him without damaging our relationship. The conversation is surface ("Lord, please bless this food"), and we avoid spending time with Him ("I just don't have time for my devotions").

The main prerequisite for experiencing fellowship with Jesus is following Him and obeying His commands. It's like when Peter and the disciples were fishing, and the Lord told them to cast their nets on the right side of the boat. When Peter obeyed, something greater than catching a boatload of fish happened—he saw Jesus. What followed was an intimate meal, a sweet time of fellowship with the Lord. Fellowship follows obedience.

If you're feeling out of fellowship with Jesus, the chances are good that you've either stopped following or started disobeying.

JOURNALING

Remember His marvelous works which He has done, His wonders, and the judgments of His mouth.
1 CHRONICLES 16:12

Jim Elliot was an intensely committed missionary who was killed in 1956 by the Ecuadorian Indians he was trying to reach. Indians were not his only challenge: "My devotional reading pattern was broken. I have never restored it. . . . Prayer as a single man was difficult. . . . Now it's too hard to get out of bed in the morning. . . . I've made resolutions on this score before now but not followed them up."

Jim Elliot was a godly young missionary who struggled with spiritual disciplines like every believer. But unlike most, he kept a written record of spiritual defeats as well as victories in his journal. Keeping a journal can help us remember God's works, retain our honesty, reflect on our hearts, register our progress, regain lost momentum, reject bad habits, reinforce good habits, and reach our spiritual goals. What other discipline offers such benefits? Consider making a journal your personal place to be honest with God and yourself. You, and perhaps others, will benefit from your faithfulness.

A journal is a record of a journey, a written account of your travels on the road to heaven.

GIVING TO THE GIVER

For all things come from You, and of Your own we have given You.
1 CHRONICLES 29:14

Sixteen of Jesus' thirty-eight parables were concerned with how to handle money and possessions. In the four Gospels, one out of every ten verses deals directly with the subject of money. The Bible has five hundred verses on prayer, less than five hundred verses on faith, but more than two thousand verses on money and possessions.

Do you think God is trying to tell us something? It seems to be a truism in life that generous people are comfortable talking about money and even more comfortable giving it away. Stingy people, on the other hand, obsess over keeping what they have and how to get more. Maybe that's why Jesus, the most generous person in history, spoke so much about money—He understood its source, its use, and who owns it all.

Jesus' ancestor David understood those same things. King David gave generously to build the temple and left us the basis for understanding money and material possessions: all things come from God, and from His gifts to us we give back to Him. When we get comfortable with that truth, we will be comfortable in giving generously as He directs.

If you are uncomfortable with giving, you may be opening your Bible less often than your checkbook!

CARELESS TALK

Let your speech always be with grace, seasoned with salt, that you may know how you ought to answer each one.
COLOSSIANS 4:6

Have you noticed the similarities between the New Testament letters of Ephesians and Colossians? Many verses in Colossians have a parallel in Ephesians. For example, notice how Colossians 4:6 corresponds with Ephesians 4:29, which says: "Let no corrupt word proceed out of your mouth, but what is good for necessary edification, that it might impart grace to the hearers."

Our words shouldn't be "salty," but seasoned with salt—tasteful and appropriate, useful for helping others and building them up.

The Chinese Christian leader Watchman Nee devoted a chapter in his book *The Normal Christian Worker* to this subject. He writes, "Because of unrestrained speech, the usefulness of many Christian workers is seriously curtailed. Instead of being powerful instruments in the Lord's service, their ministry makes little impact on account of the constant leakage of power through their careless talk."

If you're in need of wiser, more gracious, salt-seasoned speech, here's a prayer for you: "Set a guard, O LORD, over my mouth; keep watch over the door of my lips" (Psalm 141:3).

Every Single Law

Submit yourselves to every ordinance of man for the Lord's sake.
1 Peter 2:13

Georgi Vins, a pastor in Russia before the fall of Soviet Communism, was severely persecuted for his faith. But no matter how severe the repression and mistreatment became, he and his fellow Christians determined they were going to obey every single law on the Russian books, just or unjust. With the exception of laws that would force them to cease worship or disobey God's Word, these brave pastors bent over backward to be good citizens. Even in concentration camps, they obeyed the rules unless these rules conflicted with their worship or directly countermanded a truth in the Word of God.

Their example made them heroes not only among the Christians but among the citizens of Russia. In the eyes of the world, the cause of Christ was advanced.

Both Peter and Paul told their readers (who were living under the tyranny of the Roman government) to obey the laws of the land, respect civil authority, and pay their taxes (Romans 13:1; 1 Peter 2:13). God ordained human government for our good, and He desires us to obey even those laws that we dislike. He will bless us as we do so.

WHY WORSHIP?

Because He is your Lord, worship Him.
PSALM 45:11

An old gospel song goes like this:

> Jesus, I'll never forget what You've done for me,
> Jesus, I'll never forget how You set me free,
> Jesus, I'll never forget how You brought me out,
> Jesus, I'll never forget, no never!

The song goes on to proclaim, "He's done so much for me, I cannot tell it all, He's taken all my sins away!"

Whether we worship God for His attributes (who He is) or His actions (what He has done), worship is our response to Him. Worship is a measure of our perception, appreciation, or understanding of who God is and what He has done.

When a child erupts with squeals of delight and hugs of affection upon receiving a surprise, we are seeing the response of joy. In a similar way, because God's mercies are new every morning to us (Lamentations 3:22–23), we have good reason never to stop worshiping Him. A good exercise for the Christian is to spend some time remembering the things God has done, which flow from who He is. If we consider carefully, we will agree with the songwriter: "He's done so much for me, I cannot tell it all."

To remember God's greatness and goodness is to respond with a heart of gratitude.

THE VALUE OF UNIQUENESS

But one and the same Spirit works all these things, distributing to each one individually as He wills.
1 CORINTHIANS 12:11

Author Stu Weber's two oldest sons did well in high school athletics. To encourage his youngest son, Ryan, to find his niche, Stu spent lots of time camping and hiking in the outdoors with him. Ryan's identity developed around a favorite pocketknife he always carried on their trips. But the real value of the knife was revealed the day Ryan gave it to his dad as a birthday gift.

What Ryan Weber did for his dad is a reflection of what Jesus Christ has done for us. Jesus, by His Holy Spirit, has given every believer a personal spiritual gift especially suited for who we are. Jesus gave up His physical ministry on this earth when He returned to heaven, then He distributed His ministry to us to help carry out for Him.

That's what spiritual gifts are—individual portions of the ministry of Jesus with which each individual Christian has been gifted. Others may have the same gift as you, but no one else will be led to use that gift in the same unique way. Excitement and joy in ministry come from recognizing how special the gift of God to us really is.

The combination of you and your spiritual gift occurs nowhere else in the world.

The Essence of Aging

You shall come to the grave at a full age, as a sheaf of grain ripens in its season.
Job 5:26

Ben Patterson says old age has a way of whittling a person down to his or her bare essence—what is left of us is what we were all along. He cites his wife's grandmother, who, in her eighties, couldn't remember family names, but her prayers were heaven on earth. A distant uncle, on the other hand, spent his life making money and was obsessed with it at the end of his life.

When mind and muscle leave us, what remains is who we really are. Some of us, like Moses, will minister right up to the end (Deuteronomy 34:7). But for most of us, aging will take its toll. If Patterson is right, and what remains is the essence of who we are . . . what will stand out in your life?

Abraham and Sarah were just getting started when they hit the century mark. They had their first child together and set out to build a nation that would cover the earth like the sand on the seashore. That's called walking by faith, and the older we get the more it ought to characterize our life.

If today were your last day on earth and the essence of your life was revealed, what would it be? Start building a life of faith so that when all else passes away, your legacy of faith will remain.

For the Christian, growing old gracefully means growing old, full of grace.

Delayed Dreams

God meant it for good.
Genesis 50:20

Are you wrestling with disappointment, a broken dream, or a setback in life? Think of Joseph. His brothers called him a "dreamer" (Genesis 37:19), but all his dreams died—or seemed to—in an act of brotherly betrayal that led to Egyptian imprisonment.

God's heroes have always been dreamers, men and women who sensed what God wanted them to do and who were willing to trust Him to perform it. But sometimes those dreams have died. Perhaps yours have too.

We must remember that when God seems to say no, there is still a lot left, a lot to be thankful for, and a lot to do for Him. We should learn to say, "I don't understand why my dream hasn't come true, but thank God for all He's done for me anyway."

And we must go on dreaming and persevering. When Joseph's dreams seemed to have died, he remained faithful anyway. He decided to bloom where he was planted, even if it was in a filthy jail, falsely accused as a rapist. Later, in God's own mysterious way, He took Joseph from the prison to the palace, and all Joseph's God-given dreams were fulfilled.

If your dream has been set aside by God, don't quit. Seek out what God has for you in the days ahead. Trust Him, and keep dreaming.

DON'T BE SURPRISED

We are hard-pressed on every side.
2 CORINTHIANS 4:8

I don't know why this is happening," Jill cried. "Just a month ago, I turned my life over to Christ. Now my car has died, my child has mononucleosis, and my promotion at work fell through."

While it seems logical that God would shield us from all pain, that isn't the way He worked in the Bible. Study the great biblical heroes—Abraham, Joseph, Moses, David, Peter, Paul—and trace their trials and tribulations. Despite what certain false teachers say, the Christian life is not unbridled health and wealth. Jesus put it bluntly when He said, "In the world you will have tribulation; but be of good cheer, I have overcome the world" (John 16:33).

In other words, we shouldn't be surprised when, in seeking to do God's will, we find ourselves in painful, frightening, difficult, or impossible situations. God hasn't promised us exemption from the trial but grace in the trial. He has promised never to leave us nor forsake us, and to work all things together for our good. Peter said, "Beloved, do not think it strange concerning the fiery trial . . . as though some strange thing happened to you; but rejoice . . . be glad with exceeding joy" (1 Peter 4:12–13).

The Lord will see you through.

STOP THE WORLD!

Finally, my brethren, be strong in the Lord.
EPHESIANS 6:10

Ever wonder if you can press on? Life is difficult, and we often feel like saying, in the words of the old musical, "Stop the world—I want to get off!" It's hard to bear up under chronic pain, to keep going against constant opposition, and to remain joyful in cheerless surroundings. Within ourselves, we haven't sufficient courage or morale.

But we can be strong in the Lord. When our strength is gone, His is ready to be tapped. We can give Him our burdens, trust Him with our hurts, tell Him our cares, and claim the promises of His Word. As J. B. Phillips put it in his paraphrase of Ephesians 6:10: "Be strong—not in yourselves but in the Lord, in the power of his boundless resource."

Commentator Matthew Henry says about this verse: "We have no sufficient strength of our own. Our natural courage is as perfect cowardice, and our natural strength as perfect weakness; but all our sufficiency is of God. In His strength we must go forth and go on."

Focus your mind today on the strength of our Lord Jesus Christ. Tell Him you feel weak, but don't dwell on that. Don't dwell on your problems either. Dwell on Christ. Let Him be your strength and solution today.

CHRISTIAN BOOKS

Bring the cloak that I left with Carpus at Troas when you come—and the books, especially the parchments.
2 TIMOTHY 4:13

The *Left Behind* series of Christian novels has sold tens of millions of copies, and *The Prayer of Jabez* was the best-selling nonfiction book in America in 2001. So strong is the Christian publishing market that some major evangelical publishers have been sought by secular media companies.

If there is a danger in the rise of Christian publishing in recent years, it is the temptation to read more books about the Bible than the Bible itself. But keeping all things in balance, the wealth of good resources for Christians is a modern blessing that believers ought to take advantage of. For instance, try a good biography of a famous saint to find a stimulating role model or a devotional classic to keep you in the Word daily. Or perhaps you'd enjoy a missionary tale or exciting novel with biblical themes to read aloud as a family. Reading good Christian books can reinforce and illustrate the themes we read in Scripture. What are you reading this week?

Looking for dependable guidelines for choosing books to read along with the Bible? Check out Philippians 4:8.

God with Us

. . . Christ in you, the hope of glory.
Colossians 1:27

Patrick was born in what is now called Scotland. He was kidnapped by pirates as a lad and enslaved in Ireland, but after a dramatic escape, he returned home to Ireland as an evangelist. During his ministry, he planted about two hundred churches and baptized one hundred thousand converts.

Patrick once said this about the Lord Jesus: "Christ with me, Christ before me, Christ behind me, Christ in me, Christ beneath me, Christ above me, Christ on my right, Christ on my left, Christ when I lie down, Christ when I sit down, Christ when I arise, Christ in the heart of every man who thinks of me, Christ in the mouth of everyone who speaks of me, Christ in every eye that sees me, Christ in every ear that hears me."

All the promises of our almighty Father can be encapsulated in the name prescribed for the Lord Jesus at His birth—Emmanuel, God with us. Jesus Christ is the embodiment of all His grace, the fulfillment of all His promises, the satisfaction of all our needs.

The reliability of God's promises to us is found in the presence of Christ among us. When He is near, we have all we need.

Peculiar People

The LORD hath chosen thee to be a peculiar people.
Deuteronomy 14:2 KJV

When the older translations talk about us being "peculiar" people, they mean we're to be different from everyone else on earth, caring little for the things of the world and living instead for Jesus alone. That sometimes makes us seem peculiar—and some Christians really are.

The nineteenth-century backwoods evangelist Bob Sheffey is a good example. He was known for the unique nature of his prayers, which were often answered in astonishing ways. On one occasion, encountering moonshiners in the mountains, "Uncle Bob" dismounted, knelt, and offered a long prayer for God to "smash the still into smithereens." He rose, smoothed his trousers, and continued his journey. A heavy tree fell on the still, wrecking it. The owner rebuilt it, and Sheffey prayed again. This time a flash flood did the job. Sheffey's unorthodox prayers and sermons made him seem peculiar, but they ushered many mountaineers into the kingdom of God.

While we don't want to be peculiar in a negative sense, we are to be separate from the world, different, living for Christ alone. Is your Christianity enough to make you peculiar?

Make the Connection

For since the creation of the world His invisible attributes are clearly seen . . . even His eternal power and Godhead.
Romans 1:20

In a seminary missions class, Herbert Jackson told about a car he was given as a new missionary. Because the car would not start without a push, for two years he made a habit of always parking on a hill—or just leaving the car running. When he left that mission assignment, he passed the car on to his replacement. Curious about the starting problem, the new missionary raised the hood, twisted a wire, turned the key, and the car roared to life!

Failing to take advantage of a car's power for two years is bad enough, but not nearly as bad as living a lifetime without God's power. Look at the evidences of God's power all around us. From the countless galaxies in the universe to the tiniest atoms of which they are made, from the marvelous complexity of the human body to the stunning simplicity of a one-cell bacterium, from the grandeur of the Himalayas to the mysteries of the ocean floor—God's power is clearly seen wherever we look. Are you connected to God as your power source, or do you need a push just to get started every day?

Don't let a loose connection with God leave you powerless in this life.

SAVING VERSUS SPENDING

Wealth gained by dishonesty will be diminished, but he who gathers by labor will increase.
PROVERBS 13:11

Albert Einstein believed the rule of seventy-two (the compounding of interest) was a more important discovery than his theory of relativity. Here's the rule: divide seventy-two by the interest rate of your savings to discover the number of years in which your savings will double. For instance, one thousand dollars saved at 6 percent interest becomes two thousand dollars in twelve years. No wonder compound interest is called the eighth wonder of the world!

But credit card issuers also know the rule of seventy-two. If you make a one thousand dollar purchase on a credit card at 18 percent interest and don't pay it off, that balance becomes two thousand in four years (72 ÷ 18 = 4). Instead of earning you money, your one thousand dollars is earning big bucks for the credit card company.

Saving versus spending is a daily battle in a wealthy and materialistic economy. But God's economy is designed to repay savings. Save and sow a single tomato seed, and you'll get thousands in return—it's only a matter of time. And it's the same with money. Take time today to evaluate your savings practices. Remember: a penny saved is (another) penny earned!

The very day we think we can't afford to save is the day we can't afford not to!

DEFENDING THE CHILDREN

And give my son Solomon a loyal heart to keep Your commandments and Your testimonies and Your statutes.
1 CHRONICLES 29:19

Irene Park is a committed Christian with a tragic background: she was a high witch in the state of Florida, seducing boys and girls into abusive occult activities. She has stated that the only children she could never reach were those who had Christian parents who protected their children by pleading the blood of Christ over them in prayer.

Today, occultism has made its way directly into the public school systems of our land under the guise of the New Age movement. Well-meaning parents provide children every kind of protection possible—cell phones, pagers, nannies, cars—but too often fail to provide the most powerful defense of all: prayer in the name and through the blood of Jesus. Technology will never overcome Satan like the blood of Jesus can (Revelation 12:11). As you pray for your own children this week, pray for their teachers, schools, and classmates as well. The devil will take a foothold wherever he can.

What a tragedy to think of a single child walking through today's world without the protection of praying parents.

Home Run

One's life does not consist in the abundance of the things he possesses.
Luke 12:15

In a *Sports Illustrated* interview, baseball hero Mickey Mantle once described his long battle with alcohol and his heartbreaking problems with his family. The interviewer then asked, "So how are things going with you today, Mickey?"

"Better," was the reply. "I haven't had a drink in eight months. I'm starting to get my life back together, but I just feel like there's something missing."

Here was a living legend who had played 2,401 games for the New York Yankees from 1951 to 1968, hit a record eighteen homers in twelve World Series, and had entered baseball's Hall of Fame in 1974. But he felt empty inside, for the accumulation of wealth, fame, and accomplishment didn't satisfy.

Is something missing in your life?

Near the end of his life, Mickey Mantle found what he had always been looking for—Jesus Christ. Another former baseball player, Bobby Richardson, led him to Christ. At Mantle's funeral, Richardson told of helping Mantle receive the Lord Jesus as his personal Savior. "I am trusting Christ's death for me to take me to heaven," Mickey Mantle said on his deathbed.

Only in Jesus Christ can we find our true identity. He alone gives us a fulfilled, abundant life.

INVESTOR OR TRADER?

On the first day of the week let each one of you lay something aside, storing up as he may prosper.
1 CORINTHIANS 16:2

In the volatile world of commodity futures trading, investors rely on a critical document called the Commitment of Traders Report. This document reveals what large commercial corporations are buying (for example, how much wheat General Mills is securing for its cereal production), which gives smaller investors an indication of a particular market's direction.

Once a huge corporation makes a commitment to buy a commodity like wheat, cotton, or lumber, its action sets a course for the rest of the market. An investment is a long-term proposition that requires careful consideration. And with millions of dollars at stake, companies make such decisions for the long-term only.

If a "Commitment of Christians Report" were issued on your life, what long-term investment decisions would it reveal? Would it show investments of time, talent, and treasure for the kingdom of God? Can others look at your life and get direction for their own?

The church needs long-term investors with commitment, not day-traders who are in the market and then out. God rewards patient commitment in every realm of life.

Imperfect Saints

Lord, I believe; help my unbelief!
Mark 9:24

None of the "heroes of the faith" described in Hebrews 11 was perfect. They all had lapses in their faith. Take Abraham. When a famine struck Canaan, he rushed to Egypt, where he became so fearful he lied about his wife (Genesis 12:10–20). How did Abraham recover? In Genesis 13:1–4, he returned to his altar at Bethel, "and there Abram called on the name of the LORD."

When we realize our faith is faltering, we need to go back to our Bethel, to our place of commitment, and call on the name of our Lord.

The Christian statesman George Müller was a spiritual giant, but this is what he once said about his faith:

"My faith is the same faith which is found in every believer. It has been increased little by little for the last 26 years. Many times when I could have gone insane from worry, I was at peace because my soul believed the truth of God's promises. God's word, together with the whole character of God, as He has revealed Himself, settles all questions. His unchangeable love and His infinite wisdom calmed me. I knew, 'God is able and willing to deliver me.' It is written, 'He who did not spare His own Son, but delivered Him up for us all, how shall He not with Him also freely give us all things?' [Romans 8:32]."

THE BIGGEST LIE

Get behind Me, Satan!
LUKE 4:8

A store manager heard his clerk tell a customer, "No, ma'am, we haven't had any for a while, and it doesn't look as if we'll be getting any soon." Horrified, the manager came running over to the customer and said, "Of course we'll have some soon. We placed an order last week." Then the manager drew the clerk aside. "Never," he snarled, "never say we're out of anything—say we've got it on order and it's coming. Now what was it she wanted?" The clerk replied, "Rain."

As absurd as it is to order rain for a customer, it is equally absurd to believe Satan's lies compared to God's truth. Satan wants us to believe that there is a sin that can separate us from God. But in John 8:44, Jesus reminds us, "He [Satan] is a liar and the father of lies" (NIV).

Satan used lies to trick Eve and to tempt Jesus, and today he tests our wills with his lies. But we can trust God. When Christ was being tempted, He fought back by quoting scripture. Today, we have the power to ignore Satan's ploys by focusing on God's Word and prayer.

Don't forget that Jesus is the only way, the truth, and the life.

A TIME FOR CELEBRATING

. . . absent from the body . . . present with the Lord.
2 CORINTHIANS 5:8

When Christian author and speaker Dr. Bob Hill was seventy-one, his mother passed away. She was nearly ninety-four. Family and friends gathered in St. Louis for the memorial service, and Bob rose to open the funeral. "Friends," he said with a smile, "this is not a time for grieving but a time for celebration." At that moment, Bob suffered a massive brain hemorrhage and slumped to the floor. As his wife and children rushed to the platform and gathered around him, he slipped into glory.

Bob had written sixty books and had preached hundreds of times, but his last words were perhaps his most memorable. He had intended for them to be about his mother, but they became instead a comfort to those he himself left behind.

While it's necessary and normal for us to grieve, we also sense a celebration going on in heaven when a loved one falls asleep in Jesus, and we sorrow not as those who have no hope (1 Thessalonians 4:13). But such an occasion also causes us to revisit our own lives and reexamine our walk with the Lord.

Are we really living a life worth living? Are we doing those things that when we stand before the Lord, we'll wish we had been doing?

HARMONY

Finally, all of you, live in harmony with one another; be sympathetic, love as brothers, be compassionate and humble.
1 PETER 3:8 NIV

A fifth-grade music teacher asked her class to sing "Do Re Mi," a song about the musical scale that was made popular in the movie *The Sound of Music.* The children did so in unison, all singing the same notes as they worked their way up the scale. Then the teacher asked half the class to sing the song again while she led the remaining students in singing up the C-major scale, holding each note until it was time to go on to the next. In that way, she taught the class two-part harmony.

A lot of us need to learn the difference between unison and harmony. The Bible doesn't tell us to live our lives in unison. Your friends, family, and fellow believers all have different personalities, backgrounds, and opinions. We have different levels of spiritual maturity, different strengths and weaknesses, and different gifts. We aren't all going to agree about everything.

Instead of being argumentative, learn the secret of harmony. Respect the opinions and personalities of those the Lord has placed in your life, and don't always expect to have your own way or have the last word. Live in harmony with one another.

TRUE SPIRITUALITY

God is Spirit, and those who worship Him must worship in spirit and truth.
JOHN 4:24

Congressman J. C. Watts, Jr. (Republican, Oklahoma) made the statement famous in his speech at the 1996 Republican Convention, while one of the earliest references to it comes from the nineteenth-century evangelist, D. L. Moody. Since Moody's day, and Congressman Watts's day, and up to the present day, this statement continues to ring true: "Character is what you are when no one is looking."

The issue, of course, is double-mindedness. Are we really who we say we are? If so, what is the essence of a Christian—that is, the true nature and character of a follower of Jesus Christ? One of the surest ways to discover the essence of true spirituality is to pull back the curtain on heaven and see what occupies its residents. Since we leave everything else behind when we enter heaven, perhaps whatever we take with us is close to the definition of true spirituality.

The Book of Revelation suggests that one thing dominates heaven: worship (Revelation 4:8, 11; 5:9–10, 13–14; 7:11–12; 11:15–18; 15:3–4; 19:1–8). When we are stripped of all we pretend to be, worship is what will endure for eternity.

For the Christian, worship is what we should do even when no one sees us except God.

Bearing and Sharing Fruit

Therefore by their fruits you will know them.
Matthew 7:20

You drive up to a local roadside produce market with your heart set on buying a load of fresh summer vegetables. You see homegrown tomatoes, squash, cucumbers, and several varieties of peppers—everything you need and more. Just as you start to select your items, the farmer who owns the stand says, "Sorry, ma'am; this produce isn't for sale. I just like to grow it and enjoy looking at it until it rots. Then I throw it away."

Huh? You likely haven't encountered such an absurd situation, and probably never will. Farmers and consumers know that produce is for consuming. Sure, it's beautiful to look at, but its God-ordained purpose is to bring nutrition and health to people. Fruit that isn't consumed is no better than fruit that was never grown.

Similarly, if Christians aren't manifesting fruit in their lives that benefit other people, something's wrong. The fruit of the Spirit, as well as the good works we were made to walk in (Ephesians 2:10), are not for analyzing, discussing, and admiring. They're for sharing with others! Not to bear and share fruit in the Christian life is to keep others from being blessed as God intended.

Bearing fruit and sharing fruit are two sides of the same spiritual coin.

CHANGE YOUR WORLD

These who have turned the world upside down have come here too.
ACTS 17:6

Quick—name five Christians who literally changed the world by their presence (or, as young people might say, five Christians who "rocked their world"). Think about Martin Luther and the Reformation, John Wesley and holiness, William Wilberforce and slavery, C. S. Lewis and apologetics, and Billy Graham and evangelism. None of these men set out to change the world; they set out to obey God one step at a time.

That could also be said of the man who, besides Jesus Christ, is the greatest world-changer in history—the apostle Paul. Ironically, Paul set out to keep his world from being changed. He was content with being a Pharisee—keeping the Law and making sure others did too. He didn't like the changes the itinerant preacher Jesus of Nazareth was proposing. But when confronted by Jesus in all His glory, Paul's world was changed—and the whole world was changed as well.

What does it take to impact your part of the world, or the whole world, for Christ? If we use Paul as an example, we would have to say unreserved obedience. Jesus told Paul to take the gospel to the Gentile world, and that's exactly what he did.

What has God directed you to do? Remember: your world has to change before you can change the world.

YE OF MUCH FAITH

But Peter and the other apostles answered and said: "We ought to obey God rather than men."
ACTS 5:29

The seventeenth-century Scottish pastor and theologian Samuel Rutherford wrote an important book in Christian history: *Lex, Rex, or The Law and the Prince: A Dispute for the Just Prerogative of King and People.* In this book, he argued that the laws of man can never supercede the laws of God; any just human law will be consistent with God's law.

It took faith for Rutherford to write that book, since he had already spent two years in a Scottish prison for his nonconformist views. He would have found a cellmate in the apostle Peter, who also spent time in a Jewish jail in Jerusalem for advocating Rutherford-like views. Peter, remember, had been "O ye of little faith" (Matthew 6:30 KJV) just before Jesus' crucifixion, unwilling to even be named as a follower of Jesus. But the coming of the Holy Spirit changed him completely. He was full of faith and the rest of the fruit of the Spirit as well. When told to stop preaching, Peter said, "Not so fast—we have a higher command than yours to obey."

When was the last time your faith brought you into conflict with society's values, norms, or laws? Were you "of little faith" or "of much faith"?

It takes faith to obey—and faith to trust God with the outcome.

April

Father Knows Best

For this child I prayed. . . . I also have lent him to the LORD; as long as he lives he shall be lent to the LORD.
1 Samuel 1:27–28

Carman, the well-known Christian performer, credits his parents with dedicating him to Christ as a child. "My parents held me up in a Bible study and dedicated my life to the Lord so that, whatever happened, my life would be used for the service of God," he writes. "I guess that commitment really stuck because the presence of Jesus haunted me until I finally succumbed [to Christ] when I was twenty years old."

When we dedicate our children to God, we're saying, "Lord, this is the child You have loaned me, and I understand he belongs to You. I'll do everything I can as a mother (or father) to see that he grows up to know, love, and serve You." When you do that, you're giving your child back to the Lord.

What if God wants him to be a missionary in a faraway land? What if He wants your child to do something difficult? God's plan is always best—best for your child and best for you. You can trust your child to Him, for the Father knows best.

Faith Over Reason

But without faith it is impossible to please Him, for he who comes to God must believe that He is, and that He is a rewarder of those who diligently seek Him.
Hebrews 11:6

Author Marshall Shelley suffered the deaths of two of his children—and grew in faith. As a child reading novels, he learned not to be confused by the introduction of many different characters, events, and subplots introduced in early chapters. He learned that, if the author was skilled, all the disparate parts would come together by the end of the book. Thus, he said about his life, "I choose to trust that before the book closes, the Author will make things clear."

Who can understand the death of one child, much less two? How far can human reasoning go in explaining the facts, much less in healing the hurting heart? Because we possess strong minds, as those created in the image of God, our natural tendency is to seek solutions first in reason. But reason is not all the mind is good for. The spiritually minded have "the mind of Christ," which is first and foremost a mind of faith (1 Corinthians 2:16). Our challenge in the spiritual life is to be faithful first and reasonable second.

The Author of the story of your life has a plot in progress that will leave no question unanswered.

Casting Out Fear

God has not given us a spirit of fear, but of . . . a sound mind.
2 Timothy 1:7

Missionary Isobel Kuhn found herself imperiled when the Communists overran China. Taking her young son, Danny, she escaped on foot across the snow-covered Pienma Pass, arriving in Myitkyina in Burma. There she was stranded at world's end with no money and no way to get home. "I cannot tell you the dismay and alarm that filled me," she later wrote.

But she made two decisions. "The first thing is to cast out fear," she said. "The only fear a Christian should entertain is the fear of sin. All other fears are from Satan sent to confuse and weaken us. How often the Lord reiterated to His disciples, 'Be not afraid!'" So Isobel prayerfully trusted God and rejected panic. Second, she sought light for the next step, and she eventually arrived home safely.

Anxiety disorders are at an all-time high in America. How prone we are to panic in a crisis! Fear comes so powerfully and naturally.

Yet the Bible tells us, as God's children, to fret not (Psalm 37:1), faint not (Deuteronomy 20:3), and fear not (Isaiah 41:10). With God's strength, we can learn to handle crises with sound counsel and calm faith.

Perhaps you're in a difficult spot today. By His grace, cast out fear and seek light for the next step.

EQUIPPED FOR SUCCESS

You have made known to me the ways of life; You will make me full of joy in Your presence.
ACTS 2:28

Former U.S. senator Mark Hatfield tells of touring Calcutta with Mother Teresa and visiting the so-called House of Dying, where sick children are cared for in their last days, and the dispensary, where the poor line up by the hundreds to receive medical attention. Watching Mother Teresa minister to these people, feeding and nursing those left by others to die, Hatfield was overwhelmed by the sheer magnitude of the suffering she and her co-workers faced daily. "How can you bear the load without being crushed by it?" he asked. Mother Teresa replied, "My dear Senator, I am not called to be successful, I am called to be faithful."

God has given us the tools to succeed. First Samuel 18:14 says, "In everything he did he had great success, because the LORD was with him" (NIV). When we are faced with overwhelming or seemingly impossible situations, it is our duty to remain faithful and to leave the definition of success to God.

How do you define success? Does it line up with the will of God? Meditate on these questions as you go through your day.

Are You a Learner?

The disciples were first called Christians in Antioch.
Acts 11:26

We're prone to think of disciples as turbocharged Christians, but originally the terms *disciple* and *Christian* were synonymous. Differentiating between the two has had the effect of watering down the original demands of following Christ.

Dallas Willard puts it this way: "The word *disciple* occurs 269 times in the New Testament. *Christian* is found three times, and was first introduced to refer precisely to the disciples. The disciple of Jesus is not the deluxe or heavy-duty model of the Christian—especially padded, textured, streamlined, and empowered for the fast lane of the straight and narrow way. He stands on the pages of the New Testament as the first level of basic transportation in the Kingdom of God."

Modern Christians don't often think of using the term *disciple* to describe themselves, but Jesus never put the terms of discipleship in small print. He's not content for us to be distant followers, and He will not rest until we learn to take His yoke upon us and learn from Him (Matthew 11:29).

The word *disciple* means learner, and it refers to someone who is committed to learning to live the Christ-life in conscious, daily obedience. Is that you?

The Knowledge of Love

Knowledge puffs up, but love edifies.
1 Corinthians 8:1

Dr. Albert Schweitzer earned doctorates in philosophy and medicine and received a half-dozen additional honorary doctorates in medicine, theology, and music. He was an authority on Bach and won the Nobel Peace Prize in 1952. Yet despite his brilliance and acclaim, he is best known as a humble doctor who labored for decades in the equatorial jungles of Africa, bringing health and hope to the spiritually and physically needy.

When Albert Schweitzer dispensed medicine or performed surgery on a hurting African man or woman, they did not know how many languages Dr. Schweitzer could read and speak or how many academic degrees he possessed. They only knew him as the kind and gentle doctor who seemed to have a reverence for all of God's creation, whose words to them were comforting and encouraging.

In many ways, Albert Schweitzer was like the apostle Paul, who said we amount to nothing if our great knowledge is not couched in love (1 Corinthians 13:2). We can become more like Paul, who himself was like Jesus, when people discover first how much we care. Only then will they care how much we know.

People will always have a greater appreciation for your head once they appreciate your heart.

Student of the Scriptures

All Scripture is God-breathed and is useful for teaching, rebuking, correcting and training in righteousness, so that the man of God may be thoroughly equipped for every good work.
2 Timothy 3:16–17 NIV

When their son left for his freshman year at Duke University, his parents gave him a Bible, assuring him it would be a great help. Later, as he began sending them letters asking for money, they would write back telling him to read his Bible, citing chapter and verse. He would reply that he was reading the Bible, but he still needed money. When he came home for a semester break, his parents told him they knew he had not been reading his Bible. How? They had tucked ten and twenty dollar bills by the verses they had cited in their letters.

The rewards of Bible study are life-changing—even if there is no money between the pages. It is vital to spend time in God's Word because it is the guide to help you prosper in everything you do. Create new ways to revitalize your walk with the Lord—invest in new study materials, find an accountability partner, or rearrange your schedule to include a different environment in which to meet with God.

When you commit to reaching out to God, He has already committed to meeting you where you are.

The Velvet Ant

Satan . . . transforms himself into an angel of light.
2 Corinthians 11:14

There's a strange little insect called the velvet ant—attractive, as ants go—garbed in a thick coat of tiny hairs that feel smooth and velvety. But it's all a disguise. This tiny creature isn't an ant at all, but a wingless wasp with a nasty sting. After injecting its victims with venom, it lays its eggs in their incapacitated bodies.

How like Satan! He's a venomous impostor who wants to implant his warped ideas into the dulled hearts of his victims. One of his cleverest strategies is to make evil seem desirable. Just consider today's movies. Sexual sin of every type is glamorized and glorified. Profanity appears as righteous indignation. Fame captivates. Fortune beguiles. Violence titillates.

Or take modern faith fads. Satan doesn't mind if we become religious, just so long as it remains politically incorrect to proclaim Jesus Christ as the only name under heaven whereby we must be saved.

Paul told the Corinthians, "I fear, lest somehow, as the serpent deceived Eve by his craftiness, so your minds may be corrupted from the simplicity that is in Christ" (2 Corinthians 11:3).

Be on guard! Don't fall for Satan's frauds.

SPOUSES WHO NEVER GIVE IN

Tribulation produces perseverance; and perseverance, character; and character hope.
ROMANS 5:3–4

On October 29, 1941, when England was being mercilessly attacked by German rockets and planes, Winston Churchill visited his alma mater. A verse honoring him had been added to one of the school songs; it spoke of "darker days." Churchill asked that it be changed to "sterner days." The days of the war were stern but not dark, he said. Churchill was committed to seeing the light of England's glory shine yet again.

Many marriages today are under attack by enemies such as discouragement, infidelity, unforgiveness, and bitterness. Spouses find themselves wandering through dark days, ready to declare defeat. What they need is a Churchill-like, biblical kind of commitment and perseverance. Marriages can go through stern days without entering dark nights if the partners enter their marriage committed to defeating any enemy that comes against them. When your marriage encounters a stern enemy, recommit yourself to your partner—and never give up.

Don't be committed to commitment. Be committed to the partner you told "til death do us part."

The Right to Sacrifice

All things are lawful for me, but not all things are helpful.
1 Corinthians 10:23

One of the biggest issues facing lawmakers today is whether there should be limits on damages awarded in lawsuits where injury has occurred. Opponents of tort reform say it's impossible to place a limitation of value on personal injury. Proponents say the lack of limits is driving doctors out of business, since they can't afford the premiums on malpractice insurance.

Whose rights are more important? A citizen's right not to be permanently injured? A doctor's right not to be driven out of business? A lawyer's right to profit? Or a jury's right to decide what's "right"? The pursuit of rights has made America the most litigious society in the world. What ever happened to people giving up their rights for a greater good?

The apostle Paul said everything is "lawful," but not everything is helpful. For instance, Paul had the right to be paid by those he served. But he gave up that right, and others, for the sake of spreading the gospel without criticism from others. Look at your rights and see if limiting them would give you a greater voice with those you seek to serve.

A right is only a right until we discover it makes us wrong.

Impact

Follow Me.
Mark 1:17

John Wesley once said, "If I had three hundred men who feared nothing but God, hated nothing but sin, and determined to know nothing among men but Christ and Him crucified, I would set the world on fire."

Missionary Jim Elliot said, "He is no fool who gives what he cannot keep to gain what he cannot lose."

Jonathan Edwards, whose ministry sparked the Great Awakening, made this his life's motto: "Resolved: To follow God with all my heart. Resolved also: Whether others do or not, I will."

John Eliot, early missionary to the American Indians, said, "I can do little; yet I am resolved through the grace of Christ, I will never give over the work, so long as I have legs to go."

C. T. Studd, one of England's greatest athletes, shocked the world when he gave up fame and fortune to be a missionary to China. "If Jesus Christ be God and died for me, then no sacrifice can be too great for me to make for Him," he explained.

What would be the impact of your life if you were totally yielded to God?

SHORT-TERM MISSIONS TRIPS

So Jesus said to them again, "Peace to you! As the Father has sent Me, I also send you."
JOHN 20:21

William Carey is often called the father of modern missions. The number of his accomplishments in India was almost equaled by the number of obstacles he overcame to get there. He was told by a group of English ministers, "If God wants to save the heathen, young man, He will do it without your help or ours."

When he developed a burden for the lost in India, William Carey was not a career missionary. He was a young Englishman in poor health with a pregnant wife and small children underfoot. That is, he was a lot like the average Christian today—just trying to make ends meet and keep life together. But he also had something else, a burning question he could not escape: "Who will reach the lost if I don't go?" He ultimately became a career missionary, but he started by saying yes to God.

From high schoolers to retirees, Christians today are discovering the blessing of sharing the gospel and doing good works in other lands. Take a short-term missions trip, and see how God can change your life.

A career missionary is nothing more than a short-term missionary who keeps saying yes to God.

The Heart of Worship

My heart greatly rejoices, and with my song I will praise Him.
Psalm 28:7

In *Meditations from a Prison Cell*, F. Olin Stockwell, one of the last missionaries to leave Communist China, wrote about his imprisonment at a center where the Communist leaders were indoctrinating young people in Marxist ideology. Every afternoon and evening, the leaders would teach the young people and then set the teachings to music. China was singing herself into the Communist worldview, Stockwell wrote.

Everyone has had the experience of hearing a song on the radio or a hymn from childhood and being able to sing along "by heart." While it's our mind that remembers, we say "by heart" because of the emotional "hooks" these songs set in us. And it is from an emotional level—the level of the heart—that God wants us to worship Him as well as from the mind.

Some of the most heartfelt and theologically oriented worship in the Bible is found in the Psalms, the hymnbook of Israel. With the abundance of edifying Christian music available today in varying audio formats, there is no reason for the home and heart of every Christian not to be filled with worshipful songs.

Since God knows you "by heart," make sure yours is a heart of rejoicing.

WHY?

Peace I leave with you, My peace I give to you; not as the world gives do I give to you. Let not your heart be troubled, neither let it be afraid.

JOHN 14:27

There are six interrogative words commonly used in discourse between people: *Who? What? When? Where? Why?* and *How?* Of these six, one is used more frequently than the others in times of personal anguish: *Why?* It is human nature to want to know why things happen the way they do. And for Christians, *Why*? means, "Why did God allow it?"

The disciples of Jesus surely asked *Why*? questions more than once in their relationship with Jesus. But at no time did they wonder why more seriously than when their lives were in peril on the Sea of Galilee. A huge storm had come up while they and Jesus were crossing the water. While they feared for their lives, Jesus napped calmly in the back of the boat. They wondered, "Why doesn't Jesus do something?" When Jesus finally calmed the storm, He had a *Why*? question for them: why did they let their faith be overcome by fear (Mark 4:40)?

If you've been asking God *Why?* questions lately and receiving no answers, stay focused by faith on Jesus. He will still the storm at the right time.

It's okay to ask God why. It's even better to wait for the answer in faith instead of fear.

APRIL 15

TRUSTING IN GOD FOR FRIENDS

There is a friend who sticks closer than a brother.
PROVERBS 18:24

Two young men, best friends since childhood, enlisted together in World War I. Their outfit came under a withering attack, and one of the men was mortally wounded. His friend crawled out amid the fire to rescue him and was mortally wounded himself. When he made it back to the trenches with the body of his friend, the rescuer was told he had wasted his life to reach a dead man. "It was worth it," he said. "The last thing my friend said before he died was, 'I knew you'd come, Jim.'"

These two men had the kind of friendship that Proverbs speaks about and that Jesus made reference to: "Greater love has no one than this, than to lay down one's life for his friends" (John 15:13). Those closest to God, like Abraham and the disciples of Jesus, were referred to as "friends" (James 2:23; John 15:15). In both cases, friendship meant being told the very plans and purposes of God. And in both cases, these friends repaid God's friendship with the highest human value: loving loyalty. Gaining loyal friends takes time, but you can start today by being a loyal friend yourself.

How good a friend are you? Think of a way this week to confirm your loyalty to those you value most.

The Surprise Gift

[They] were astonished . . . because the gift of the Holy Spirit had been poured out on the Gentiles also.
Acts 10:45

C. S. Lewis's personal story in *Surprised by Joy* chronicles his journey to faith in Christ. The title reflects what he discovered: he was surprised by the joy he experienced once he received the free gift of salvation. He hadn't realized that joy would come as a result of faith.

The Bible is filled with examples of how God surprised people. The apostle Peter was certainly surprised when he learned it was God's intention to offer salvation through the gift of the Holy Spirit to Gentiles as well as Jews (Acts 10). And every Christian who truly understands the mercy and grace of God must stand amazed at the forgiveness God offers in Christ.

That we are accepted into, instead of banished from, God's presence is perhaps His biggest surprise ever. Knowing how good surprises feel, have you surprised anyone lately with a gift of grace, appreciation, encouragement, forgiveness? Give someone today the pleasure of being surprised by your unexpected gift of love.

The better people know our faults, the more meaningful are the surprise gifts we receive from them.

The Persistent Mercy of God

Through the LORD's mercies we are not consumed, because His compassions fail not. They are new every morning.
Lamentations 3:22–23

Francis Thompson was a nineteenth-century English poet who failed at early ventures and ended up destitute until taken in by a benefactor who was impressed with his poetry. "The Hound of Heaven" is his most famous work, telling of God's persistent pursuit of him until finally Thompson surrenders to His love.

"Ah, fondest, blindest, weakest, I am He Whom thou seekest," says the Hound of Heaven to the object of His pursuit. The persistent mercy of God is what finally captured the poet's heart.

God's relentless grace is also what saved Lot, the nephew of Abraham, in the wicked city of Sodom. Before God judged the city, He gave Lot repeated opportunities to escape. Lot, his wife, and two daughters were finally dragged—kicking and screaming, as it were—from the city of sin. God's mercy was greater than Lot's own spiritual reasonableness, as is often the case with us as well.

Only heaven will tell how many times God has saved us from ourselves by working harder at our salvation and deliverance than we did. Have you thanked God recently for His persistent mercy?

Fortunately, our resistance is not as great as God's persistence.

Every Day

Every day of my life was recorded in your book. Every moment was laid out before a single day had passed.
Psalm 139:16 NLT

While Elvis Presley was filming *Roustabout*, he met Larry Geller, a hairdresser with whom he developed a close friendship. The two discussed spiritual issues and Eastern religions. "What you're talking about," Elvis told Geller, "is what I secretly think about all the time." While discussing Elvis's purpose in life, the singer admitted he felt "chosen" but didn't know why. "Why was I plucked out of all of the millions of millions of lives to be Elvis?" he asked. We don't know if he ever found the answer.

The Bible teaches that God has a life purpose for us, and we discover it only through our relationship with Christ. He has something for us to do, something special for us to do today. If God were finished with us, He'd take us immediately to heaven. But He saved us, not just to take us to heaven but to use us on earth. Every day we should be looking into His face, saying, "Lord, what do You want me to do? How can I advance Your work today? How can I serve You now?"

Give this day to the Lord, and ask for His will to be done in your life. Use every moment to fulfill His great purpose for you.

ONLY ONE MISSIONARY

I thank Christ Jesus our Lord who has enabled me.
1 TIMOTHY 1:12

Because of her father's drinking problem, eleven-year-old Mary Slessor was putting in twelve-hour shifts in the mills, helping her family pay their bills. She found she could prop books on her loom while working. As she read about the land of Calabar (modern Nigeria), Mary grew convinced she should go there as a missionary. In 1876, she sailed for West Africa aboard the SS *Ethiopia*, which, ironically, was loaded with hundreds of barrels of whiskey. Remembering how alcohol had hurt her family, she said, "Scores of barrels of whiskey, and only one missionary."

But what a missionary! Mary was a combination circuit preacher, village teacher, nurse, nanny, and negotiator who single-handedly transformed three pagan areas by preaching the gospel. She diverted tribal wars and rescued women and children by the hundreds. For forty years, she labored as God enabled her.

If you feel like you're the only Christian at your school, office, or factory, rejoice! Don't underestimate how God can use you. One plus God is a majority in any setting.

It Takes an Expert to Tell

[The Bereans] . . . searched the Scriptures daily to find out whether these things were so.
Acts 17:11

Lots of people who want to adorn themselves with diamonds use the classic counterfeit—cubic zirconium. While it's pretty easy to tell the imitations from real diamonds, scientists have devised a way to actually create real diamonds in the laboratory. These lab creations are so good that gemologists have a hard time distinguishing manufactured diamonds from mined ones.

To tell the difference, an expert's checklist is applied: color, intensity, weight, brilliance, and hardness. Without it, an imposter could pass off a two-day-old diamond for one that took thousands of years to develop. The same is true with spiritual truth. If Christians don't know their Bibles, spiritual imposters can pass off all manner of lies as truth. It's not enough for someone to do miracles in Jesus' name. Even Satan can disguise himself as an angel of light. We have to own, use, and study our Bibles so that we can know the truth. We have to have the desire of an expert—a desire not to be deceived.

If study and care are taken in determining the quality of a precious stone, how much more should the same effort be applied to the precious Word of God?

It's All His

He who is faithful in what is least is faithful also in much.
Luke 16:10–15

A few years ago, the *Wall Street Journal* changed its format, adding a section devoted to personal money and life management, entitled "Personal Journal." The paper realized that many of the leaders of America's top companies are skillfully handling their companies, but their personal lives are in turmoil.

The word *manage* comes from the Latin word *manus*, meaning hand. It has to do with handling things. For the Christian, that means handling God's things. The concept of stewardship has to do with wise management of our lives—recognizing we don't own anything. God owns it all; we simply manage it on His behalf.

Tithing, for example, is my acknowledgment that all my money is His and that I'm managing it well enough to return at least 10 percent into the work of His kingdom. As someone has said, the real question is not, "Should I give God 10 percent of my money?" but "Should I keep 90 percent of His money for myself?"

The earth is the Lord's and the fullness thereof. We are not our own; we are bought with a price (Psalm 24:1; 1 Corinthians 6:19–20). Let's manage wisely what He has entrusted to us, that His work and Word might advance.

THE REFRESHMENT OF GRACE

The words of a wise man's mouth are gracious, but the lips of a fool shall swallow him up.
ECCLESIASTES 10:12

The most unsettling TV commercial in 1999 showed closeups of three individuals bearing noticeable physical injuries and scars. There was no explanation—only a familiar logo at the end and the words, "Just do it." What made the commercial moving was the Joe Cocker song playing throughout in the background: "You are so beautiful ...to me."

Granted, the commercial was for shoes. But there was another message as well: true beauty and grace is not a matter of physical perfection. Some of the most refreshing people to be around are those who have overcome serious limitations in their lives. Their gracious attitude seems to say, "I may not have everything that's possible, but I'm doing everything possible with what I have been given."

There should be no bounds to the graciousness of those who know Christ since God has made all grace abound to us to make us sufficient in all things (2 Corinthians 9:8). Wherever we go as Christians, we should take with us the refreshment of the gospel of grace.

Instead of "Just do it," Christians should "Just dispense it"—the grace of God, that is.

Meeting God Anywhere

Then the king said to me, "What do you request?" So I prayed to the God of heaven.
Nehemiah 2:4

A woman was in the habit of praying while ironing. One day, she was thinking about the different kinds of lines—bus lines, clotheslines, fishing lines, telephone lines. "Why not a prayer line?" she asked herself. So she strung a short rope with names of people she knew needed prayer. Now as she irons, she prays for each person by name. Not surprisingly, she gets regular requests to "hang me on your prayer line."

Prayer is a conversation with God. It doesn't matter where you are or what you are doing; you can meet with Him and pour out your heart in prayer. Most dictionaries define prayer as a reverent petition made to God, a god, or another object of worship. So how do you define prayer in your daily routine? Do you come to God with your petitions, thanksgiving, and praise each morning and evening? While you are driving your car or taking a break at work?

Creating habits with prayer helps you meet with God no matter where you are or how hectic your schedule is.

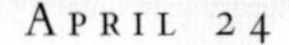

Ecology of the Heart

Keep your heart with all diligence, for out of it spring the issues of life.
Proverbs 4:23

Increasing importance is being placed every year in America on cleaning up our environment—and rightly so. As stewards of God's creation, we have not always done the best job of preserving and protecting His handiwork. But Jesus talked about a different kind of ecosystem that deserves an even higher priority—cultivating the soil of the heart.

Jesus told a parable of a sower, seed, and soil. But as any good gardener will tell you, the effectiveness of the sower and his seed is totally dependent on the condition of the soil. In fact, Jesus said this was a key to understanding all His other parables (Mark 4:13). The parable of the soils says this: when God's Word is sown into heart-soil that is prepared, and that seed springs up and the new life is nurtured, salvation is the result. But if kingdom truth is sown onto hard heart-soil, or if the soil dries up or is rocky, it stands little chance of saving the soul.

The parable of the sower and soils is not just about being saved; it's also about living as saved. Because seeds of God's truth come continually to our hearts, our hearts must be continually kept soft and fertile.

The first order of Christian ecology is the purity of the heart.

READING GOD'S WORD

As newborn babes, desire the pure milk of the word, that you may grow thereby.
1 PETER 2:2

Bible scholar Wilber Smith once wrote, "One single, normal issue of *The Saturday Evening Post* contains as much reading matter as the entire New Testament. Thousands of people read *The Saturday Evening Post* through every week. The number of Christians who read the New Testament through every week, or even one whole book...are so few that we need not talk about it."

When Josiah became king in Jerusalem, he assigned workers to repair the temple. There they discovered a copy of the Law in the ruins. No one had seen it in years! Josiah quickly reasoned that Judah's idolatry was directly tied to the absence of the reading of God's Word. So he gathered all the people of Judah together, personally read to them the Law of God, and led them in a rededication to live according to God's Word (2 Chronicles 34).

What connections can you make between your spiritual life and your consistency in studying God's Word? If you are not consistently in the Bible, it will be impossible for the Bible to be consistently in you.

A Barnyard of Pigs

Always be ready to give a defense to everyone who asks you a reason for the hope that is in you.
1 Peter 3:15

Without Christ, we're left with nothing but despair. William Lane Craig, the brilliant professor, said that a worldview that omits God is tragic. "Mankind is a doomed race in a dying universe," he writes, "Because the human race will eventually cease to exist, it makes no ultimate difference whether it ever did exist. Mankind is thus no more significant than a swarm of mosquitoes or a barnyard of pigs, for their end is all the same. The same blind cosmic process that coughed them up in the first place will eventually swallow them all again."

We're living in a world in which several generations have been taught a philosophy of despair. If evolution is true, we're nothing more than random accidents that emerged from primordial slime. There is no basis for hope. We have no future, no everlasting life.

Look closely and you'll see despair in the eyes of those around you at school or work. But we know that there is no hope apart from God, no joy apart from Christ, and no eternal salvation apart from the gospel.

Today, let hope shine through you that others, seeing it, will ask about it. And then tell them about Christ, the King of the ages.

Pray Everywhere

And [Joseph] was there in the prison. But the LORD was with Joseph and showed him mercy, and He gave him favor in the sight of the keeper of the prison.
Genesis 39:20–21

A famous preacher tells how, when he was a child, his mother paid a neighbor girl to walk the eight blocks to school with him and back each day. He finally convinced his mother to let him walk to school and back alone.

Years later, at a family party, he bragged about his independence as a child, how he had walked to school alone. "Did you think you were alone?" his mother asked. "Those first few years, I walked behind you to and from school. You never saw me, but I was there every day just in case you needed me."

That preacher's mother might have taken a lesson from the experience of Joseph in Egypt. When Joseph was thrown into prison, being falsely accused by Potiphar's wife, the Bible says that God was with him during his two-year imprisonment.

When we find ourselves imprisoned spiritually or emotionally by our circumstances, we need to remember that God is with us. Though it is dark in prison, pray anyway, every day, for God is near you and listening to your prayers. You cannot be in a place where God isn't.

The day you stop believing God is with you is the day you stop believing God.

Rewards for Being Faithful

And your Father who sees in secret will reward you openly.
Matthew 6:4, 6, 18

An eleventh-century German king, Henry III, grew tired of ruling. He applied to a monastery to spend the rest of his life in quiet contemplation. The prior asked if he, a king, could live out a vow of complete obedience. "I will," said the king. "Then you are accepted," replied the monk. "Your first duty is to return to your throne and serve faithfully where God has placed you."

It is easy to grow weary of being a spouse, a parent, an employee, or employer. Some days we just want to quit! One woman who resisted that temptation was Abigail, the wife of Nabal (1 Samuel 25). Abigail was understanding and beautiful; Nabal was harsh and evil. Abigail even saved Nabal from the sword of David because she chose to honor her husband instead of humiliate him. She drew joy and strength from God, not her surroundings. And God rewarded her when Nabal died. David was so impressed with Abigail that he took her for his wife.

Are you tempted to leave it all behind—to throw in the towel? Don't do it. Make God your joy, and wait for His reward.

We aren't faithful to get a reward, but we are rewarded for being faithful.

AN EQUAL-OPPORTUNITY SIN

[Pilate] knew that the chief priests had handed Him over because of envy.
MARK 15:10

One of the largest and most active federal government agencies is the EEOC—the Equal Employment Opportunity Commission. They are responsible for the statement seen nearly everywhere today: ". . . does not discriminate on the basis of race, color, religion, sex, or national origin." The EEOC's goal is to make sure everyone gets treated fairly in the workplace and other public and private venues.

Many people are surprised to find that jealousy is an equal-opportunity sin. People think only the poor, the ungifted, the lower classes, the uneducated, or the common man ever get jealous. After all, of whom or what would "the rich and famous" have to be jealous?

Yet anyone can be jealous of someone who has something he or she wants but doesn't have. In Jesus' day, the Pharisees were jealous of Jesus because He was loved and appreciated by the people. Mark 15:10 says that the Pharisees handed Jesus over to Pilate "because of envy." Anyone who is dissatisfied and discontent is a prime candidate for jealousy and envy.

The strongest defense against the attacks of jealousy is a heart that is grateful for what God has done in your life and for what He is doing in the lives of others.

Rowing Upstream

Put away the foreign gods which are among you, and incline your heart to the LORD.
Joshua 24:23

As John and Debbie canoed down the Arkansas River, they decided to turn around and try rowing upstream for a while. It took about ten minutes for exhaustion to set in, and they gladly reversed course and let themselves be carried by the stream.

The current of our culture is downward, and many people just drift along with the moral flow. Living for Christ is like rowing upstream. The entertainment industry is a persuasive evangelist, churning out nonstop programs and movies designed to convert us to secular thinking.

Take romance and marriage, for example. If a visitor from space watched an evening of television, he'd think premarital sex was the greatest discovery in history. He would see divorce, cohabitation, same-sex marriage, and immodesty portrayed as glamorous and glorious.

Yet the Bible says, "Among you there must not be even a hint of sexual immorality, or of any kind of impurity, or of greed, because these are improper for God's holy people" (Ephesians 5:3 NIV). We can't escape our culture, but we don't have to be shaped by it. We have to paddle against the current, which can be lonely and laborious.

How long can we stay at the oars? The Lord strengthens those who obey Him. Trust Him today for the strength to row against the flow.

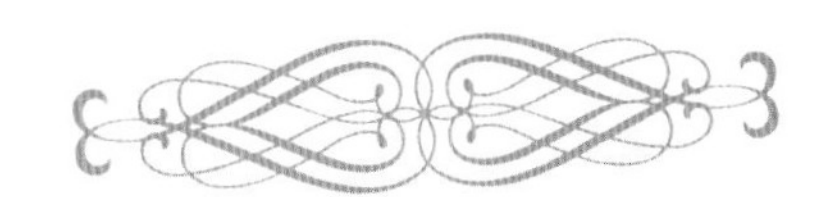

May

MAY 1

CHERISHING GOD'S WORD

How sweet are Your words to my taste, sweeter than honey to my mouth!
PSALM 119:103

In his famous volume *How to Read a Book*, Mortimer Adler notes the one time when everyone reads as they should: when reading a love letter. They read it over and over, between the lines and in the margins, taking into account context, insinuation, and implication. Words, phrases, punctuation, and style—all are important to the person in love. A love letter is the most cherished writing in the world.

Isn't it ironic that the world's greatest love letter has not been more cherished by those to whom it was written? The Bible can be rightly viewed as God's love letter to mankind—a disclosure of His love, a record of His sacrifice for His beloved bride, a promise of His faithfulness and fidelity.

How many of us still have shoeboxes filled with letters and cards from the days of our courtship, still savored after so many years? Our hearts and passions are stirred afresh when we read them, just as they would be if we pored over God's letter to us with equal fervor.

Next time you open your Bible, read it as a love letter from God to you and see what a difference it makes. To give God's words the honor they are due is to cherish them above all others.

SUCCEEDING AT FAILING

Get Mark and bring him with you, for he is useful to me for ministry.
2 TIMOTHY 4:11

One of the most unusual sets of circumstances in the New Testament is that surrounding Mark, the cousin of Barnabas. Paul and Barnabas took young Mark with them on a missionary trip, but he returned home before the end of the trip for reasons not revealed in Scripture. Whatever Mark's reasons, Paul apparently thought they were unjustified since he refused to take Mark along on a subsequent trip (Acts 15:38).

Did Mark fail at being a missionary? Judging from Paul's response, it would appear he did. While the New King James Version says Mark "departed" from Paul and Barnabas, the word probably is closer to "deserted"—a more negative connotation. It's probably reasonable to conclude that Mark did fail at being a missionary.

But did that make him a permanent failure? Apparently not, for the same apostle Paul who was so disappointed in Mark counted him a valuable coworker in ministry later in his life. This is a perfect example of how to succeed at failing: fall, get up, and continue on. The next time you fail, make sure it is a temporary experience, not a permanent label.

Don't get "failing" and "failure" confused. Failing is nothing more than the back door to success.

Law of the Harvest

Do not be deceived, God is not mocked; for whatever a man sows, that he will also reap.
Galatians 6:7

In 1687, Sir Isaac Newton set forth a theory we call the law of gravity. While revised by Einstein and others along the way, the law has remained an immutable principle of nature that governs the universe. Another immutable law, found in both the physical and spiritual realms, was cited by biblical writers centuries ago: the law of the harvest.

The law of the harvest has three parts: no reaping without sowing, reaping is in proportion to sowing; and time separates sowing and reaping. We can understand how the law of the harvest works with money by observing the law of the harvest at work in nature. No farmer expects to reap a harvest without having first sowed his seed, nor does he expect to sow sparingly and reap bountifully. And no farmer expects to reap the day after sowing.

God applies those principles to our money as well: giving precedes receiving; we receive in proportion to our giving; and God chooses when to repay our giving. Unlike farmers, we can apply the law of the harvest anytime, anywhere—even today!

We bring pain on ourselves by violating the law of gravity. Are we doing the same thing spiritually by violating God's law of the harvest?

IT TAKES TWO

As a prisoner for the Lord, then, I urge you to live a life worthy of the calling you have received.
EPHESIANS 4:1 NIV

One story in circulation claims that a mother and son were eager to attend a concert by renowned Polish pianist Ignacy Paderewski. When the house lights dimmed, the mother discovered that the child was missing. As the curtain rose, the mother noticed in horror that her little boy was sitting at the keyboard, innocently picking out "Twinkle, Twinkle Little Star." At that moment, the great piano master made his entrance, quickly moved to the piano, and whispered in the boy's ear, "Don't quit. Keep playing." Leaning over, Paderewski reached down with his left hand and began filling in a bass part. Together, the old master and the young novice transformed a tense situation into a wonderfully creative experience.

Whether this story is true or not, it is a perfect example of the relationship we have with our heavenly Father. What we can accomplish on our own is hardly noteworthy. But with the hand of the Master, our life's work can be beautiful. Next time you set out to accomplish great feats, listen for the voice of the Master, whispering in your ear, "Don't quit. Keep playing." Feel His loving arms around you. Know that His strong hands are there, turning your feeble attempts into true masterpieces.

Remember, God doesn't call the equipped; He equips the called.

A SECOND, DEEPER LOOK

It is good for me that I have been afflicted, that I may learn Your statutes.
PSALM 119:71

Many of Fred Astaire's movies rank as classics of the silver screen. But in 1932, when Astaire was just starting out in Hollywood, he went to a screen test to try out for a part. After the audition, the evaluator wrote, "Can't act. Can't sing. Can dance a little." That memo hung over the actor's fireplace in his Beverly Hills home throughout his successful career as an actor, singer, and dancer.

There is no end to the stories of people who succeeded wildly after failing miserably—often for years. The lessons are usually similar in every case: don't give up, try harder, dig deeper, don't settle for no, and winners never quit.

There's nothing wrong with such advice, but it only addresses one level of our lives. For the Christian, failure can represent an entirely different set of realities: God is at work in me for His own good pleasure (Philippians 2:13); God can take every event and cause it to work for good (Romans 8:28); God is shaping my character to be like Christ (Romans 8:29). If you have failed recently, take a second, deeper look. God is at work to accomplish what only He can.

Every time we fail, we eliminate one more option that is proven not to work.

ANOTHER KIND OF POWER

I can do all things through Christ who strengthens me.
PHILIPPIANS 4:13

In 1967, a teenage girl dove into a lake, having no idea how shallow it was. Crashing into the bottom, she broke her neck and was paralyzed from the shoulders down. For the next several years, she wrestled mightily with the person of God: What kind of God was He? Why had He allowed this to happen? And, most of all, why didn't He use His power to heal her of her disabilities?

Most Christians are familiar with Joni Eareckson Tada's life story. When all of her physical power was taken from her as a teenager, and God's power to heal seemed unavailable, she asked her friends to help her commit suicide. Fortunately, they refused. In time, God revealed an inner, spiritual power through Joni that overshadowed anything she could have accomplished physically. Books, art, music, advocacy for the disabled, films, radio, congressional testimony on cloning and human rights—God has touched more people through Joni in a wheelchair than she ever imagined He could.

Are you in a situation that is not changing for the better? Ask God to release His spiritual power through you. God has more than one kind of power. The kind He sends you is the kind you need.

FAITHFUL PROVIDER

The LORD has heard my cry for mercy; the LORD accepts my prayer.
PSALM 6:9 NIV

A little girl approached her father and asked for a nickel. The father drew out his wallet and offered her a five-dollar bill. But the little girl, not knowing what it was, would not take it. "I don't want that," she said. "I want a nickel."

Are there times when we deal with our heavenly Father as this little girl dealt with her earthly father? Do we sometimes ask for some small favor and refuse His offer of a blessing a hundred times more valuable?

When we come to God with petitions, He promises to answer. But it is not always the answer we want to hear. However, it is the answer that God knows is best for us.

We must believe that God will be a faithful provider, no matter what our circumstances. Psalm 111:5 says, "He provides food for those who fear him; he remembers his covenant forever" (NIV). What an amazing promise: He will never forget about our needs, and He will sometimes bless us beyond our wildest imagination. He will accept our prayers and our cries for mercy. What an awesome God we serve!

JOSEPH THE GENEROUS

And Joseph took the body and wrapped it in a clean linen cloth, and laid it in his own new tomb, which he had hewn out in the rock.
MATTHEW 27:59–60 NASB

Christian novelist Bodie Thoene once worked for Hollywood film star John Wayne as a scriptwriter. Wayne read an article she had written and liked it; a relationship developed, and she began writing for Wayne's production company. Later, when Thoene asked the famous actor why he had been so generous toward her, he answered, "Because somebody did it for me."

Receiving seems to stimulate giving. That was true for a man in the four Gospels, Joseph of Arimathea. He was a prominent member of the Jewish Council in Jerusalem, meaning he was wealthy and well-respected. But like another member of the Council, Nicodemus, Joseph had become a disciple of Jesus, albeit a secret one for fear of retaliation from the Jews.

But when Joseph watched Jesus suffer and die for him, he could remain a secret follower no longer. He went to Pilate and got permission to bury the body of Jesus in his own new tomb. Joseph was transformed by Jesus' generosity toward him. That ought to be true of everyone who claims to be His follower.

Generosity in giving is often a response to gratitude in receiving.

MAY 9

IT TAKES TIME

Give, and it will be given to you: good measure, pressed down, shaken together, and running over will be put into your bosom. For with the same measure that you use, it will be measured back to you.
LUKE 6:38

This is one of the Bible's most powerful verses about giving and has several important lessons for us. First, we get only if we sow. If we sow nothing, we get nothing. Second, we get only what we sow. If we sow corn, we don't get beets. Third, we also get more than we sow. Put one seed in the ground and see how it multiplies at the harvest.

Luke 6:38 also says we get later than we sow. The farmer does not reap the harvest on the day he plants the seed. It takes a while for the plants to mature and produce the harvest.

Some people tithe faithfully for a few weeks or a few months, then wonder why they aren't being financially blessed. "Where's the harvest?" they ask. The harvest comes after the sowing, and we have to be willing to wait for the interval. Ecclesiastes 11:1 says, "Cast your bread upon the waters, for you will find it after many days."

Hebrews 6:10 reminds us that "God is not unjust to forget your work and labor of love which you have shown toward His name." If you are faithful to God, He will provide for you. He has promised.

A BODY OF PRAISE

Now may the God of peace Himself sanctify you completely... spirit, soul, and body.
1 THESSALONIANS 5:23

One of the strangest individuals in early church history was Simon the Stylite. At age thirty-three, he began living atop a pillar in the desert. For thirty-six years, he lived on a platform that gradually reached a height of sixty feet. From there he preached to curiosity seekers who came by the thousands. After his death in AD 459, a monastery and sanctuary were built on the site of the pillar.

Simon the Stylite was an ascetic, a person who pursues spirituality by disavowing the material things of this world. Ascetics especially deny themselves any bodily pleasures—tasty foods, marriage, hygiene—believing that they are temptations to worldliness.

But ascetics miss an important point: the human body shares the same creation blessing as do the soul and spirit. Therefore, your body should be a medium for praise and channel for worship just as your spirit is. In fact, "your body is the temple of the Holy Spirit," Paul says (1 Corinthians 6:19). Your body is that which the Spirit animates to bring glory to God.

An offering of your body to God brings glory to its Creator and Sustainer.

SURVEY SAYS...

He hears the prayer of the righteous.
PROVERBS 15:29

The following statistics come from the Barna Research Group:

- Four out of five Americans believe that "prayer can change what happens in a person's life" (1994).
- Nine out of ten adults agree "there is a God who watches over you and answers your prayers" (1991).
- One out of five adults has a time of extended prayer with members of their household during the course of a typical week.

If someone were to take an inventory of your prayer life, how would you score? Although prayer isn't a competition between believers, it is a sign of constant communication in our relationship with God. When we don't take time to get on our knees, it is often evidence that we have strayed from our walk with Him.

So how do we approach God after being out of fellowship? Micah 6:6 says, "With what shall I come before the LORD, and bow myself before the High God?" We are to come back with praise and thanksgiving on our lips—and He will hear our prayers. It doesn't matter if you have prayed an hour before or a year before; God is waiting to hear from you.

Psalm 3:4 reminds us, "To the LORD I cry aloud, and he answers me from his holy hill" (NIV). Rewrite your survey, and be faithful in prayer.

Everybody Submits to Somebody

Let every soul be subject to the governing authorities. For there is no authority except from God, and the authorities that exist are appointed by God.
Romans 13:1

As mentioned earlier, the Scottish reformer Samuel Rutherford published *Lex, Rex, or The Law and the Prince* in 1644. In this book, he challenged the prevailing notion of the divine right of kings—that whatever the king says is the law. Rutherford reminded rulers that they are not authorities unto themselves, but they are all under God's authority. God is the ultimate source of all authority in this world.

No matter how much authority we think we have in any setting, we quickly discover there is someone with more. But no one's authority is ultimate, for all authorities are ultimately subject to God. From parents to potentates, the apostle Paul reminds us that God establishes all authorities on earth. Unless an authority requires us to break a law of God, we should make submission and honor a part of our lives (Acts 5:29).

Who are the authorities in your life? If there are some you find it difficult to submit to, make it a practice to pray diligently for them. It's hard to resist someone you're praying for.

Submission to authorities shows we understand the nature of authority.

THE RICHES OF GRACE

In Him we have redemption through His blood, the forgiveness of sins, according to the riches of His grace.
EPHESIANS 1:7

In 1997, *The New York Times* reported on a conference where Bill Gates, founder and CEO of Microsoft, gave an address. In the question-and-answer session that followed his talk, a medical doctor asked Gates whether, if he were to lose his sight, he would exchange all of his wealth to have his sight restored. Gates, who in 1997 was worth $35 billion, said he would indeed.

Microsoft's stock's highest ever selling price was $119.75. If Gates had never sold any of his original Microsoft stock, on the day of that highest share price he would have been worth $384.3 billion. We can assume he would have traded all that to regain his sight as well.

But did you know those numbers pale in comparison to another set of riches that were exchanged that we might have sight? The riches of Christ's glory in heaven were exchanged that our spiritual eyes might be opened and we may recognize the love and forgiveness of God (Philippians 2:5–8). We may never have many of this world's riches, but we have been given riches of grace beyond comparison.

The riches of grace are not affected by the stock market or economic conditions. They represent wealth we cannot lose.

A SACRIFICIAL MOTHER

When Jesus therefore saw His mother . . . He said to His mother, "Woman, behold your son!"
JOHN 19:26

She was the twenty-fifth child in the English family of a religious dissenter; she had little education and lived in a male-dominated age; she married an older man and bore him nineteen children, nine of whom died. Her house burned down, her barn fell down, her health failed, and her pastor husband was either poor, jailed, or sick much of the time. But Susanna Wesley raised two sons, named John and Charles, who changed the world. Fortunately, Susanna Wesley wasn't a woman who thought the task of mothering to be beneath her.

And fortunately, a young Jewish woman named Mary didn't consider anything more meaningful than being the mother of the Son of God. From the beginning, she knew she was irreplaceable in the life of her child, and her sacrificial love remained strong to the end as she watched Him die for her and the world's sins. Jesus' efforts to care for Mary indicate just how much she meant to Him (John 19:27).

It is the heart of mothers to sacrifice and the need of mothers to be remembered. Surprise your mother this week with an unexpected token of love.

Motherhood is best defended by children who appreciate their mother's love.

EVENTUALLY LIKE JESUS

For whom He foreknew, He also predestined to be conformed to the image of His Son, that He might be the firstborn among many brethren.
ROMANS 8:29

Jesus Christ was both God and man. While it is difficult for us to comprehend such a union, the Bible makes it clear that Christ was a man of two natures. Though He was sinless, Jesus was like us in other ways. When we fail, we can draw encouragement from Hebrews 5:8: "Though He was a Son, yet He learned obedience by the things which He suffered."

Jesus had to "learn" obedience? Who does that sound like (besides your children)? It sounds like every Christian who has ever tried, and often failed, to put off the old man and put on the new (Colossians 3:9–10). Though we don't understand how or why the Son of God learned obedience, He did. And He suffered in the process. The way we know that He learned it is because, when He faced the greatest test in His earthly life, He said to God, "Nevertheless not My will, but Yours, be done" (Luke 22:42).

Learning obedience is not easy. If you have recently chosen your will instead of God's, don't despair. You have been predestined to be conformed to the image of Jesus Christ. Let what you know you will become tomorrow keep you moving beyond what you are today.

Today Is the Day

For this cause everyone who is godly shall pray to You in a time when You may be found.
Psalm 32:6

A German farmer settled in Guatemala and became prosperous. While sailing back to Germany to visit family, he discovered that a tropical flea had taken up residence under a toenail and laid its eggs. Instead of dealing with the painful problem then and there, he let the toe fester so his family could see the foreign insect. By the time he got to Germany, blood poisoning had set in and the farmer died.

The farmer made a faulty assumption: that he had plenty of tomorrows in which to make a life-or-death decision. We are not guaranteed any set number of days on this earth, as the apostle James wrote: "[Life is] a vapor that appears for a little time and then vanishes away" (4:14).

Every person faces a life-or-death decision, spiritually speaking, and many put it off indefinitely. They think there will be plenty of time to consider God's place in their life: "I want to be saved, just not right now." Do you see the faulty assumption in that statement? None of us is guaranteed tomorrow. If you have been putting off a spiritual decision, make it today.

Today is the day of salvation for all who don't know what tomorrow holds.

STRENGTH

... strengthened with might through His Spirit in the inner man.
EPHESIANS 3:16

In 1998, after speaking at a Christian rally in New Delhi, India, Dr. P. P. Job received threats against his family. At the time, his son Michael was training at the university to be a medical missionary. One evening, a white Fiat with Delhi plates, traveling at a high speed, changed lanes, rammed into Michael, and sped away without stopping. Michael died from the injuries.

Dr. Job was inconsolable. "It happened because I am a preacher of the Word of God," he said. "I was shattered. There are no words to describe the pain I went through." But as he read his Bible, he found Philippians 1:12: "the things which happened to me have actually turned out for the furtherance of the gospel."

That verse strengthened Dr. Job's faith, imparting courage to advance the gospel. Today there is a Michael Job Orphanage, a Michael Job High School, a Michael Job Residential Art and Training College, and a Michael Job Memorial Chapel. Multitudes have been inspired by this story, and God is gaining glory for Himself throughout India because a father was inwardly strengthened by the Holy Spirit.

Ask God for His inner strength to meet the challenges of your life too.

The Real Meaning of Sharing

Rejoice with those who rejoice, and weep with those who weep.
Romans 12:15

Just before speed skater Dan Jansen was to race at the 1988 Winter Olympics, he received word his sister had succumbed to her yearlong battle with leukemia. He fell in that race and again in his second race four days later. Returning home, one of many letters of consolation he received was from a thirty-year-old medal winner in the Special Olympics, who wrote: "I want to share one of my gold medals with you because I don't like to see you not get one. Try again in four more years."

For Dan Jansen, receiving that medal from a fellow athlete must have come close to winning one of his own. That's an example of the *koinonia*—the oneness, the unity—that athletes share.

Christians are to share that same kind of oneness, which is the true meaning of *koinonia*, or what we call "fellowship." If a fellow Christian is suffering, then the rest of the church suffers. If we are rejoicing, then we're blessed when other believers rejoice with us. Because we are all part of one body, the experiences of one member of the body—whether joy or sorrow—are experienced by all.

God never intended for any of His children to laugh or cry alone.

STRONG ENOUGH TO BE GENTLE

Blessed are the meek, for they shall inherit the earth.
MATTHEW 5:5

George Washington Carver, the scientist who developed hundreds of useful products from the peanut, said, "When I was young, I said to God, 'God, tell me the mystery of the universe.' But God answered, 'That knowledge is reserved for Me alone.' So I said, 'God, tell me the mystery of the peanut.' Then God said, 'Well, George, that's more nearly your size.' And He told me."

Meekness is having a patient and humble outlook on life. Meekness is being mild of temper, not easily provoked or irritated; patient under injuries, not vain, haughty, or resentful; forbearing; submissive.

This character trait seems like a tall order and hardly applicable to daily life. Meekness is truly hard work; it's being strong enough to be gentle in whatever situation you are placed. When you understand the importance and power of meekness, God can use you to glorify Him as well as be useful to others.

James 3:13 says, "Who is wise and understanding among you? Let him show by good conduct that his works are done in the meekness of wisdom." It doesn't matter so much what your position in life is—it matters how you respond to your position. And when you have the attitude of meekness, you are sure to succeed in the eyes of the Lord.

Home Security System

Go, show your love to your wife.
Hosea 3:1 NIV

The United States now has a Department of Homeland Security to help ensure the safety of our American homes. It's an important safeguard against terrorism, but a lesson might be learned from the Great Wall of China, one of the wonders of history. Upon its completion, the Chinese emperors expected never again to worry about security. No enemy could ever get past the forty-five-hundred-mile defensive wall, or so they thought. But the enemy did invade—by bribing the guardians of the gates and walking in.

Our government is doing its best to protect our nation's homeland, but the real enemy—Satan—is effectively slipping into our homes. Almost everyone has been touched by divorce in one way or another, and America now has the highest divorce rate in the world.

Many divorces could be prevented if husbands and wives committed their homes to Christ and took time to build a spiritual friendship, one that included daily Bible study and prayer together. The hectic demands of our society make it important to spend time together having fun, going out to eat, taking in a ball game, chatting over tea, or enjoying a weekend getaway. Go, show your love to your husband or wife.

The enemy has a hard time bribing the guards in a marriage like that.

KNOCKOFFS

Take heed to yourself and to the doctrine.
1 TIMOTHY 4:16

They're called "knockoffs"—counterfeit watches, sunglasses, pens, and ties, all sporting a designer label. "Counterfeiting is a booming international business," reported *The New York Times*, "accounting for an estimated 5 to 7 percent of global trade." Some people buy phony goods for fun because they enjoy sporting a "Rolex" watch or "Louis Vuitton" purse, but others are fleeced of their hard-earned money.

There are a lot of counterfeit religions being peddled today too. Visit any large bookstore, and peruse the titles in the religion/spirituality section. Surf through the channels on your television. Scan the religion section of your newspaper.

How can you tell the truth from the knockoffs? The best way is to carefully study the genuine article. It's easy to spot fakes if you know the authentic. That's why it's important to read the Scriptures and divide them rightly. It's important to listen to the sermons and study the writings of trustworthy pastors and teachers.

The apostle Paul warned Timothy to reject the claims of false teachers, "rightly dividing" the Word of God for himself (2 Timothy 2:15). Don't fall for the phony. Take heed to yourself and to the doctrine.

SUNDAY AND BEYOND

I beseech you . . . that you present your bodies a living sacrifice, holy, acceptable to God.
ROMANS 12:1

Since the Reformation, Protestant churches have included two sacraments in their worship: baptism and the Lord's Supper. In both of these observances, the Christian worships with his body, physically participating in the ordinances of the Lord.

In the Old Testament, believers worshiped with their bodies by bringing offerings to the Lord as sacrifices and by participating in the various festivals throughout the Jewish year. Participation in appointed worship is important, but the New Testament gives a brand-new mandate to Christians: take your worship beyond the meeting of the church. Instead of only participating in sacraments, become a sacrament. Instead of bringing a sacrifice to God, be the sacrifice.

Offer your whole life to God in daily service. Like Jesus, there shouldn't be a time when we aren't serving the Lord (John 5:19; 8:28). Make a conscious effort this week to view every day as "the Lord's day." Instead of looking for a sacrifice to bring, look for ways to live sacrificially for Christ.

Think of the impact on the world if every Christian began worshiping God every day of the week.

Y

TREASURE IN HEAVEN

By faith Moses . . . [esteemed] the reproach of Christ greater riches than the treasures in Egypt; for he looked to the reward.
HEBREWS 11:24, 26

Scott Adams, creator of the popular *Dilbert* comic strip, creates his cartoons from his own experience as a corporate cubicle dweller: "I don't think I'll ever forget what it feels like to sit in a cubicle and realize . . . everything you did today will become unimportant in the next [corporate] reorganization."

That's not to say, of course, that working at a corporate job is not without eternal significance. However, it does highlight the fact that every aspect of our lives has both a temporal and an eternal aspect. And it's learning to invest our lives—our time, talent, and treasure—for eternity that is the goal of life.

At work, seeing a co-worker come to Christ through your witness adds an eternal dimension to what may be a mundane job. And investing the earnings from your job in the lives of a missionary family engaged in cross-cultural evangelism adds an eternal perspective to temporal work. In how many ways is eternity benefiting from your investments of time, talent, and treasure?

The reason you never see a hearse pulling a trailer is because investing in heaven must be done now, not later.

JESUS WITH SKIN ON

I have been crucified with Christ; it is no longer I who live, but Christ lives in me.
GALATIANS 2:20

The story is told of a small boy who was terrified of thunderstorms at night. Whenever the lightning and thunder would begin, he would invariably end up at his parents' bedside saying, "I'm scared." On one particular night, his father told him, "You don't need to be afraid of the storm; Jesus is there with you." "I know He is," the boy replied, "but I need a Jesus with skin on."

Out of the mouths of babes, right? The phrase "Jesus with skin on" is not found in the New Testament, but it definitely expresses a biblical reality: Christ living His life through the heart and hands of the Christian. A Christian, to put it in a child's terms, is the Holy Spirit with skin on. Isn't that what Paul said in Galatians 2:20: "it is no longer I who live, but Christ lives in me"? We ought to ask ourselves, "Who do people see when they look at me?" If they see love, joy, peace, longsuffering, kindness, goodness, faithfulness, gentleness, and self-control, then they're seeing Jesus through the Holy Spirit in us (Galatians 5:22–23).

Just as a dirty window conceals what's on the inside, so an unclean life keeps Jesus from being seen in us.

Y

May 25

Memorizing God's Word

Your word I have hidden in my heart, that I might not sin against You.
Psalm 119:11

Seneca, the ancient Greek teacher of rhetoric, would impress his class of two hundred by asking each student to recite a favorite line of poetry. He would then recite all two hundred lines from memory in reverse order. St. Augustine had a friend who could recite all the poet Virgil's works—backward!

Okay, maybe those guys were gifted—but there are lots of things each of us can recite from memory too. Family members' names, birthdays, and other important dates; numerous phone numbers and addresses; and our Social Security, checking account, credit card, and driver's license numbers. And what about popular songs from high school, songs from summer camp, and favorite hymns?

These items have two characteristics in common: frequent use and indispensability. We've memorized them because we use them so often and because we can't get along without them. What would happen to our efforts at scripture memory if we viewed the Bible the same way?

Try this: pick a passage of scripture that addresses a need you face (indispensability), and read it once a day (frequency). Before long, you'll know it by heart!

THE VALUE OF PERSECUTION

Our God whom we serve is able to deliver us.
DANIEL 3:17

On July 15, 2002, a seventeen-year-old Christian Pakistani girl resisted the sexual advances of a Muslim man in her workplace. Angry at her refusal, the man returned and doused her with acid. She was burned severely on her face and chest and lost sight in her right eye. The International Christian Concern lists sixty-eight countries around the world where there is severe persecution or discrimination against Christians.

When we read stories in the Bible of believers being thrown to the lions, put into a fiery furnace, stoned, beaten, or made to suffer other forms of torture (Hebrews 11:35–38), we tend to think in historical terms only. But the truth is, millions of saints around the world today live in daily fear of persecution, simply for identifying themselves as Christians. And it is even happening in America, though in much more subtle ways.

The irony associated with persecution is striking: historically, there has been a direct correlation between the growth of the church and the degree of persecution it suffers. God is never so present in our lives as when we suffer in His name.

It's Never Too Late to Begin!

For we must all appear before the judgment seat of Christ.
2 Corinthians 5:10

In 1980, a young woman named Rosie Ruiz was declared the winner of the women's division of the Boston Marathon—but not for long. It was discovered this was only her second marathon, she never practiced, and none of the other runners had seen her during the race. She had ridden a subway sixteen miles, entered the race near the end, and crossed the finish line first.

Perhaps as the marathon approached, Ms. Ruiz realized she had waited too late to begin training. Instead of cheating, she should have run the best race she could and gained the prize of satisfaction and a clear conscience.

Like the Boston Marathon, the Christian life is a long-distance race (2 Timothy 4:7; Hebrews 12:1). Every participant will stand before the final Judge, Jesus Christ, and be evaluated on how he or she has run. But unlike the Boston Marathon, the Christian life is a "grace race." We will be judged not on being first but on being faithful. Did we use time, talent, and treasure for His glory? Did we run the best race we could with the gifts we have?

Regardless of how you've run in the past, today is the day to get in the race! Don't worry about where you place. Just be there at the end!

WILLING TO BE WOUNDED

Faithful are the wounds of a friend.
PROVERBS 27:6

When George Whitefield, the eighteenth-century British evangelist, first sailed to America, he wrote in his journal that the ship's cook had a drinking problem. When he was reproved about his sins, the cook boasted that he planned to reform his life two years before he died, but not before. Whitefield noted that the cook died six hours later.

No one likes to be reproved about sin, but a wise person listens and repents. Indeed, Solomon said, "Open rebuke is better than love carefully concealed" (Proverbs 27:5). Not surprisingly, most of us love to give reproof more than we like to receive it. But Solomon also said that the person who receives correction is considered wise (Proverbs 15:5).

As a Christian, humility is perhaps the top priority in being open to reproof. God says He gives grace to the humble but resists the proud (James 4:6). That doesn't mean we have to be a doormat, but it means we are willing to receive godly reproof without becoming defensive and resentful. If you were lost on a journey, wouldn't you appreciate the person who pointed you in the right direction?

Receiving reproof could be the first step in reaching the goals you've set for your life.

THE GREAT MULTIPLIER

Who has despised the day of small things?
ZECHARIAH 4:10

In 1912, Dr. Russell Conwell, pastor of Grace Baptist Church in Philadelphia, had a young student in Sunday school named Hattie May Wiatt. The church was crowded, and one day Dr. Conwell told Hattie May that he would love to have buildings large enough for everyone to attend.

When Hattie May became ill and died, Rev. Conwell was asked to preach the funeral. The girl's mother told him Hattie May had been saving her money to help build a bigger church. Hattie's purse contained coins amounting to fifty-seven cents. Taking the coins to the bank, Conwell exchanged them for fifty-seven pennies, which he put on display and "sold." With the proceeds, a nearby house was purchased for a children's wing for the church. Inspired by Hattie's story, more money came in, and out of her fifty-seven cents eventually came the buildings of Temple Baptist Church, Temple University, and Good Samaritan Hospital.

Perhaps you feel your gifts, your time, your talents, and your efforts are too small to make a difference. But have you ever given them to God completely and asked Him to bless them richly? He's the Great Mathematician, and He can take our words of witness, our undertakings, and our gifts and multiply them beyond anything we can ask or imagine.

The Soil of Your Soul

Examine me, O LORD, and prove me; try my mind and my heart.
Psalm 26:2

Topsoil—that luxurious layer of soil in which plant life thrives—is disappearing in America. As modern agricultural and commercial development has spread, wind and water have removed more than a foot of this precious resource. Yet when soil leaves one grain at a time, it's hard to see it happening.

The erosion of one's spiritual life happens like the erosion of topsoil—one sin at a time. Erosion and sin are deceptive. A grain of soil breaks free, weakening others that soon follow. A sin is willingly committed and unconfessed, and others are likely to follow.

That's what happened to Saul, the king of Israel. He grew impatient for the prophet Samuel to come to Gilgal to offer a sacrifice before battle, and so he offered the sacrifice himself—a sin in God's sight (1 Samuel 13). He gave himself permission to sin once, and it became ever easier to sin again.

If you have sinned, repent quickly. The same clay that makes bricks to build a cathedral can create a gully by its absence. Don't let sin wash away the soil of your soul.

MAY 31

FLEE IMMORALITY

But immorality or any impurity or greed must not even be named among you, as is proper among saints.
EPHESIANS 5:3 NASB

L. M. Clymer was president of the Holiday Inn hotel chain when the corporate board made a decision to invest $25 million in a gambling casino in Atlantic City. As a committed Christian, he had protested the decision to invest in the gambling industry but was overruled. As a result of the decision, Clymer resigned his position as president of the company, being unwilling to compromise his moral and spiritual convictions.

Godly men and women cannot be content in the presence of wickedness. Some would say to Mr. Clymer, "You can't help what the board decides. Besides, *you're* not gambling; *you're* not doing anything wrong." But the apostle Paul told the Roman Christians that God's judgment is upon those who not only sin themselves but give approval to others who sin (Romans 1:32).

If our failure to speak out against wickedness can in any way be interpreted as approval of the practice, then we are guilty as well. Look around—is there sin surrounding you to which you have grown accustomed? Are you willing to take a stand regardless of the cost?

A voice of dissent unheard speaks as loud as any shout of approval.

JUNE

FIRE AND FENCE

Daniel purposed in his heart that he would not defile himself.
DANIEL 1:8

F. Scott Fitzgerald wrote, "At 18 our convictions are hills from which we look; at 45 they are caves in which we hide." Another analogy would be: convictions are the fires that propel us and the fences that protect us.

Our inner convictions propel us to action. If I have a deep conviction the world is lost without Christ, I'm going to be a witness. If I have a deep conviction God answers prayer, I'm going to pray. If I deeply believe I should help the helpless, I'm going to get involved.

At the same time, convictions erect boundaries around our lives that protect us from sudden temptation. The backseat of a car is no place to decide what we believe about morality and purity. We'd better know about that before we get into such a situation. Convictions need to develop in our lives so that when pressure comes, we'll know what to do.

What are the boundaries in your life? How far will you go in a business deal to make a little extra money when you know in your heart you're violating something deep within your own soul? Do you have a set of convictions that you've thought out clearly so you'll know what to do when temptation comes?

FAITH GROWS

We . . . thank God always for you . . . because your faith grows exceedingly.
2 THESSALONIANS 1:3

If faith dispels worry, anxiety, fear, and depression, then why am I worried, anxious, fearful, and depressed?" asked Jamie. "Why do I react so suddenly to life's punches? Why can't I trust God more?"

If you've ever asked such questions, you're in good company. Take the disciples, for example. They trusted Christ enough to leave their homes and livelihoods, to follow Him despite persecution and opposition. Yet when they faltered during the storm, He bemoaned their "little faith."

Fast-forward a few years. Those same disciples were braving prison, beatings, and death to take the gospel of the kingdom to the ends of the earth. Their faith had grown strong.

The simple fact is that faith is a growing thing. Paul said, "Faith grows" (2 Thessalonians 1:3). It grows as we find and claim specific promises during times of need. It grows as we ask God to increase our faith and as we advance in our understanding of the trustworthiness of our Lord.

Remember, it's not great faith you need—but faith in a great God.

IMITATORS OF GOD

Therefore be imitators of God as dear children.
EPHESIANS 5:1

President Calvin Coolidge invited some people from his hometown to dinner at the White House. When the time came for serving coffee, the president poured his coffee into a saucer. As soon as his guests saw it, they did the same. Next, the president poured some milk and added a little sugar to the coffee in the saucer. The home folks did the same. They thought that surely the next step would be for the president to take the saucer with the coffee and begin sipping it. But the president didn't do so. He leaned over, placed the saucer on the floor, and called the cat.

Although you may never find yourself in the position of imitating the president at a dinner in the White House, you are called to be imitators of God every day. The story in Genesis tells of humans being created in God's image, and we are to be reflectors of Him to the world. How have you reflected His image to the world recently?

When you make decisions based on the Bible and prayer, when you love your neighbor as yourself, when you strive to lead a life that is pleasing to Christ in all that you do, then you are truly being an imitator of your Maker.

WHIRLWIND OF WISDOM

Then the LORD answered Job out of the whirlwind.
JOB 38:1

Missionaries Martin and Gracia Burnham, seized by guerrillas in the Philippines in May 2001, were held captive for 376 days. Just before a military raid led to Martin's death and Gracia's freedom, Martin said, "The Bible says to serve the Lord with gladness. Let's go out all the way. Let's serve Him all the way with gladness."

How can someone talk of joy while in deadly peril?—of serving the Lord with gladness while in captivity? It's because of God's wisdom. His infinite brilliance looks at everything with perfect understanding. God's wisdom is revealed in the Bible and imparted to us by the Holy Spirit as we study His Word.

This was the wisdom Job discovered. Overwhelmed with life, he had tried to sort out his troubles, aided by three friends whose insights were even more misguided than his own. But after human wisdom was exhausted, God spoke to Job out of a whirlwind: "Where were you when I laid the foundation of the earth?" God demanded. "Who laid its cornerstone?" (Job 38:4, 6).

We may not have all the answers to life, but the Lord does. We can defer to His wisdom and trust Him to understand things that make no sense to us.

MY ROCK AND REFUGE

I will say to God my Rock, "Why have You forgotten me? Why do I go mourning because of the oppression of the enemy?"
PSALM 42:9

In 1174, the Italian architect Bonnano Pisano began work on what would become his most famous project: a separately standing bell tower for the cathedral of the city of Pisa. There was just one "little" problem. Builders quickly discovered that the soil was much softer than they had anticipated, and the foundation was far too shallow to adequately hold the structure! Sure enough, before long the whole structure began to tilt . . . and it continued to tilt . . . until finally the architect and the builders realized that nothing could be done to make the "leaning tower" straight again.

If only the tower had been built on the right foundation. What is the foundation of your life? If it isn't God, chances are you're tilting one way or another. Isaiah 33:6 says, "He will be your sure foundation, providing a rich store of salvation, wisdom, and knowledge. The fear of the LORD is the key to this treasure" (NLT).

Make God the rock and foundation that your life is built upon.

JUNE 6

THE RISKY BUSINESS OF RECONCILIATION

Blessed are the peacemakers, for they shall be called sons of God.
MATTHEW 5:9

Novelist John Grisham recalled a conversation with a friend who died of cancer at the age of twenty-five. When told of the diagnosis, Grisham asked, "What do you do when you are about to die?" The sick man replied, "You get right with God, spend time with those you love, and settle up with everybody else." Then he said, "Really, you ought to live every day like you have only a few more days to live."

It's one thing to "settle up" with others when facing death. But for most people, living with the possibility of rejection is a formidable burden to consider carrying the rest of their lives. Reconciliation is a risky business. Where there has been a rift in a relationship, there are no guarantees as to how the other party might respond to your efforts; that person might still be angry, hurt, and nonresponsive. On the other hand, that person may embrace you fully and the relationship be restored.

The only way the distance between two people can be bridged is by someone taking the first step. If needed, be a peacemaker and close the gap between yourself and another.

Reconciliation is a form of investing in the future. The greater the risk, the greater the reward.

PRAISE TODAY

Enter into His . . . courts with praise.
PSALM 100:4

Is there a sequence to follow in prayer? Prayer should be a natural conversation between us and our Father, and no specific order is required. On the other hand, prayer is our highest activity, and we shouldn't do it thoughtlessly. Would you enter the presence of a king and just start babbling?

Isaac Watts, the father of English hymnody, once wrote a little poem about the order of prayer:

> Call upon God, adore, confess,
> Petition, plead, and then declare
> You are the Lord's, give thanks and bless,
> And let Amen confirm the prayer.

Begin prayer with adoration and praise. Some people use a hymnbook and begin their time with the Lord by singing. Others keep a "praise list" in their prayer journal.

You might develop the habit of pausing as you leave your house each morning to gaze into the sky and thank God for the beauty of that day. How often do you see the blue sky, the gentle rain, or the rising sun without acknowledging His creative genius? Other people begin the day by reciting: "This is the day the LORD has made; [I] will rejoice and be glad in it" (Psalm 118:24).

However you do it, praise God today.

Heaven on Earth

For the things which are seen are temporary, but the things which are not seen are eternal.
2 Corinthians 4:18

Do a survey of today's local newspaper, or pay close attention to the evening news broadcast on television. Here's what you'll likely find: stories on the U.S. economy, ongoing military efforts against terrorism, medical and technological advances, and other such stories. Here's what you will likely not find: news reports about heaven.

Let's face it: the world we live in is not focused on heaven. Atheists, agnostics, and pagans aren't concerned with heaven at all, and we can understand their inattention. The surprising reality is that many Christians hardly give heaven a second thought either. We live as if this world is the real thing, that which defines who and what we are.

In fact, just the opposite is true. This world is a very temporary parentheses in the eternal plan of God. Christians' citizenship is heavenly, not earthly. While on earth, the way we keep our eyes focused on heaven is to live in the presence of God through continual worship and communion with Him.

Though the media is full of news, don't let it distract you from the good news of the gospel.

PUT DOWN THE HAMMER!

Put on the full armor of God so that you can take your stand against the devil's schemes.
EPHESIANS 6:11 NIV

In her "Autobiography in Five Short Chapters," Portia Nelson writes:

Chapter 1: I walk down the street. There is a deep hole in the sidewalk. I fall in. It isn't my fault. It takes forever to find a way out.

Chapter 2: I walk down the same street. There is a deep hole in the sidewalk. I pretend I don't see it. I fall in again...but it isn't my fault. It still takes a long time to get out.

Chapter 3: I walk down the same street. There is a deep hole in the sidewalk. I see it is there. I still fall in. . . . My eyes are open. I know where I am. It is my fault. I get out immediately.

Chapter 4: I walk down the same street. There is a deep hole in the sidewalk. I walk around it.

Chapter 5: I walk down another street.

Satan has his schemes and tactics, and we need to devise ours to defend ourselves from his temptations. If you know there is a temptation down one street, take a different one!

Clothing yourself in the armor of God is step one in devising strategies to resist the devil's schemes.

I'D RATHER BE A DOG

And when He had given thanks . . .
JOHN 6:11

Rev. William Biederwolf once shocked his audience by saying, "I'd rather be a dog with gratitude enough to wag his tail . . . than to be a man with a soul so contemptibly mean as to sit down at the table three times a day and gulp down the food God has provided and never once lift my heart in thanksgiving."

We might not put it like that, but the point is well taken. When Jesus told us to pray, "Give us this day our daily bread," He was teaching us dependence upon Him for daily provision (Matthew 6:11). Even our Lord paused to give thanks before breaking the bread in John 6.

"Saying grace" shouldn't be a perfunctory act, and we shouldn't use the same words each time. Try praying an original prayer at each meal. At breakfast: "Lord, thanks for giving someone enough wisdom to invent high-fiber cereal." At lunch: "Lord, thanks for this food, but keep me from eating too much of it." And at supper? Well, you could say: "Lord, I'd rather be a dog than fail to thank You for this meatloaf."

Whatever words you use, learn to thank God for giving you this day your daily bread.

God's Estate Plan

I pray also that the eyes of your heart may be enlightened in order that you may know the hope to which he has called you, the riches of his glorious inheritance in the saints.
Ephesians 1:18 NIV

The reading of a deceased person's will is a stereotypically comic event seen less often in real life than in the movies. The deceased is absent, the heirs are nervous and competitive, and the content of the will is unknown. Not a happy scene—and totally removed from the joy of a Christian's spiritual inheritance.

Christians are heirs of God and joint heirs with Jesus Christ (Romans 8:17). And there is great joy in heaven whenever one lost soul turns to God and receives his inheritance (Luke 15:10). God, the benefactor, has joy. Christians, the heirs, have joy as well.

Our inheritance is clearly spelled out. But the joy of our inheritance extends beyond this age to the "ages to come" (Ephesians 2:7). God's "estate plan" makes provision for us to enjoy Him, and for Him to enjoy us, forever. Never doubt whether there is anyone who longs to be with you. God does, and He plans to spend eternity with you, His heir.

Being an heir of God means that the Benefactor, heir, and inheritance are not separated but united in mutual joy forever.

Fearing Fear Itself

For God has not given us a spirit of fear, but of power and of love and of a sound mind.
2 Timothy 1:7

The Great Depression began in October 1929, and began to turn around with the inauguration of Franklin D. Roosevelt as president in 1933. In his inaugural address, FDR lifted the spirit of America with these words: "Let me assert my firm belief that the only thing we have to fear is fear itself—nameless, unreasoning, unjustified terror which paralyzes needed efforts to convert retreat into advance."

God says, "Fear not" (Isaiah 41:10)—don't fear anything. The Christian has no fear that faith cannot cancel (Luke 8:25). Fear paralyzes. It stops us in our tracks and halts the advance of the kingdom of God into the kingdom of Satan, the kingdom of light into the kingdom of darkness (Colossians 1:12–14).

Satan wants nothing more than to paralyze God's saints—to halt their progress in holiness and to stop the spread of the gospel. If you are paralyzed by fear, ask God to deliver you. Say, "Lord, I'm afraid! Deliver me from evil. Deliver me from all my fears."

Power, love, and the mind of Christ advance the kingdom of God; fear turns advance into retreat.

Staying Spiritually Solvent

As iron sharpens iron, so a man sharpens the countenance of his friend.
Proverbs 27:17

On February 26, 1995, Barings Bank, England's oldest, declared bankruptcy after losing nearly one billion dollars. How could such a thing happen? Lack of accountability. A twenty-eight-year-old Barings trader in Singapore had been given too much authority—like letting a schoolboy grade his own tests. He lost money in stock trades, and no one knew about it—until all of the bank's money was gone.

If that trader had been surrounded by associates who were closer to him, his failures might have been caught before they turned into a freefall. It's hard to overestimate the positive influence that good and godly friends, mentors, and role models can have on our lives—or the negative results that accrue when we have a "lone ranger" mentality. Not only can friends keep us from going astray, they can move us in the right direction as well.

Surveys have shown that in our disconnected culture, most people have few, if any, close friends. How about you? Don't be a stranger! Be a good friend, and you'll have good friends who can help you find, and stay on, the right path.

Peer pressure can have a negative or positive effect. Make sure your peers are of the positive kind.

BENEFITS OF BOUNDARIES

. . . having predestined us to adoption as sons by Jesus Christ to Himself, according to the good pleasure of His will.
EPHESIANS 1:5

In *Knowledge of the Holy*, A. W. Tozer illustrates freedom and boundaries: an ocean liner leaves New York bound for England, piloted by a captain and crew who will not be taken off course. The passengers are free to roam the giant boat and do whatever they like—within the confines of the ship. They exercise their freedoms while all the time being moved toward an ultimate destination.

God's adoption of Christians into His family reflects the same two dynamics: freedom of movement within safe boundaries, while moving toward an ultimate destination. The word *predestination* in Scripture has the idea of boundaries in its meaning. When God predestined us to adoption as His children, He set boundaries around us that gradually conform us to the image of His Son (Romans 8:29). Like children, we may chafe at times against the boundaries of our spiritual family, but they are for our good. Think how much safer you feel now than when you were lost and without hope in the world (Ephesians 2:12).

God's boundaries tell us we are on His ship, heading for a heavenly port. Without boundaries, we would be lost forever.

ONLY A GYPSY BOY

Not many noble, are called.
1 CORINTHIANS 1:26

Some are still around who heard the inimitable preacher, Rodney (Gipsy) Smith. He was born among the gypsies in England. His mother died when he was young; and his father, Cornelius, was imprisoned for debts. But after his release, Cornelius took his children to Latimer Road Mission, where, as worshipers sang, "There Is a Fountain Filled with Blood," Cornelius suddenly fell to the floor. Soon he jumped up, shouting, "I'm converted! Children, God has made a new man of me!" Young Rodney ran from the church terrified.

But at age sixteen, Rodney himself asked Christ into his heart. Someone nearby whispered, "Oh, it's only a gypsy boy." Undeterred, Rodney acquired a Bible and began preaching. Thus began seventy years of worldwide evangelistic work. He became one of the greatest preachers of his age.

Don't worry if you haven't a lot of education, a fistful of money, or a prestigious background. God takes us as we are and makes us what He wants us to be. He uses the weakest people to do His greatest work, "that no one may boast before him" (1 Corinthians 1:29 NIV).

Follow the Leader

For to this you were called, because Christ also suffered for us, leaving us an example, that you should follow His steps.
1 Peter 2:21

You show up bright and early for the first day of your new job and sit down with your boss to review your job responsibilities. Everything looks good—meet deadlines for reports, monitor departmental budget, supervise junior staff—until you get to the last item: "Suffer extreme persecution, harassment, and loss of some privilege for the sake of the company."

Whoa! Are they serious? Not many people in today's world would agree to a job that required them to suffer for the sake of the company. Yet, in a manner of speaking, that's what Christians are asked to do. For instance, when Paul met the Lord Jesus Christ on the Damascus road, Jesus said He was about to show Paul "how many things he must suffer for My name's sake" (Acts 9:16). And Paul never wavered throughout his life.

We are not promised deliverance from every hardship in this life. In fact, we are told that we will suffer. How often are you surprised at the suffering you experience in this life?

Following Jesus means imitating His example in all things—even suffering for the sake of the gospel.

THE EXPRESSING OF GRACE

Having then gifts differing according to the grace that is given to us, let us use them.
ROMANS 12:6

When David Livingstone volunteered as a missionary with the London Missionary Society, they asked him where he wanted to go. He replied, "Anywhere, so long as it is forward." After he had reached Africa, he recorded his impressions, saying that he was haunted by the smoke of a thousand villages stretching off into the distance. David Livingstone had the heart of a missionary.

Should every Christian have the heart of a missionary? Yes and no. In the sense of being as sure of one's calling as most missionaries are—willing to sacrifice and endure hardship—absolutely yes. But in being an actual missionary who goes to a foreign land for a lifetime of service—only if God clearly directs.

Scripture is clear that the grace of God is expressed differently through different members of the body. We do not all have the same gifts and calling. But we all do have the grace of God, which is sufficient to carry out our particular ministry with a Livingstone-like vision and commitment. What is the measure of God's grace you have received?

Zealous ministry for God is nothing more than the expression of the powerful grace of God deposited in us.

CONFESSION IS GOOD FOR THE SOUL

If I regard iniquity in my heart, the Lord will not hear.
PSALM 66:18

In pre-Revolution Russia, one of the most influential people in Czar Nicholas II's court was a wandering Orthodox monk named Grigori Rasputin. Empress Alexandra fell under Rasputin's spell and his doctrine of immorality—that it is the believer's responsibility to sin with abandon in order to experience the joy of repentance. The greater the sin, the greater the joy.

Rasputin clearly had not read Romans 6:1–2: "What shall we say then? Shall we continue in sin that grace may abound? Certainly not! How shall we who died to sin live any longer in it?" And had he read Psalm 32:3–4, he would have discovered that David found no pleasure in sin: "My bones grew old through my groaning all the day long. For day and night Your hand was heavy upon me; my vitality was turned into the drought of summer." The Bible is clear that sin is what separates us from God. Choosing not to confess our sin and turn from it is like cutting the communication lines with God.

Confession means to say the same thing about our sin that God says about it. And agreeing with God is always good for the soul.

How Did We Know?

The LORD has appeared of old to me, saying: "Yes, I have loved you with an everlasting love; therefore with lovingkindness I have drawn you."
Jeremiah 31:3

Comedian Jonathan Winters said in an interview that his life was scarred by the cruel things his parents said to him in childhood. "I'm no crybaby, but I remember things with almost total recall—there's a lot of pain there." His father once told him, "You're the dumbest kid I know."

When he joined the marines and went off to the South Pacific during World War II, Jonathan felt no support from his mother. When he came back home, he discovered that she had given away the precious, personal things he had stored in the attic. He was upset, but her response was, "How did we know you were going to live?"

Many people have scars caused by people's words. If that has happened to you, there's another voice you should hear. The Lord's words are stronger than anyone else's. He has words of love and life, words of affirmation. "I have loved you with an everlasting love," says the Father.

God loves you so much, and He desires a deep and delightful relationship with you. Don't be discouraged by the words of others. You are special in God's eyes.

THE JOB OF THANKSGIVING

Heman and Jeduthun . . . were designated by name, to give thanks to the LORD.
1 CHRONICLES 16:41

Perhaps you've never heard of these two men; they're among the Bible's more obscure characters. Yet their role was paramount. In the great worship choirs of King David, they were appointed to give thanks. Jeduthun and Heman "were under the authority of the king," says 1 Chronicles 25:6. And they were designated by name to give thanks. It was their job!

Giving thanks is our job too. We're under the authority of a King who commands: "Be thankful" . . . "Offer to God thanksgiving"... "Come before His presence with thanksgiving" . . . "Enter into His gates with thanksgiving"... "In everything give thanks; for this is the will of God in Christ Jesus for you" (Colossians 3:15; Psalm 50:14; 95:2; 100:4; 1 Thessalonians 5:18, respectively).

This is one of God's commands for healthy living. The Creator of the soul is the Master Psychologist. He knows that thanksgiving is not only appropriate but therapeutic. It's hard to be both thankful and, at the same time, grumpy, cantankerous, critical, or ill-tempered.

Be a Heman. Be a Jeduthun. We are appointed by the King to praise His name and to thank Him every day.

CHILDLIKE FAITH

So the Lord said, "If you have faith as a mustard seed . . ."
LUKE 17:6

A man approached a Little League baseball game one afternoon while strolling through a park. He stopped and asked a boy in the dugout what the score was. The boy responded, "Eighteen to nothing—we're behind."

"Boy," said the spectator, "I'll bet you're discouraged."

"Why should I be discouraged?" replied the little boy. "We haven't even gotten up to bat yet!"

What a difference an optimistic attitude makes! As Christians, we have the ultimate comfort that we are blessed with the ultimate win—eternal life in heaven with God. But until then, how are we supposed to face the discouragements of this world? Job 16:5 says, "But my mouth would encourage you; comfort from my lips would bring you relief" (NIV).

God is our great encourager. He reminds us that with His help, anything is possible. It is a matter of perspective that determines the productivity of our actions. Childlike faith is the way to success in this world. Do you believe that the Lord will be faithful to provide for your needs and your desires? He is waiting to hear and see your enthusiasm for life; He is waiting to bless a childlike faith.

BELIEVE ME WHEN I SAY

So will the Son of Man be three days and three nights in the heart of the earth.
MATTHEW 12:40

A little boy walked up to a lady sitting under an umbrella on the beach: "Are you a Christian?" "Yes, I am," she replied. "Do you read your Bible every day?" "Yes, I do." "Do you pray often?" Yes, again. "Well," the lad concluded, "will you hold my quarter while I go swimming?"

Trustworthiness is developed by telling the truth and, more importantly, never failing to do what has been promised. It only takes one unkept promise or one lie to destroy credibility and become an untrustworthy person.

Take the resurrection of Jesus, for instance. Many times during His three-year ministry on earth He foretold that He would be killed but would rise from the dead after three days. And that's exactly what happened! That may be the most astounding self-fulfilled prediction ever made. The fact that Jesus was raised from the dead exactly as He foretold gives us confidence in everything else He said.

If there is anything Jesus said that you are tempted to question, remember the Resurrection. He proved His word is good.

To be trustworthy in the hardest thing is to be trustworthy in everything.

THE REASON WE SERVE

And whatever you do in word or deed, do all in the name of the Lord Jesus, giving thanks to God the Father through Him.
COLOSSIANS 3:17

Josh McDowell, who has spoken to millions of university students worldwide and authored scores of books, began his lifetime of service to Christ in a more humble fashion. His first assignment at the headquarters of Campus Crusade for Christ was scrubbing the main entryway floor. He wasn't meeting with the ministry's leaders; he was scrubbing up the dirt from their shoes.

Biblically, Josh's introduction to ministry was the equivalent of the guy in the Old Testament who carried the tent pegs when they moved the tabernacle from place to place. That is not exactly a high-profile task. Without a proper perspective on and motivation for ministry, it would be easy to get our feathers ruffled when given a lowly assignment.

So how do we stay motivated about serving God? By the promise that we will one day reap what we sow. God has promised to reward our faithful service at the judgment seat of Christ. If you are serving God, keep your heart focused on faithfulness instead of prominence.

When it comes to our rewards, motive will be determined by how much of what we did was for Jesus' sake.

DEFENSE AGAINST DISTRACTIONS

Above all else, guard your heart, for it is the wellspring of life.
PROVERBS 4:23 NIV

Perhaps they didn't get enough sleep the night before; maybe they were worn out from a hard day's work. Or maybe the clock ticked "bedtime." We've all been victims of drowsiness, so we shouldn't be surprised the three young men fell asleep. But we are! We're shocked because it was such an important night. This night, more than any other, required disciplined vigilance.

Jesus, about to begin His journey to the cross, asked the disciples to pray for Him. Imagine His disappointment when He found Peter, James, and John sleeping instead. Victims of drooping eyelids, the disciples missed an opportunity to encourage and strengthen Jesus in His moment of greatest need. And they missed the opportunity to strengthen themselves through prayer as well.

Satan knows if he can keep us from worship, he can keep us from spiritual power. He is the master distracter, able to deter us from worship with his tactics. How many times have we been distracted from our private worship by the TV, the telephone, a messy house, our to-do list, a wandering mind, or heavy eyelids?

When we prepare our hearts for personal worship, we must remember to guard our hearts from the distractions of Satan.

THE RIGHT LOOK

As water reflects a face, so a man's heart reflects the man.
PROVERBS 27:19 NIV

You can tell a lot about a man by the way he dresses. Consider the family portrait. Each family member spends hours in front of the mirror trying to look just right. Then, in front of the camera, they are all on their best behavior with their largest smiles across their faces.

What if someone followed you around every day with a camera? It would make an impact, but it is up to you what kind of impact. Charles Spurgeon once said, "A man's life is always more forcible than his speech. When men take stock of him, they reckon his deeds as dollars and his words as pennies. If his life and doctrine disagree, the mass of onlookers accept his practice and reject his preaching."

Does your appearance reflect the transformation that Christ has done in your heart? First Peter 3:3–4 says, "Your beauty should not come from outward adornment. . . . Instead, it should be that of your inner self . . . which is of great worth in God's sight" (NIV).

Hold your head up high, and make the spiritual family portrait more beautiful from the inside out.

Comprehension

For we are not ignorant of his [Satan's] devices.
2 Corinthians 2:11

There's nothing wrong with eating a piece of bread, but Jesus, seeing through the devil's scheme at the Temptation, refused to partake. He said, "It is written, 'Man shall not live by bread alone, but by every word that proceeds from the mouth of God'" (Matthew 4:4).

There may be nothing wrong with repeating that story, attending that play, making that purchase, or saying those words. But sometimes there is something wrong with doing those things if we'll just have the discernment to recognize it.

One of Satan's oldest tricks is to confuse our values so that good appears to be evil, and evil appears as good. He is the deceiver, and his deadliest tools often appear to be innocent pleasures. The Bible tells us to "put on the whole armor of God, that you may be able to stand against the wiles of the devil" (Ephesians 6:11).

Where do we find the needed wisdom to spot Satan's ploys? Only a close walk with God, a deep study of Scripture, and an intense prayer life will supply the special discernment to see through his devices.

Ask God for wisdom. Ask Him to guard your mind, your mouth, and your morals. Ask Him to open your eyes and to deliver you from evil. And keep your armor on!

STAYING POWER

A new commandment I give to you, that you love one another.
JOHN 13:34

A cartoon in a national magazine showed a couple standing before a minister during their wedding. The minister, looking at the bride, said, "The correct response is 'I do'—not 'It's worth a try.'"

Love—in marriage and in other relationships—requires dogged commitment on our part. Contrary to popular opinion, love doesn't come naturally for us humans. Love is others-centered and self-sacrificing. We are self-centered; and, in our own natural selves, we care little about sacrifice unless powerfully motivated.

In fact, the Bible teaches that only someone who really knows God through Jesus is capable of the kind of love the Bible describes. John wrote, "Love comes from God. Everyone who loves has been born of God and knows God. Whoever does not love does not know God, because God is love" (1 John 4:7–8 NIV).

Paul taught that God's love is "poured out in our hearts by the Holy Spirit" (Romans 5:5), and Jesus said that the world would recognize that we are Christians by our love (John 13:35). Love grows as we nurture it. It develops as we feed it. It expands as we persist in it. That kind of love has staying power.

The Queen's Fast

Fast for me . . . And so I will go.
Esther 4:16

There may be times in life when we must say no to our physical desires so we can focus on spiritual needs. Fasting can express our fervency in prayer and therefore prepare us to meet challenges.

Esther's life provides a good example of the importance of fasting, especially when approaching an important moment. In Esther 4:4–16, Queen Esther became so deeply distressed about the fate of her people that she stopped eating or drinking and told all the Jews not to eat or drink for three days. The king had been tricked into signing an order for the annihilation of the Jewish nation. Knowing that it could mean her death, the queen approached the king to plead for the lives of her people. Instead of killing her, the king offered her half his kingdom because "she found favor in his sight" (5:2).

Esther prayed and fasted to save her people, and God saved them. If you are facing a critical decision, practice the spiritual discipline of fasting. Your single-mindedness will help you focus on earnestly seeking God.

GIVING CREDIT WHERE IT'S DUE

I am the LORD, that is My name; and My glory I will not give to another.
ISAIAH 42:8

Evangelist Billy Graham is well known for his humility. Despite worldwide fame, he still finds it difficult to say no to anyone approaching him, he is unfailingly pleasant to strangers, and he always credits God with the success of his ministry. His guiding verse on the subject of personal humility has been Isaiah 42:8: "I am the LORD...My glory I will not give to another."

Tragically, success often changes people. We see it especially in the athletic world. Someone gets to the top, makes the starting team, and experiences fame. Suddenly he changes. His humble, submissive attitude is gone.

Can you be humble in the face of success? Humility doesn't imply a lack of self-confidence, nor does it make us a doormat for others to walk on. It isn't having a low self-image or thinking poorly of oneself. Humility means not thinking of oneself very much at all, but thinking of Jesus Christ more and more.

Whatever we accomplish is due to His blessings. Whatever we gain comes from Him, for "every good and perfect gift is from above" (James 1:17 NIV). Remember to give Him the glory, honor, and praise for any success that comes your way.

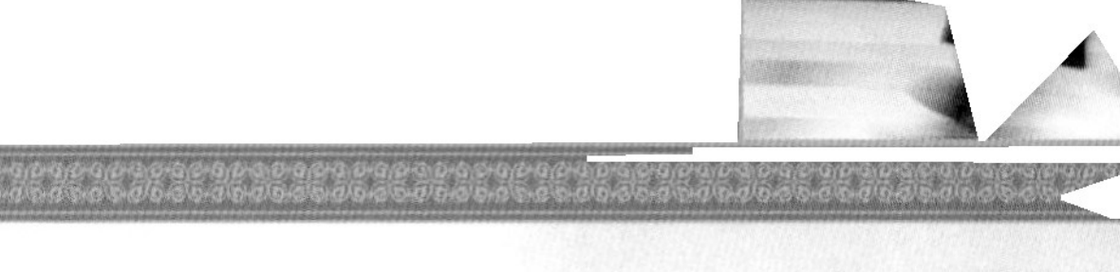

FREEDOM TO LOVE

Love does no harm to a neighbor; therefore love is the fulfillment of the law.
ROMANS 13:10

The famous nineteenth-century preacher Charles H. Spurgeon was fond of smoking cigars. Because this was before the days of research into the effects of tobacco, he saw nothing wrong with the practice. Until, that is, he passed a tobacco shop with a sign advertising a particular cigar for sale: "The cigar smoked by C. H. Spurgeon." That was the last day Spurgeon ever smoked a cigar.

Charles Spurgeon recognized that something he had a right to engage in might be viewed as a vice by other believers. He didn't want his actions to be a stumbling block for others; his love for people was greater than his love for cigars.

Spurgeon learned this spiritual lesson in love from the apostle Paul, who counseled first-century Christians to be self-sacrificing in their love for one another. While "all things are lawful," he wrote, "all things are not helpful" (1 Corinthians 6:12). Freedom in Christ does not mean we have the right to do anything we want. Rather, it means we have the power to do everything we ought.

If there is any right you love more than a brother's or sister's progress toward holiness, it is a right that is best left unexercised.

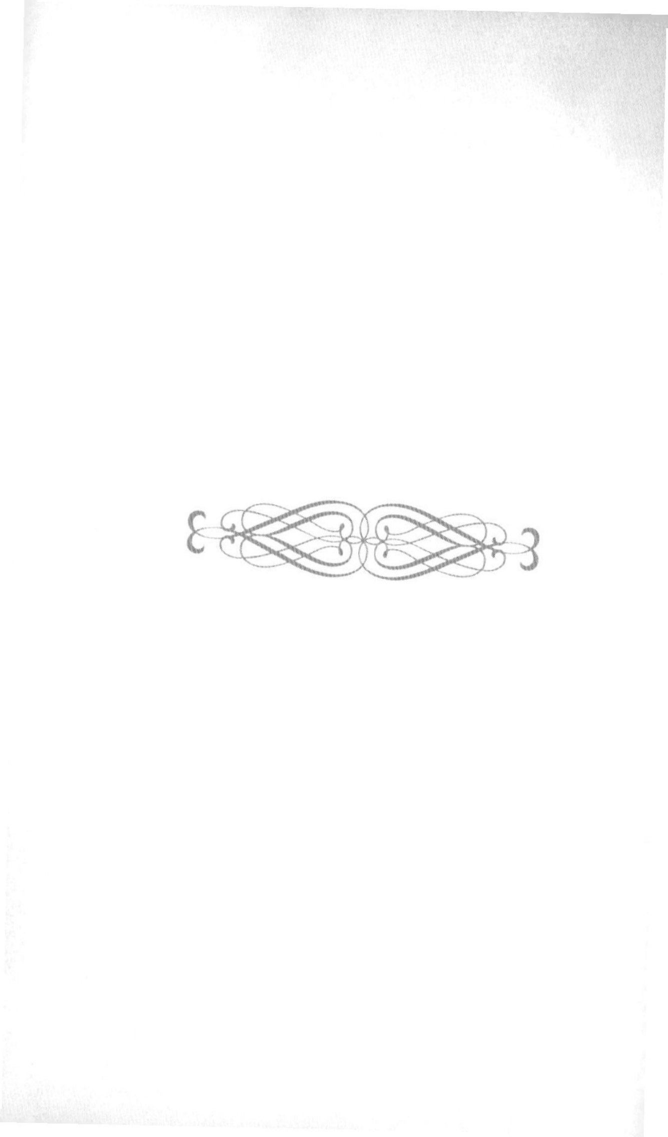

JULY

WHEN GIVING EQUALS LIVING

For the love of money is a root of all kinds of evil.
1 TIMOTHY 6:10

The Italian city of Pompeii was destroyed by the eruption of the volcano Mount Vesuvius in AD 79. When modern excavators began digging in the ruins, among the many bodies found frozen in time was that of a woman whose feet faced the city gate but whose hand was reaching back for a bag of pearls. Her effort to save her wealth was rewarded with death.

Perhaps the woman dropped the pearls when fleeing the city, or perhaps the pearls had been dropped by another. In any case, she wanted them. Two people died that day: a person who loved life and a person who loved wealth. In her case, wealth won and life lost.

If we pursue righteousness and greed together, our destination is disaster (Matthew 6:24). The Pharisees discovered this when they refused to support their own parents by claiming that all their funds had been dedicated to the Lord's work (Mark 7:9–13). The idea that God would be pleased with such hypocrisy shows how little the Pharisees knew of Him. Greed will make hypocrites out of the pseudorighteous before they have time to say, "I wanted to give more but . . ."

The righteous live and give the same way. Make sure you don't lose something eternal while grasping for something temporal.

REVIVE US AGAIN

Will You not revive us again, that Your people may rejoice in You?
PSALM 85:6

Only a revival of biblical proportions can restore America to moral decency and spiritual strength. Don't think that such a revival is impossible; it has happened before, and it can happen again. God often sends revival when times are at their worst.

The mood of America was grim during the mid-1850s. In New York City, a layman named Jeremiah C. Lanphier announced a series of noontime prayer meetings to begin September 23, 1857, at the Old Dutch Church on Fulton Street. When the hour came, Lanphier found himself alone. Finally, one man showed up, then a few others.

The next week, twenty came. The third week, forty. Other churches opened their doors. The revival spread to other cities. Offices and stores closed for prayer at noon. Newspapers spread the story, and even telegraph companies set aside certain hours during which businessmen could wire one another with news of the revival. The revival, sometimes called the Third Great Awakening, lasted nearly two years, and between five hundred thousand and one million people were said to have been converted.

Ask God to revive us again, and let it begin with you.

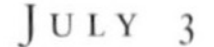

JULY 3

PRESIDENTIAL PRAYERS

I exhort first of all that supplications, prayers, intercessions, and giving of thanks be made for all men, for kings and all who are in authority.

1 TIMOTHY 2:1–2

On January 20, 1953, the newly sworn-in president, Dwight D. Eisenhower, surprised America by opening his inaugural address with prayer. "My friends," he said, "before I begin . . . would you permit me the privilege of uttering a little private prayer of my own? And I ask that you bow your heads."

He then prayed: "Almighty God, as we stand here at this moment, my future associates in the executive branch of government join me in beseeching that Thou will make full and complete our dedication to the service of the people in this throng. . . . Give us . . . the power to discern clearly right from wrong, and allow all our words and actions to be governed thereby."

Have you prayed today for your national, state, and local leaders? Presidents, prime ministers, and leaders everywhere need our prayers. Our senators, representatives, governors, mayors, and aldermen can be guided and influenced by prayer. Take a page from Eisenhower's speech, and ask God to give our leaders the ability to discern right from wrong—and to choose the right.

FREEDOM!

If the Son makes you free, you shall be free indeed.
JOHN 8:36

John Witherspoon, one of the signers of the Declaration of Independence, had been a Presbyterian leader in Scotland when called to become president of the College of New Jersey (now Princeton). Despite his wife's terror at crossing the ocean, they accepted the call and arrived in America in 1768.

In May 1776, as the United Colonies readied for war, Witherspoon gave a famous sermon entitled "The Dominion of Providence," saying, "This is the first time of my introducing any political subject into the pulpit." He insisted the cause of freedom was just and God-blessed, but most of his message begged his hearers to give their hearts to Christ.

While independence is important, he said, the eternal state of souls is even more so. "There can be no true religion till there be a discovery of your lost state by nature and practice, and an unfeigned acceptance of Christ Jesus, as He is offered in the Gospel. Unhappy are they who either despise His mercy or are ashamed of His cross. Believe it, there is no salvation in any other."

We thank God for our freedom today. But are you "free indeed"? Have you received eternal life in the Lord Jesus Christ?

Let Freedom Ring!

And you shall know the truth, and the truth shall make you free.
John 8:32

We hold these truths to be self-evident, that all men are created equal, that they are endowed by their Creator with certain unalienable Rights, that among these are Life, Liberty, and the pursuit of Happiness." So states America's Declaration of Independence. A foundational truth, being watered down in history textbooks with every succeeding generation, is that America's Founding Fathers saw liberty as a God-given right.

America is not the symbol of liberty to the whole world by accident. This nation was designed to reflect, corporately and individually, a principle found only in the Bible—that man was created to be free. Nothing was to hinder the creature's relationship with his Creator—not kings, or governments, or tyranny, or the will of man. In a day when American soldiers are defending our right to live free from terrorism, it is incumbent upon us to thank God for a land in which freedom's bell has rung for 229 years. Will prayers of thanksgiving for freedom be heard in your home today?

Those who take freedom for granted are also in danger of taking for granted the Author of freedom Himself.

WORSHIP THE KING

The Lamb will overcome them, for He is Lord of lords and King of kings.
REVELATION 17:14

People often ask why the audience stands during the singing of the "Hallelujah Chorus" portion of Handel's *Messiah*. The custom dates back to the 1740s, when England's King George II heard the presentation for the first time. He was so moved by the "Hallelujah Chorus" that he stood to his feet in honor of the King of kings and Lord of lords. Since no one remains seated when royalty stands, the rest of the audience stood as well—and audiences have stood ever since.

In the ancient Near East, the superlative form of an adjective or adverb was not described in one word, as it is in English (such as best, brightest, or funniest). The best song was "the song of songs," and the greatest king was "the king of kings." Artaxerxes, king of Persia, referred to himself as the "king of kings" (Ezra 7:12), and God gave Nebuchadnezzar of Babylon the same title (Ezekiel 26:7).

A day is coming when the whole world will recognize the true "King of kings," Jesus Christ. If He is not the king you worship, wouldn't now be the time to worship Him as the King of kings?

Whether standing or bowing, worship is due the King of kings.

FREEDOM AND SECURITY

But seek first the kingdom of God and His righteousness, and all these things shall be added to you.
MATTHEW 6:33

Compare the oyster and the eagle. The oyster has a rock-hard home to protect it from predators and opens its shell whenever it wants nourishment. The eagle resides on freezing and exposed mountain crags and flies through miles of dangerous weather in search of food. The oyster is completely secure, while the eagle is completely free. Which did America choose as its national symbol?

Animals don't choose their lifestyles; they just follow their God-given instincts. So we can't be too critical of one over the other. But all too often, we see humans who choose worldly security over spiritual freedom. They invest all their time and talent in laying up treasures on earth. Security against the unexpected becomes their obsession.

There's nothing wrong with security, of course. The question is, where do we seek it: in God or in the things of this world? Do a security check in your own life. Wherever you find some insecurities, look at them against the backdrop of God's great resources, not your own.

Oysters may be secure and eagles may be free, but Christians are both secure and free when they live in dependence on God.

Guard and Guide

And the Angel of God, who went before the camp of Israel . . . gave light by night.
Exodus 14:19–20

It was the Lord Himself—a pillar of fire—who ushered the Israelites through the Red Sea. His presence cast darkness on the Egyptians but light on the children of Israel. What a perfect description of our Lord Jesus, who gives light to those who trust Him; but to those who reject Him, utter darkness. He comforts the one and confounds the other. He is a Savior to the one and a Judge to the other.

For His children, the Lord is both guard and guide. He precedes us and protects us. He is simultaneously our shepherd and shield. He is Alpha and Omega, the first and the last, the One who goes before and the One who goes behind, gathering up our debris and our failures, blessing us, and leaving a blessing behind us for others.

When you feel the enemy on your heels, remember that He who is a pillar of fire goes with you. He's "a very present help in trouble" (Psalm 46:1).

DON'T LEAVE HOME WITHOUT HIM

For through Him we both have access by one Spirit to the Father.
EPHESIANS 2:18

Competing credit-card companies love to one-up each other by announcing the remote, exotic, or unique places on earth where their card is accepted—and where the competition's is not. A credit card becomes like a universal economic passport. Meet a merchant in an out-of-the-way place who accepts your credit card, and you are family! You are united by financial bonds that cross all cultural and geographic boundaries.

Well, maybe not family—but that's how the companies want us to think of ourselves if we use their cards. Go anywhere, meet anyone, buy whatever you want—your credit card is your link to the world. That may be true, but it's a shallow form of unity: an inch deep and a world wide.

A much deeper sense of belonging is provided by another type of identity: possession of the Holy Spirit. Travel anywhere in the world, meet a fellow believer in Christ, and there is instant fellowship. Next time you make a new Christian friend, skip the formalities and polite introductions—you're family!

To be filled with the Spirit as you travel through life gives access to the most meaningful network on earth: the body of Christ.

THE MEYER METHOD

Envy is rottenness to the bones.
PROVERBS 14:30

Everyone is vulnerable to jealousy. The famous Bible teacher F. B. Meyer, who struggled with it, found only one solution. Meyer often preached at D. L. Moody's Bible Conference in Northfield, Massachusetts, where he was popular and drew large crowds. But one day another well-known Bible teacher, Dr. G. Campbell Morgan, was invited to preach at Northfield.

To Meyer's consternation, Morgan's audiences were larger. Meyer confessed to his friends that he was tempted to feel envious of Morgan, but he said, "The only way I can conquer my feelings is to pray for him daily, which I do."

Why is it we feel a secret inner cringing when our close friend wins a free trip to Hawaii? When our coworker gets a raise? When our buddy wins the MVP trophy? When our best friend's child gets the starring role in the play?

Envy isn't just an inner emotion; it's a sinful attitude. Mark tells us that the chief priests handed Jesus over to be crucified "because of envy" (Mark 15:10). If you're envious of someone today, try the Meyer method—pray for that person. It's hard to envy someone while asking God to bless him!

DON'T FUMBLE YOUR FAITH

Be sober, be vigilant; because your adversary the devil walks about like a roaring lion, seeking whom he may devour.
1 PETER 5:8

Running back Rashaan Salaam won the Heisman Trophy in 1994 as the best player in college football. But in his rookie season with the NFL's Chicago Bears, he fumbled the ball nine times. To prevent future fumbles, the coaches fixed a tether to the football. When Salaam ran with it in practice, someone ran behind him jerking on the tether, forcing Salaam to grasp the ball more tightly. As his grip grew stronger, his fumbles grew fewer.

The Bible is clear that God does not tempt anyone to sin (James 1:13). But it is also clear that God allows us to be tempted. Have you ever wondered why? Just as having someone try to jerk the ball out of his hands caused a star football player to stop fumbling, so God allows Satan to attempt to steal our faith so we'll learn to grasp it tighter. Often we don't realize the value of something we have until someone attempts to steal it from us. Your faith is a treasure delivered to you for safekeeping by God. Hold it tight regardless of how hard you're hit by the opposition.

View temptations as your heavenly Coach's way to keep you from fumbling your faith.

THE POWER OF THE WORD

And daily in the temple, and in every house, they did not cease teaching and preaching Jesus as the Christ.
ACTS 5:42

Alexander Smith was the sole survivor of the band of mutineers who took the English ship *Bounty* from its captain, William Bligh, in 1787. The community of natives for which Smith found himself responsible on Pitcairn Island were defeated, diseased, and despondent—until he discovered the *Bounty's* Bible, which he began to teach them. Twenty years later, a visiting ship found a thriving Christian community, the fruit of the Word of God.

Because the Word of God is living and active (Hebrews 4:12), and because it never fails to accomplish the purposes for which it was given (Isaiah 55:10–11), we should not be surprised when we read stories like that of Alexander Smith. Multitudes of lives throughout history—including yours?—have been transformed by responding to the teaching of Scripture. Some Christians have the spiritual gift of teaching, but all Christians are responsible for knowing God's truth and communicating it to others as the Spirit gives opportunity.

God has chosen preaching and teaching the Bible as the means for announcing the good news of salvation. How shall people otherwise hear (Romans 10:14)?

ACCEPT ONE ANOTHER

Therefore receive one another, just as Christ also received us, to the glory of God.
ROMANS 15:7

Author and Nobel laureate Elie Wiesel worked in New York City after World War II as a correspondent for a French newspaper. His travel permit expired, and he was told at the French consulate that he would have to return to France to have it renewed, which he could not afford to do. At the U.S. immigration office, an official kindly said to him, "Why don't you become a U.S. resident and apply for citizenship?" So he did. Years later, when offered French citizenship, Wiesel declined. When he needed a homeland, it was America that had offered him one.

People often gravitate to where they are accepted. When we were lost, "having no hope and without God in the world" (Ephesians 2:12), it was God who "accepted [us] in the Beloved" (Ephesians 1:6). Once accepted by Him, we remain because of the riches of grace He bestows upon us. Millions of wandering souls have found welcome refuge in America, but millions more have found welcome acceptance in the kingdom of God. If you know people who are looking for acceptance, why not model God's acceptance by extending them yours?

Accepting people as they are is the first step toward helping them find out who they can become.

The Benchmark of Our Faith

And if Christ is not risen, then our preaching is empty and your faith is also empty.
1 Corinthians 15:14

The Christian apologist and author C. S. Lewis made an interesting observation about Jesus' practice of saying to people, "I forgive you." It is natural for us to forgive people for things they have done to us. But what would you say if someone cheated you out of ten dollars and I say, "That's all right; I forgive him"?

When a person goes around forgiving people who haven't done anything to harm that person, something seems amiss. The Pharisees caught the problem immediately when they once said to Jesus, "Hold on there—who are you to say 'I forgive you?' No one but God can forgive sins" (Mark 2:7, paraphrased). Exactly. So Jesus was saying He was God.

Now anyone could make that claim, and many have. What's needed is something to back up those claims. Jesus did many such things, all of which led up to the greatest proof of all: His resurrection from the dead. There are some things only God can do—like forgiving sin and conquering death. And Jesus did them all. The Resurrection is the ultimate, historical benchmark for your faith. Jesus is God—the Resurrection proves it.

Your faith can remain full because Jesus' grave remains empty.

SUNDAYS

Continuing daily with one accord in the temple, and breaking bread from house to house . . .
ACTS 2:46

Evangelist Vance Havner wrote, "My father was faithful to the house of God. When he felt like it and when he didn't, when the preaching was good and when it wasn't, my father was there."

Today's crowd isn't quite so faithful, nor is our society very helpful. A group of churches in New Jersey issued an appeal to public and private sports leagues to refrain from scheduling games before noon on Sunday. Fewer and fewer families were in church because of children's sporting events.

A congregation in Andover, Massachusetts, conducted a marketing survey to find out when people could attend church. The most common response: Saturday at 5:00 p.m., because their Sundays were booked.

We need to be in church for many reasons, not the least of which is the mutual fellowship we have with other Christians. The body of Christ is a family whose members are involved with each other—encouraging and building up one another. The early Christians couldn't seem to be together enough. They continued daily with one accord in the temple and from house to house.

Be in church this Sunday.

Rules or Relationships?

For the kingdom of God is not eating and drinking, but righteousness and peace and joy in the Holy Spirit.
Romans 14:17

Bible scholars have attempted to count all the laws and commandments given by God in the Old Testament—635 is one such suggested total. Regardless of the exact number, life under the law was a life of rules and regulations. Worship, food, sacrifices, clothing, diseases, marriage . . . every aspect of life was the subject of a rule.

God's rules were given for a purpose—they paved the road to a relationship. Paul says that "the law was our tutor to bring us to Christ" (Galatians 3:24). God gave rules to show us our need for Jesus. When it became apparent over centuries of trying that Israel couldn't keep God's rules by herself, God unveiled a relationship with Jesus the Messiah. That relationship offered what rules never could: "righteousness and peace and joy in the Holy Spirit." Rules can establish boundaries for a relationship, but they cannot be the soul of it. If you tend to focus on rules, it might explain the absence of peace and joy.

Rules are like the skeleton, and relationships are like the heart. Both are important, but life depends on one more than the other.

Photos of Forgiveness

Forgive us our debts.
Matthew 6:12

Some people don't pray as they should because they feel unworthy to come before a pure and holy God. But Jesus taught us to include confession as a part of our prayers: "Forgive us our debts." When we pray in obedience, we must confess our sins; and when we pray in faith, we must trust God to fully forgive.

If you're having trouble with this, utilize some Bible visuals. Isaiah 1:18 tells us that when God forgives us, we are whiter than snow. Micah 7:19 says He casts our sins into the depths of the sea. Psalm 103:12 says He removes them as far from us as east from west.

Isaiah 38:17 says God casts our sins behind His back. In Matthew 18:21–35, Jesus compared our sins to a great debt cancelled by a gracious king. Psalm 51 talks about being washed and cleansed, and about God's hiding His face from our sins and blotting out our transgressions.

God provided this assortment of images because we need to visualize the vast, many dimensions of His grace. So when you pray, confess your sins specifically and claim God's forgiveness. Then go on and pray as one who is righteous in God's sight through the grace of our Lord Jesus.

He doesn't want you to continue feeling guilty. He wants you to pray.

A Heart Like God's

I have found David the son of Jesse, a man after My own heart, who will do all My will.
Acts 13:22

Imagine that you purchased a house and the previous owner gave you keys to all the rooms except one; he reserved the right to come and go as he pleased in that one room. That brings to mind how the founder of the Salvation Army, William Booth, answered Queen Victoria when she asked the secret of his ministry: "I guess the reason is because God has all there is of me."

Robert Boyd Munger wrote a famous tract titled *My Heart, Christ's Home*, in which he likened his heart to the rooms in a house. If your heart were divided into rooms, is there any one to which you would not give Christ the key? Or, like William Booth, does He have all there is of you?

When God chose a man to succeed Saul as king of Israel, He chose David. And the primary reason given in Scripture is that David was a man after God's own heart. That means that God would be just as comfortable in the house of David's heart as in His own. No surprises, no dark corners, no hidden passageways not revealed to the light. Our goal should be to create the kind of heart-home that Jesus would love to come to—a heart like God's own.

God is still looking today for hearts that are loyal to Him (2 Chronicles 16:9). Has he found yours?

AN ENCOURAGING PROMISE

Jesus answered him, "Where I am going you cannot follow Me now, but you shall follow Me afterward."
JOHN 13:36

An observer asked a foreman overseeing a demolition crew if he had to hire highly skilled men to tear the building down. "Not really," the foreman replied. "I just need strong men—men who can tear down in a matter of days something that took years to build." It never takes as long to destroy something as it took to put it together.

Jesus Christ spent three years building up a group of twelve disciples. They had high hopes and expectations that He would bring in the kingdom and rule of God to restore Israel to her former glory. While they grew steadily in their understanding of who Jesus was, it was harder for them to understand fully that He had to suffer and leave them before God's kingdom would be established on earth. Had Jesus not prepared the disciples for His going away, He could easily have crushed their spirits and undone all He had built into their lives. He chose to encourage them before the fact, not just after.

If you know someone who is about to face a potential disappointment or challenge, build him or her up beforehand with a preparatory word of encouragement. Encouragement in anticipation of disappointment may keep the latter from ever happening.

NEHEMIAH THE THANKSGIVER

So I . . . appointed two large thanksgiving choirs.
NEHEMIAH 12:31

Nehemiah is the Bible's great wall builder. His Old Testament book tells of the masterful way in which he prayerfully led his people to repair Jerusalem's broken-down defenses despite danger, discouragement, and insufficiency. At the dedication of the rebuilt walls, Nehemiah appointed two great thanksgiving choirs, made up of Levites having both musical skills and grateful souls (Nehemiah 12:8, 31). They were appointed to "praise and give thanks, group alternating with group" (v. 24). They were armed with strong voices, and with "cymbals and stringed instruments and harps . . . [and] trumpets" (vv. 27, 35).

Positioned on opposite walls, these thanksgiving choirs burst into praise and thanksgiving at the appointed moment, "for God had made them rejoice with great joy . . . so that the joy of Jerusalem was heard afar off" (v. 43).

There's a thanksgiving choir inside you. Look around at the beauty of God's creation, the power of His promises, and the record of His care over your life. Lift up your heart, and let the strains of thanksgiving pour forth from the ramparts of your soul.

THE ART OF HEALTHY LIVING

Revive me according to Your word.
PSALM 119:25

The Bible...is a book in which [a person] may learn from his Creator the art of healthy living," said Swiss physician Dr. Paul Tournier.

Hymnist Fanny Crosby gave this testimony: "This Book is to me God's treasure house. It is my bread of life, the anchor of my home, my pillar of fire by night, my pillar of cloud by day. It is the lantern that lights my pathway to my paradise home."

Missionary Amy Carmichael wrote, "Have you noticed this? Whatever need or trouble you are in, there is always something to help you in your Bible, if only you go on reading 'til you come to the word God specially has for you."

Doctors tell us that many lung diseases are caused by shallow breathing. We don't open up our lungs and deeply inhale the life-giving oxygen God has placed in our atmosphere. In the same way, many spiritual and emotional diseases are caused by shallow reading. We skim over favorite passages, but we don't set aside the necessary time to dig deeply into God's Word.

The Lord has given us the Bible to help us through the challenges of life. Breathe deeply of its oxygen. Feast richly on its truths. Read, study, memorize, and meditate on its verses. There you'll find the art of healthy living.

THE STRENGTH OF THE CHURCH

You also, as living stones, are being built up a spiritual house, a holy priesthood.
1 PETER 2:5

Whenever we hear about earthquakes in underdeveloped nations, the loss of life seems disproportionately large. Disaster experts usually cite a primary cause: the quality of building materials. It doesn't take much of a quake to bring down buildings made out of poor-quality bricks, mortar, and concrete.

Good mortar, often lacking in poorer parts of the world, has to have several ingredients to be strong: lime, cement, sand, and water. Often, small pebbles or steel bars are put in the mortar for added reinforcement. To the degree any of these elements are missing, the strength of the building is compromised.

Likewise, the "living stones" of the church need a mix of elements in order for the body to be edified, or strengthened: love, encouragement, love, correction, love, wisdom, love, service . . . and don't forget love. These, and more, make up the mortar that binds living stones to one another to withstand the assaults of the "gates of Hades" (Matthew 16:18). Make sure you add something to the mix this week to build up a brother or sister in Christ.

Dying to self is the only way living stones can strengthen one another.

Riches Untold

The blessing of the LORD makes one rich.
Proverbs 10:22

The cost of refurbishing Michelangelo's painted ceiling in the Sistine Chapel was $4.3 million. Not many of us can afford a ceiling like that. But God has placed an ever-changing fresco over our heads every day. The sky-blue ceiling and the star-spangled heavens are priceless yet free.

Van Gogh's "Portrait of Dr. Gachet" brought $82.5 million at Christie's, but God gives us His beautiful world to enjoy at no charge. Have you paid your water bill recently? Your electric bill? The Lord gives us the warmth of His sunshine, the cool of His breezes, the irrigation of His rain without cost. At a political fundraiser, VIPs who gave $4,000 each had their pictures taken with the president. But the King of kings welcomes us into His presence anytime, free of charge.

Charles Spurgeon said, "Scripture is the bank of heaven. You may draw from it as much as you please, without interference or hindrance." God cares about our needs, and He is interested in the "little things" of our lives. He wants to give us a life that's abundant, and He wants us to share abundantly with others. He wants us to freely receive and freely give. Trust Him with your needs, and learn to appreciate the riches of His grace.

How to Miss a Blessing

They immediately left their nets and followed Him.
Matthew 4:20

When writer, congresswoman, and ambassador Clare Booth Luce was seventy-five, she was asked whether she had any regrets. She said, "Sometimes I wake up in the middle of the night, and I remember a girlhood friend of mine who had a brain tumor and called me three times to come and see her. I was always too busy, and when she died, I was profoundly ashamed. I still remember that after fifty-six years."

Is there anything you have been putting off which, once the opportunity has passed, you will regret not having done? Procrastinating about service to others is a double-edged sword: not only do we fail to extend a blessing, but we miss the blessing that comes with being a blessing! Instead of a double blessing, procrastination results in no blessings at all.

When Jesus was calling His disciples, the original twelve left "immediately" to follow Him. Later, others said, "Let me first go and [do this or that important thing]" (Luke 9:59, 61). Guess who ended up changing the world and being blessed in the process? If God has put an opportunity for service in front of you, don't fail to take it—to bless and be blessed at the same time.

Remember: today is the day you thought about yesterday when you said, "I can do that tomorrow."

But in Everything by Prayer

Be anxious for nothing, but in everything by prayer and supplication, with thanksgiving, let your requests be made known to God.
Philippians 4:6

Do you have a prayer list? One young girl knew the power of specific prayer when she faced death head-on. In the midst of her sickness, she went to her pastor and asked what more she could do for Jesus in the short time she had to live. He suggested that she make a list of people in their small town who needed Christ, and pray that they would find salvation. She took his advice and prayed often for each person.

Some time later, God began to stir a revival in the village. Only after the girl died was her prayer list with the names of fifty-six people found under her pillow. All had put their faith in Christ—the last one on the night before her death.

Such is the power of definite, specific, fervent prayer. When we actively seek the Lord in prayer, He will answer. James 5:16 reminds us, "The prayer of a righteous man is powerful and effective" (NIV). Do not doubt the power of prayer in your life—it is truly a great adventure with God that is meant to bring you closer to Him.

The Deity Is in the Details

Put my tears into Your bottle; are they not in Your book?
Psalm 56:8

An apocryphal story is told about the filming of the legendary movie *The Bridge on the River Kwai*. The director was preparing for the epic shot of a locomotive and train falling from an exploding bridge into a river gorge below. Three cameras were assigned to shoot the scene. After the shot, the director radioed each camera operator. "Sorry, sir—my camera jammed," said the first. "Left my lens cap on," said the second. The director nearly fainted when the third said, "Ready when you are, sir!"

With one-time opportunities, details matter. Not even enthusiasm can make up for a lack of attention to details. Modern culture likes to say "the devil's in the details." Wrong! It is our God who is at work in even the smallest parts of life.

Daniel the prophet discovered this when God showed him a preview of world history: "There shall be seven weeks and sixty-two weeks" (Daniel 9:25). Not eight and sixty-three or six and sixty-one. God knows every detail of the past, present, and future of the world—and of your life. He counts your tears and knows the number of hairs on your head. How comforting to know our God has overlooked nothing.

Because God is in the details, He is always ready when you are.

TINY CAUSES, HUGE EFFECTS

Let the words of my mouth and the meditation of my heart be acceptable in Your sight, O LORD, my strength and my Redeemer.

PSALM 19:14

In 1996, Manila, capital city of the Philippines, suffered an outbreak of cholera due to a proliferation of flies and cockroaches. The mayor announced a bounty on the bugs, dead or alive, and thousands were brought in by citizens who were paid on the spot. Health officials knew that huge problems could be prevented by dealing with tiny causes.

Stopping that cholera outbreak was an example of the law of the harvest: sow a tiny cure and reap a huge benefit. Just as removing tiny bugs saved a city, so a tiny thought in our minds can have huge results. That's why Proverbs says to "keep your heart with all diligence . . . [and] put away from you a deceitful mouth" (4:23–24).

Thoughts and words are powerful. What we meditate on and speak can do great good or great harm. In the Bible, the Christian has access to the most powerful living words ever written, words that can renew the mind. Make sure this week that you spend time sowing seeds in your mind that will bear godly fruit in your life.

History's worst acts began with a tiny, unguarded thought that yielded an ungodly harvest of destruction.

FOURTEEN HUNDRED PENNIES

Let your requests be made known to God.
PHILIPPIANS 4:6

In his book *Master Secrets of Prayer*, Cameron V. Thompson says we should pray specifically. He wrote that when his daughter, Joy, was a small child, she set her heart on a certain present. Asking her sisters how many pennies it would take to buy it, she prayed for fourteen hundred pennies. A few days later, some friends came by with a jar of coins they had been saving. It contained slightly more than fourteen hundred pennies.

"Vague praying is lazy praying," said Thompson.

We must let our requests be made known to God and then remember to thank Him when the answers come. Toward that end, many Christians keep a prayer list or devotional notebook to record their prayer requests. Others use the flyleaf of their Bibles for this, though one soon runs out of room.

Make specific requests to God for your husband or wife, your children, your financial needs, your job, your friends, and for those who don't know Christ. Pray specifically for our local and national leaders. Pray in detail for the needs of overseas missionaries. As Philippians 4:6 says in the Phillips version: "Don't worry over anything whatever, tell God every detail."

GETTING BACK ON THE ALTAR

I beseech you therefore, brethren, by the mercies of God, that you present your bodies a living sacrifice, holy, acceptable to God, which is your reasonable service.

ROMANS 12:1

Genesis 22 contains one of the most famous stories in the Bible—indeed, in all of literature. It is the account of God commanding Abraham to offer his son Isaac as a sacrifice. This was the supreme test of Abraham's obedience, and he did not hesitate. Because of his obedience, Isaac was spared moments before the sacrifice was completed.

Consider this: what if God had told Isaac to take himself up to Mount Moriah; to build an altar; to climb upon the altar; and, with his own knife, to offer himself as a sacrifice to God? The Old Testament sacrificial rituals prepared people to offer animals as sacrifices; a sacrifice was something other than yourself. That tradition did not prepare the early church for what Paul instructed them to do: offer yourself as a living sacrifice to God.

Living sacrifices don't die physically, but they must die spiritually every day. As someone has well said, "The problem with living sacrifices is they keep crawling off the altar."

Look around—if you're standing on the ground, it's time to get back on the altar.

HOLES IN THE CARPET

Teach me Your way, O LORD.
PSALM 27:11

The village of Clifton Springs is situated in the Finger Lakes district of New York, known for its rolling hills and tranquil waters. In 1849, Dr. Henry Foster, a dedicated Christian, arrived there, looking for a place to practice medicine. He felt that many sick and exhausted people could be restored to active living through a combination of physical and spiritual treatment. From around the world, people trekked to his Clifton Springs Sanitarium to regain their health.

After Dr. Foster's death, visitors to the sanitarium would often ask one of his coworkers for the secret of the man's life and wisdom. Dr. Foster had exhibited an unusual grip on God's will and ways. The coworker would take the visitors upstairs to Dr. Foster's former office and, pointing to two ragged holes in the carpet worn out by the doctor's knees, say, "That, sir, was the secret of Henry Foster's power and wisdom in the things of God and man."

God often imparts His will to us in an atmosphere of prayer. Guidance doesn't usually come on the run. We must wait before the Lord until He teaches us His marvelous ways.

First Things First

All things are lawful for me, but all things are not helpful. All things are lawful for me, but I will not be brought under the power of any.

1 Corinthians 6:12

A godly seminary professor once told his students about spending the summer in Jerusalem working on a new Bible translation. While the students were envious of such a spiritual assignment, they were shocked to hear the professor say it had been one of the most unfruitful and carnal summers he had ever experienced!

How could studying and translating the Bible result in carnality and spiritual frustration? The professor reported that their scholarly efforts became mechanical and academic. In the midst of their dictionaries and texts, they lost sight of the One they were there to serve.

Christian service is important, but it can actually draw us away from the Savior if we let it. We can become so focused on meeting goals and achieving objectives that we don't notice ourselves drifting away from the Lord. Like Paul, we need to differentiate between the good, better, and best. Is there anything—even a good thing—that is keeping you from the Best?

Just because something can be done is not enough of a reason that it *should* be done.

AUGUST

AN ENCOURAGING PARDON

Then He said to Thomas, "Reach your finger here, and look at My hands; and reach your hand here, and put it into My side. Do not be unbelieving, but believing."
JOHN 20:27

While we say, "There's no such thing as a stupid question," we don't always act that way. Who hasn't found himself wanting to ask a question but feeling too afraid? We think everyone else already knows the answer (they usually don't) and that everyone else will make fun of us (they probably will).

Among Jesus' disciples, there was one man who wasn't afraid to ask: Thomas. In fact, history remembers him as "doubting Thomas" because of his refusal to believe that which he hadn't personally proven to be true. He was as discouraged as the rest of the disciples about Jesus' death, but eight days after the Resurrection, he still wouldn't take their word for it. (He was absent on Resurrection evening when Jesus appeared to the group.)

When he finally met Jesus face to face, Thomas found the Lord forgiving, not belittling. He allowed Thomas to come to faith in his own way and at his own pace. Jesus does the same with us. If you have a question, ask Him—you'll see.

Thankfully, Jesus makes fun of no one—even those of shaky faith.

Careless Words

Let no corrupt word proceed out of your mouth, but what is good for necessary edification.
Ephesians 4:29

It's right there on page sixty-four. A filthy word that occurs in a children's book entitled *The Canning Season*, along with quite a few other profanities and obscenities. And this isn't just an obscure book for kids. *The Canning Season* was glowingly reviewed in *The New York Times Book Review*, and it won the 2003 National Book Award for Young People's Literature.

Is there anything more out of place than profanity in a children's book?

Yes. Profanity in the mouth of someone who claims to follow the Lord Jesus Christ. The Bible warns that we can grieve the Holy Spirit by the words we say. Paul wrote that we should avoid filthiness, foolish talk, and coarse jesting. Our mouths should be full of thanksgiving instead (Ephesians 5:4–5).

Have you allowed some careless words to slip into your vocabulary? Have you grown used to hearing profanity on television, in novels, and, yes, even in today's children's entertainment? Rededicate yourself to obedience in this area, and let no corrupt communication proceed from your mouth.

ONE-TIME REWARDS

And whatever you do, do it heartily, as to the Lord and not to men.
COLOSSIANS 3:23

Years ago, a popular auto product commercial on television said, "You can pay me now, or you can pay me later." The idea was that it makes more sense to pay for an oil change now than to pay to have the whole engine rebuilt later. You don't have to pay twice—for oil changes and a rebuilt engine. You just pay once, and you pick the time and the amount.

There is an aspect of that theme that is consistent with Jesus' teaching on rewards for faithfulness in the spiritual life. In essence, He said, "You will be rewarded for the spiritual acts you undertake, but you'll only be rewarded once. You can either do your acts for men and get your rewards from them, or do your acts for God and get your rewards from Him." In other words, "Get your rewards now or get your rewards later—your choice."

Why would anyone choose to forego the eternal riches of God's rewards for the temporal rewards of man? Praise, notoriety, glory, and prominence—these are powerful and tempting inducements to work for man and be rewarded immediately. But a greater motivation for working only for God is the idea of being rewarded by Him alone with rewards that will never fade away.

Remember, we only get rewarded once. Choose the rewards that will last the longest and mean the most—those that come from God.

MAKEOVER PRIORITIES

For the LORD does not see as man sees; for man looks at the outward appearance, but the Lord looks at the heart.
1 SAMUEL 16:7

America has gone "makeover" crazy! You can't watch prime-time television very long on a weeknight without seeing a commercial for a makeover show—they're even making over houses. Whether the focus is on home or homely, the idea is the same: the exterior is all-important. Tear down the old, build up the new, and life will be better.

While exterior makeovers probably bring happiness to some, success isn't guaranteed. Studies have discovered a high degree of depression in post-makeover women because their plastic surgery didn't bring them the happiness they thought it would.

Isn't it great that we don't have to have a physical makeover to be attractive to God? The prophet Samuel said that God looks on the heart above all (1 Samuel 16:7), Jesus said it's what's on the inside of a person that's most important (Matthew 15:11), and Peter said wives are most attractive when they have a beautiful spirit (1 Peter 3:1–6). If you've been thinking about a makeover lately, start with the heart. Beauty on the interior can make us more attractive than rearranging the exterior.

A surgeon can make over the body, but only God can make over the heart.

Freedom Not to Sin

Having been set free from sin, you became slaves of righteousness.
Romans 6:18

In *The Grace Awakening*, Charles Swindoll recounts the first time his father let him take the family car out by himself for two hours. He thought of all the things he could do with his freedom—speeding, a quick trip out of town, showing off for his friends—and did none of them. Out of respect for his father's trust, he drove around safely and returned home early.

What would you do if you were granted unlimited freedom from any consequences for your actions? And how often do you find yourself angry with someone who has taken away your freedom (freedom to peace and quiet, freedom to a parking space, freedom to spend your money as you like)? It's easy, living in the "land of the free," to misunderstand the true meaning of spiritual freedom.

When we are born again through faith in Christ, we are given the power to be freed from the destructive compulsions and tendencies that can hurt us and others, and we are given new power to do what is best in life. We're given power to do those things that God created us to do, power to deny the demands of our old sin nature.

If there is a sin you're having trouble saying no to, ask God to give you a fresh glimpse of what it means to be free.

ASKING FOR DIRECTIONS

Whoever gives heed to instruction prospers, and blessed is he who trusts in the LORD.
PROVERBS 16:20 NIV

An old sailor repeatedly got lost at sea, so his friends gave him a compass and urged him to use it. The next time he went out in his boat, he followed their advice and took the compass with him, but he still got lost.

Finally, he was rescued by his friends. Disgusted and impatient with him, they asked, "Why didn't you use that compass we gave you? You could have saved us a lot of trouble!" The sailor responded, "I didn't dare to! I wanted to go north, but as hard as I tried to make the needle aim in that direction, it just kept on pointing southeast." The old sailor was so certain he knew which direction was north that he stubbornly tried to force his own personal persuasion on his compass. Unable to do so, he tossed it aside as worthless and failed to benefit from the guidance it offered.

God's Word is your compass. Use it on a daily basis to check in, to make sure that you are going in the right direction. Stubbornness and busyness can take you off course, but God's Word is right there waiting for your return. Don't be afraid to ask God for directions.

THE HANDS OF JESUS

Now God worked unusual miracles by the hands of Paul.
ACTS 19:11

After World War II, a group of German students volunteered to rebuild a severely damaged cathedral. A large statue of Jesus, with outstretched arms and the words "Come unto Me" inscribed on it was missing both hands. Since it proved impossible to reattach the hands, they decided to leave them off. And they changed the inscription to read, "Christ has no hands but ours."

The most well-known metaphor used by the apostle Paul for the followers of Jesus was "the body of Christ." First, though Jesus' literal body is absent from the earth, He is still ministering through the corporate body of His followers. Second, a body has many unique parts, which the New Testament writers compared to individual Christians. Some are ears, some are hands, some are feet—all working in harmony to do the work of Jesus in the world.

If you are a follower of Jesus, you have been given grace (a spiritual gift), through the Holy Spirit, to do something that Jesus would do if He were here personally. Through you, the hands of Jesus are ministering daily to others.

The person touched by Christ's follower is being touched by Christ Himself.

WHEN CRITICISM COMES

Each one should test his own actions. Then he can take pride in himself, without comparing himself to somebody else.
GALATIANS 6:4 NIV

The Chinese Christian, Watchman Nee, died for his faith in a communist prison. During his lifetime, he was roundly criticized by the government. Smear campaigns were employed to discredit him, but he never responded to critics and never defended himself. Asked about it, he said, "Brothers, if people trust us, there is no need to explain; and if they don't trust us, there is no use in explaining."

The apostle Paul said about his critics: "It matters very little to me what you think of me, even less where I rank in popular opinion. I don't even rank myself. . . . The Master makes that judgment" (1 Corinthians 4:3–4 MSG).

How do we respond to unfair criticism and unkind words? Our natural reaction is to feel indignant and defensive, to try to straighten everyone out. But we need thick skin, soft hearts, and an absolute trust in the Lord to give us favor in the sight of God and man as He chooses. There may be times to defend ourselves or offer an explanation, but we must guard against taking criticism too seriously. We're responsible for our character, but we can leave our reputation in His hands.

Mother's Sacrifice

Let your father and your mother be glad, and let her who bore you rejoice.
Proverbs 23:25

A teacher asked a boy this question: "Suppose your mother baked a pie and there were seven of you—your parents and five children. What part of the pie would you get?" "A sixth," replied the boy. "I'm afraid you don't know your fractions," said the teacher. "Remember, there are seven of you." "Yes, Teacher," said the boy, "but you don't know my mother. Mother would say she didn't want any pie."

One of the most amazing character traits of a mother is her willingness to sacrifice her own desires for her family. The word *sacrifice* means forfeiture of something highly valued for the sake of one considered to have a greater value or claim. Whether it's a piece of pie or valuable time, all mothers give up what they want for the benefit of their children. But the giving of themselves is not done in vain; there are great rewards. Having a servant's heart is a theme throughout the entire Bible.

There is no greater reward than reaping the benefits of sacrificing personal needs for those of others. A mother's commitment, sacrifice, and prayer can be the foundation that directs her children into a lifelong journey with God.

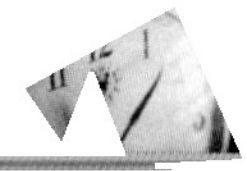

THE WOLF OF DEATH

Then they will call on me, but I will not answer; they will seek me diligently, but they will not find me.
PROVERBS 1:28

One of Aesop's fables is about a shepherd boy who was watching a flock of sheep. Wanting to play a trick on the villagers, several times he cried out, "Wolf! Wolf!" and then laughed at the villagers who rushed to his aid. When a wolf actually came to attack his flock, the boy cried out in earnest but was ignored. His game-playing proved his undoing when death was at his door.

Picture the shepherd boy as the nominal religious person of our day and the villagers as the God of Scripture. Some people are going through life treating it as a game, playing at religion, believing that when the day of judgment comes, God will save them from destruction. They think about the gospel in their idle moments or when small crises occur, but they never really commit themselves to a saving relationship with Christ.

If you have been living life on the periphery of faith, don't wait until the last day. Call out for Christ by faith before it is too late. Better to call out for Jesus while you have your breath than in the day you lose it.

Seeking Godly Counsel

Listen to advice and accept instruction, that you may gain wisdom for the future.
Proverbs 19:20 RSV

Automaker Henry Ford asked electrical genius Charlie Steinmetz to build the generators for his factory. One day the generators ground to a halt, and the repairmen couldn't find the problem. So Ford called Steinmetz, who tinkered with the machines for a few hours and then threw the switch. The generators whirred to life. Then Ford got a bill for $10,000 from Steinmetz. Flabbergasted, the rather tightfisted carmaker inquired why the bill was so high when it took so little time. Steinmetz's reply: "For tinkering with the generators, $10. For knowing where to tinker, $9,990." Ford paid the bill.

Obtaining wisdom and godly advice is priceless and hard to find in today's society. There are plenty of people who want to give their opinion, but the Bible is the ultimate guidebook on wisdom. One place you might not have thought of is your local church. Most churches offer mentoring programs, counseling, and the chance to meet one-on-one with the pastor.

Take this into consideration the next time you are making big decisions or are confused about an issue. Proverbs 15:22 says, "Plans fail for lack of counsel, but with many advisers they succeed" (NIV).

Forgiveness That Heals

Be kind and compassionate to one another, forgiving each other, just as in Christ God forgave you.
Ephesians 4:32 NIV

A Spanish father and son had become estranged after years of fighting. The son ran away, and the father set out to find him. He searched for months to no avail. Finally, in a last desperate effort to find him, the father put an ad in a Madrid newspaper. The ad read: "Dear Paco, meet me in front of this newspaper office at noon on Saturday. All is forgiven. I love you. Your father." On Saturday, eight hundred Pacos showed up, looking for forgiveness and love from their fathers.

People are not perfect. That is why God sent His Son to earth—to forgive us of our sins. But forgiveness doesn't stop there; it is just the beginning. Matthew 6:14 says, "For if you forgive men when they sin against you, your heavenly Father will also forgive you" (NIV). The act of forgiveness is not easy, but the Bible calls us to put aside our pride and forgive one another.

Is there someone in your life who needs your forgiveness? Is there a family member or friend who needs to forgive you? There is no better time than right now to make those relationships right.

AUGUST 13

DELETING THE VIRUS OF SIN

A little leaven leavens the whole lump.
GALATIANS 5:9

Almost weekly, we hear about a new computer virus that is spreading around the world—deleting files, crashing hard drives, and souring attitudes. Software viruses act like their biological cousins—they spread from one computer to another. The surest way to prevent them from infecting other computers is to delete them as soon as they're discovered.

Hitting the delete button on a computer is a simple and effective way of staying virus free. But the language of the New Testament pictures staying sin-free as a little more involved. Paul describes sin almost like a virus. He calls it leaven, the bacteria that makes bread dough rise. Once leaven gets in a lump of dough . . . well, getting it out takes some effort.

It's far better never to let sin get into our lives to begin with. But if it does, what do we do then? First, we must repent—that is, make up our minds to go a different way. Then, we confess—agree with God about what we've done, and receive His forgiveness. Finally, we put on the armor of God: faith, righteousness, and the Word of God. Don't let the virus of sin multiply in your life.

It is far better to deal with our own sin than to have God deal with it for us.

REJECTION

The stone which the builders rejected has become the chief cornerstone.
PSALM 118:22

Miriam's heart sank as she stood by her locker reading a letter her school counselor had just handed her. She'd been rejected by the university she wanted to attend. Across the hall, Martin was experiencing the same feeling, having been cut from the high school basketball team. His buddy, Thomas, had stayed home from school that day, literally sick because his girlfriend had broken up with him.

Rejection is one of the hardest burdens we're ever called on to bear. It undercuts our self-confidence and damages our sense of well-being. But it helps to remember that our Lord Himself understands the pain of rejection. Isaiah 53:3 says, "He is despised and rejected by men, a Man of sorrows and acquainted with grief. And we hid, as it were, our faces from Him." Jesus said, "The Son of Man must suffer many things, and be rejected" (Luke 9:22).

Because He was rejected, we can be accepted. Ephesians 1:6 says that it is God's grace "by which He made us accepted in the Beloved."

If you're facing the pain of rejection today, remember that Jesus Himself understands, He cares, and He is waiting to embrace your hurts and encourage your heart.

AMAZING MERCY AND GRACE

Therefore, I urge you, brothers, in view of God's mercy, to offer your bodies as living sacrifices.
ROMANS 12:1 NIV

A young Englishman wanted to be a seafaring man like his father, but the British Royal Navy would not have him. He ended up in West Africa working for a slave trader, a "wretched man," as one writer called him, begging for food to stay alive. Escaping Africa, he was washed overboard in a storm and nearly drowned at sea. After being rescued, the words of Thomas à Kempis's *Imitation of Christ* came to him, and he cried out to God for salvation. Years later, John Newton wrote a hymn in praise of the "amazing grace" that saved a wretch like him.

Not all of us have experienced the depths of wretchedness John Newton did before being saved. Or King Nebuchadnezzar, for that matter. He lost his dignity and sanity—and fortunately, his pride—before coming to his senses (Daniel 4:33–37). Whether we come from a background of wickedness or willfulness, our sin merits the same response in God's sight: condemnation. It is only God's amazing mercy and grace that can save us from ourselves.

Recipients of God's grace are easy to spot—they're the ones with the grateful looks on their faces and words of thanks on their lips.

NO EXCEPTIONS

Therefore show these men the proof of your love and the reason for our pride in you, so that the churches can see it.
2 CORINTHIANS 8:24 NIV

One evening, Pastor Bill Hybels stopped by his church to encourage those rehearsing for the spring musical. He didn't intend to stay long, so he parked next to the entrance.

The next morning he received this note: "A small thing, but last night you parked in the 'No Parking' area. One of my crew (who did not recognize you) said, 'There's another jerk in the "No Parking" area!' We try hard not to allow people—even workers—to park anywhere other than the parking lots. I would appreciate your cooperation, too. Signed, a member of maintenance."

What an example from a leader! No one is exempt from church rules or God's rules. That night, Bill realized the employee didn't want him to be labeled "I'm an exception." Exemplary conduct means encouraging others to imitate us, even in small matters. Whether the leader of a church or a member of the clean-up crew, we are all to be held accountable so that we are an example of God's love.

Be aware throughout the day of the example God gave us through His Son, Jesus. And be aware of your actions and how they affect others. Be an example God would be proud of.

AUGUST 17

NEED A MIRACLE?

This beginning of signs Jesus did in Cana of Galilee, and manifested His glory; and His disciples believed in Him.
JOHN 2:11

A couple sits on opposite ends of the couch, each of them lonely. What was once a vital marriage has digressed into something neither of them ever intended. They love each other, but they both know restoring the marriage they once had would take a miracle.

Fortunately for them, and the millions like them, a miracle is not a far stretch for our God. In fact, Jesus' first miracle recorded in Scripture was performed in a home at a wedding (John 2:1–11). He came by invitation to the very ceremony where marriage is established—a reminder to us that God cares very deeply for families.

If we aren't careful, we might think God had abandoned the institution of marriage and the importance of the home altogether. Browbeaten with statistics of marital failure, many couples forget who authored the marriage relationship in the first place.

Does your home need a miracle? Invite Christ into every room. Make Him the foundation of each relationship that is built within its walls. Like the water turned to wine at the wedding in Cana, Christ's power can transform hurt into harmony.

SECRET OF CONTENTMENT

Not that I speak in regard to need, for I have learned in whatever state I am, to be content.
PHILIPPIANS 4:11

A man named Agur once prayed a prayer that most moderns would find curious: "Give me neither poverty nor riches—feed me with the food allotted to me; lest I be full and deny You, and say, 'Who is the LORD?' Or lest I be poor and steal, and profane the name of my God" (Proverbs 30:8–9).

Most people today want to avoid poverty (though not for Agur's reason), but who in our materialistic day prays to avoid riches? Agur knew something that people today have missed completely: riches have the potential for being a trap and a source of ruin.

The apostle Paul knew what Agur knew; he had learned the secret of contentment. Paul was comfortable with having little and with having a lot because he believed that God was his provider. Because his eyes were fixed on heavenly things, he could be content with whatever earthly things God gave him.

The next time you lose your material contentment, remind yourself of who owns it all and how He's promised to provide. Contentment is an excellent indicator of what we think about God and His will.

PERSISTENCE IN PRAYER

The effective, fervent prayer of a righteous man avails much.
JAMES 5:16

A devout Scottish preacher named John Welsh used to kneel at his bedside and pray for the members of his church before retiring for the night. His wife was known to say, "Come to bed, John; it's too cold." His response to her was always the same: "But dear, I have the souls of three thousand people to answer for, and I do not know how it is with many of them."

It is one thing to pray, but it is altogether another to pray without giving up until the answer to your prayers is received. Jesus taught the disciples a parable about a widow who wouldn't give a judge any peace until she got what she needed. The lesson? That people "always ought to pray and not lose heart" (Luke 18:1–8). He could easily have told them the story of Daniel who prayed for twenty-one days before he received an answer from heaven—an answer delayed by spiritual warfare in the heavenlies (Daniel 10:1–11:1).

What if Daniel had given up praying after a week? After two weeks? No wonder God blessed Daniel with an understanding of mysteries revealed to no one else. If you are praying and waiting on an answer, don't stop! The answer may be just another prayer away.

The surest way not to get an answer to prayer is not to pray!

TRUSTING GOD

They said to Joshua, "Truly the LORD has delivered all the land into our hands, for indeed all the inhabitants of the country are fainthearted because of us."
JOSHUA 2:24

When Joshua sent the spies into Jericho, he must have recalled what had happened to the twelve spies forty years earlier. This time, Joshua chose men with trusting, faithful hearts who would take God at His Word and not panic. Despite a narrow escape, the explorers returned with a good report.

The Lord is still looking for people who will trust Him. Too many of us get upset and angry in the face of pain and problems. Such reactions, though natural, are unhealthy. A recent study found hostility a bigger predictor of coronary heart disease than high cholesterol, smoking, or obesity. Those who respond to adversity with anger or acute anxiety may trigger such conditions as cardiac arrhythmia.

Faith, however, calms us. It was the inhabitants of Jericho, not the spies, who were fainthearted in this story. How wonderful to say, "With God, we can be victorious." How wonderful to live by faith, not by fear.

ONWARD CHRISTIAN SOLDIER

And whoever does not bear his cross and come after Me cannot be My disciple.
LUKE 14:27

Entering boot camp for basic military training used to mean being stripped of all your identity. Everything was taken from you—including your hair!—and you were given back only what you would need to be a good soldier. You were even told what to think. "When I want your opinion," the drill sergeant would bark, "I'll give it to you!"

Not to compare the Christian life with the military . . . but wait—even Paul drew that comparison (2 Timothy 2:3). There is discipline, training, and especially sacrifice in both the military and the Christian life. When Jesus was recruiting and training His own kingdom soldiers, He told them they would only need one thing in order to follow Him: a cross.

He didn't say to bring your checkbook, your 401(k) retirement portfolio, your dreams and aspirations, or your hobbies. He just said to take up your cross and follow Him. The point of that drastic charge was simple: following Jesus means giving up everything in order to receive from Him so much more in due time and in His way.

The Christian soldier carries only one possession into battle: the cross of self-surrender to Jesus.

LOST LOVE SOUGHT

If it is possible, as much as depends on you, live peaceably with all men.
ROMANS 12:18

Elizabeth Barrett Browning's parents so disapproved of her marriage to Robert Browning that they disowned her. For ten years, Elizabeth wrote love letters to her parents seeking reconciliation, but with no reply. Then a large box arrived in the mail from her parents. Excitedly she opened it, only to find all of her letters to her parents unopened and unread.

We know Elizabeth Browning's love letters today as some of the most beautiful in all of classical English literature. They would have been even more famous if they had stirred the reconciliation with her parents that she longed for. Given Elizabeth's experience, some might say, "See, what's the use? All that work and no results." But if only one letter out of the hundreds had been read, and it had healed the relationship between daughter and parents, all her labor would have been repaid.

Restoring relationships is not easy. It requires death to oneself, obedience to God, and love for others—just what Christ displayed when He reconciled us to the Father. Be Christlike today, and restore a lost love.

No one ever said reconciliation was easy—just desirable, possible, and much more joyful than the alternative.

FAITH VERSUS FATE

Yet who knows whether you have come to the kingdom for such a time as this?
ESTHER 4:14

The Confederate general Thomas "Stonewall" Jackson had an unswerving confidence in the plan and protection of God. Once, during a battle, he sat down to write out a message to send to a subordinate. A Union cannonball struck a large oak tree above where he sat, showering him with bark and wood chips. He brushed off his paper and continued writing, focused on his task.

Jackson might have echoed the words of Esther from the fifth century BC in Persia: "If I perish, I perish" (4:16). When Esther spoke those words, she didn't speak fatalistically; she spoke faithfully. Esther was a Jewess who was the wife of the Persian king. When she learned of a plot by a Persian official to destroy all the Jews in Persia, she took her life in her hands by daring to approach the king to save her people from destruction. Persian law said that anyone approaching the king without permission—even his wife—would die unless the king granted a pardon. Your faith in Christ may not be a life-or-death issue, but if it were, would your faith let you risk dying in order to do the will of God?

When your faith is in God, the chips can fall where they may without taking you from the task at hand.

HONOR AND BLESSING

Honor your father and your mother, that your days may be long upon the land which the LORD your God is giving you.
EXODUS 20:12

There is widespread agreement that the custom of standing during the "Hallelujah Chorus" of Handel's *Messiah* began with King George II of England. When the king stood, everyone in the room stood.

Showing respect for authorities, women, the elderly, parents, and others is fast disappearing in modern cultures. In ancient cultures, a failure to show respect could have a serious impact on one's lifespan. The fifth of the Ten Commandments promised long life in the Promised Land to Israelites who honored their parents.

Theologians refer to this law as the "law of filial obedience," and violation of this law could lead to the death of a rebellious child. Children of all ages have a biblical responsibility to honor their parents in appropriate ways, and the expectation of God's blessing upon their "filial obedience."

Honoring one's parents translates to "the fear of the LORD" (Proverbs 1:7) as we honor our own heavenly Father.

COURAGEOUS FAITH

Be strong and of good courage, do not fear nor be afraid of them; for the LORD your God, He is the One who goes with you. He will not leave you nor forsake you.
DEUTERONOMY 31:6

When Martin Luther stood before his accusers at the Diet of Worms in Germany on April 18, 1521, he epitomized courage. "My conscience is captive to the Word of God," he declared. "I cannot and will not retract anything, since it is neither safe nor right to go against conscience. I cannot do otherwise; here I stand; may God help me. Amen."

Martin Luther's courage and resolve were like those of Daniel, who found himself captive in Babylon. As a teenager, Daniel was put on a "fast track" to become a scholar in Nebuchadnezzar's court. When given Babylonian food to eat, he took a stand. The food violated Israel's dietary standards and had probably been offered to idols before being served. Fortunately, he suggested an alternative diet that increased his health and his reputation for wisdom.

When your convictions are challenged, suggest a creative alternative. But before you do, make sure you have the courage to back it up—in case the answer is no.

If you are going to have courage, you must first have a conscience nurtured by conviction.

OUR ON-TIME GOD

Your eyes saw my substance, being yet unformed. And in Your book they all were written, the days fashioned for me, when as yet there were none of them.
PSALM 139:16

In June 1926, Raymond Edman, a young missionary in Ecuador, fell ill with typhus fever. When he was finally seen by a doctor, his condition was pronounced as incurable, and funeral plans were made. Back in Boston, a friend interrupted a prayer meeting with a burden to pray for Ray Edman. Years later, in 1967, Dr. Raymond Edman, president of Wheaton College, finished addressing the student body in chapel and collapsed in death.

Raymond Edman's first brush with death was just forty-one years too soon; God had a college He wanted Edman to run before coming home to heaven. God's timetable, especially in matters of life and death, is the Christian's greatest security.

No one discovered that more than the friends and family of Lazarus. When Jesus did resurrect Lazarus, it was to the glory of God. No one but God could raise a corpse that had been dead four days (John 11:39). If you're facing a life-or-death crisis, remember: God is never early or late.

When your timetable doesn't match God's, someone is either early or late. And guess who has never been either?

Father, thank You that Your schedule is perfect, that You are always on time.

POSITIVE CHANGES

He changes the times and the seasons.
DANIEL 2:21

A cartoonist in *The New Yorker* drew a picture of a small-town general store with this banner in the window: "Going Out of Business, Slowly but Surely." Many churches and organizations go out of business slowly but surely because they resist change.

You might not like change, but I'll bet you can think of something worse—stagnation! "Stagnation can befall any kind of organization," warns consultant Jeanie Daniel Duck.

Stagnation can also befall people. We have to remember that while not all changes are good, changes from God are very good. "Wherever the Lord's Spirit is, there is freedom," wrote the apostle Paul. "As all of us reflect the Lord's glory with faces that are not covered with veils, we are being changed into His image with ever-increasing glory. This comes from the Lord, who is the Spirit" (2 Corinthians 3:18 GW).

What a mess we'd be in if we couldn't change our sinful lives, if we couldn't grow or improve, if we couldn't learn or advance. Don't be afraid of change, and don't be afraid to change. Just make sure you're changing for the better.

BE HONEST WITH YOURSELF

Let no one deceive you.
EPHESIANS 5:6

A well-known defense attorney named Charles A. Peruto Jr. was asked about the admission by Pete Rose, after fourteen years of denial, that he bet on baseball while managing the Cincinnati Reds. Peruto replied dryly, "So now 100 percent of the population knows he bet on baseball. The only person who didn't know before he confessed was him."

It's odd how easy it is to deceive ourselves. Is it possible that your husband, your wife, or your best friend has a better grasp of your strengths and weaknesses than you do? Is it possible that you're in denial about a particular weakness, insisting you don't have a problem, though it's perfectly obvious to everyone else that you do?

Those who work with addictions say that denial and self-deception are our greatest enemies. We insist we don't have a problem when it's readily apparent to everyone else that we're in deep trouble. It isn't just addictive disorders, of course. All sin is self-deceiving.

Ask God to show you if there is an area in your life that needs correction. Pray in these words from an old hymn: "Search me, O God, and know my heart today! Try me, O Father, and know my thoughts, I pray."

August 29

Do I Have Faith?

Now faith is the substance of things hoped for, the evidence of things not seen.
Hebrews 11:1

The African impala is one of the most powerful and graceful animals in Africa. It can jump to a height of more than ten feet and cover a distance of more than thirty feet in one jump. In spite of its great ability, an impala can be kept in an enclosure with a solid fence no more than three feet high. Impalas will not jump if they can't see where their feet will land. Impalas walk by sight, not faith.

Don't laugh—there are many Christians who walk the same way. Faith is "the evidence of things not seen," not the evidence of things seen. As a believer, if we are willing to take steps in life only when we can see exactly what's on the path, we don't have biblical faith.

Abraham was a man who had true faith. God called him from his home in Mesopotamia and directed him to he knew not where. Abraham just obeyed God, left his home, and walked one step at a time. Eventually, he arrived at his destination—not because he saw Canaan but because he saw the will of God for his life.

The future can only be faced in two ways: with faith or with fear. How small is the enclosure that has you penned in? If you have to see the next step before you'll move ahead, you're trusting your sight instead of your Savior.

SHARING GOD'S WORD

Those who fear You will be glad when they see me, because I have hoped in Your word.
PSALM 119:74

In 1631, an English Bible printer made a serious error: he forgot to include the "not" in one of the Ten Commandments. His version of Exodus 20:14 read, "Thou shalt commit adultery." His edition of the Bible became known as "The Wicked Bible." He was fined £300, and all the copies of his Bible were destroyed.

The moral of the story? It's wonderful to share the Bible with others, but make sure you share it accurately! Jesus compared the Word of God with seeds sown in the soil. The condition of the soil, the depth of the soil, and environmental factors will determine whether seeds spring up and ultimately bear fruit (Matthew 13:3–23). And the same is true of the Word of God. Many factors are beyond our control, but what we can control is whether the Word of God is shared with others.

Christians as well as non-Christians need the Word, so it is not just a matter of evangelism. It is a matter of being a person who speaks the Word and wisdom of God to others to address the critical needs in the world today.

When people with receptive hearts discover that your words are God's words, not the words of man, they will rejoice when they see you.

AUGUST 31

STRIFE OR LIFE?

If it is possible, as much as depends on you, live peaceably with all men.

ROMANS 12:18

Hercules, according to legend, grew increasingly irritated by a menacing animal that kept blocking his path. He angrily struck the animal with his club, killing it. As he continued on his path, he kept encountering the same animal, each time more menacing than before. At last, a friend warned Hercules to stop his furious assaults. "The monster is Strife, and you are stirring it up," said the messenger. "Just let it alone, and it will shrivel and die."

Our newspapers are full of stories about strife. We read about nations disrupted by civil strife, athletes upset by team strife, companies suffering labor strife, of homes troubled by marital strife.

The Bible uses the word *strife* many times. Solomon said, "Better is a dry morsel with quietness, than a house full of feasting with strife" (Proverbs 17:1). And Paul said, "Let us walk properly, as in the day, not in…strife and envy" (Romans 13:13).

Are you stirring up strife? We're not responsible for the actions and reactions of others, but we are responsible for our own. Put on the Lord Jesus, evict strife from your life, forgive that grudge, and seek to live peaceably with all.

SEPTEMBER

Eight o'Clock

The prayer of a righteous man is powerful and effective.
James 5:16 NIV

Howard Cadle started drinking at age twelve and was soon in the grip of every kind of addiction. He also became caught up in a sprawling Midwest crime syndicate. His worried mother could do nothing but pray. "Always remember, son," she said, "that at eight o'clock every night I'll be kneeling beside your bed, asking God to protect my precious boy."

One evening in a rampage, Howard pulled a gun on a man and squeezed the trigger. The weapon didn't fire, and someone knocked it away. It was exactly eight o'clock. Shortly afterward, Howard made his way home, penniless and ill. "Mother," he said, "I've broken your heart. I'd like to be saved, but I've sinned too much."

His mother, using Isaiah 1:18, led him to the Lord. Howard Cadle went on to become a successful businessman, Christian leader, and one of America's pioneer radio evangelists, preaching on Cincinnati's powerful WLM. "Until He calls me," Cadle once said, "I shall preach the same gospel that caused my sainted mother to pray for me."

Don't forget to pray for your children, and never give up. The prayers of a righteous parent are powerful and effective.

PICTURE OF ENCOURAGEMENT

I am sending him to you . . . that he may know . . . and comfort your hearts.

COLOSSIANS 4:8

Edward Steichen, who eventually became one of the world's most renowned photographers, almost gave up on the day he shot his first pictures. At sixteen, young Steichen bought a camera and took fifty photos. Only one turned out. Edward's father thought that was a poor showing. But his mother insisted that the one photograph was so beautiful that it more than compensated for forty-nine failures. Her encouragement convinced him not to quit. Steichen stayed with photography for all his life, but it had been a close call.

What tipped the scales? His mother's vision. She saw excellence in the midst of failure. That's what God does for us. He is our most persistent encourager, and He often uses others to encourage us.

A word of encouragement can be used of God to help a fellow believer reach spiritual success. Jesus prepared His discouraged followers with the promise that He would send them another Comforter.

Perhaps today God will direct you in being an encourager. First Thessalonians 5:11 tells us, "Comfort each other." There is no greater joy than to know the Comforter can work through you to comfort others.

WHO AND WHOSE YOU ARE

For whom the LORD loves He corrects, just as a father the son in whom he delights.
PROVERBS 3:12

Individual birth certificates are so important that state governments keep a copy in case the original is lost or destroyed. Your birth certificate proves two things about you: who you are (your name, date, and place of birth) and whose you are (your parents' names). You can't get married, obtain a passport, or receive a driver's license without a birth certificate.

For the Christian, there is a different kind of proof that tells who and whose you are, spiritually speaking: the loving discipline of a heavenly Father. In Scripture, discipline is more akin to child training than to punishment. Just as an earthly father employs numerous methods of training in raising his children, so does God in raising us as His spiritual children.

In fact, the Bible says we are illegitimate children, not really God's, if we don't experience His hand of training in our lives. God's discipline is proof that we belong to Him. Treat God's discipline in your life with as much care as you do your birth certificate.

When God's training stretches you beyond your comfort zone, be thankful that it proves who and whose you are.

LOOK AND SEE

For since the creation of the world His invisible attributes are clearly seen, being understood by the things that are made, even His eternal power and Godhead, so that they are without excuse.
ROMANS 1:20

During the early years of the space race in the 1960s, a Soviet cosmonaut proclaimed to the world that he had proved there was no God, because he had looked around in space while circling the earth and couldn't find Him. (One humorist suggested that the cosmonaut would have met Him promptly if he had just opened the hatch of the capsule!)

Several years later, on December 24, 1968, another message was boldly proclaimed by American astronauts James Lovell, Frank Borman, and William Anders as they circled the moon: "In the beginning, God created the heavens and the earth." Had our astronauts seen God in person to verify their claim? No—but they had seen evidence of Him.

The Bible tells us that one of the chief ways we know of God's existence and His love for us is by the marvels of His creation. Whether we step back and look at the way our solar system works, or step forward and look at the intricacies of nature and the miracle of human life, we see evidence of God.

The next time you need reassurance of the presence of God, venture outdoors and open your eyes wide!

IN TUNE WITH GOD

O LORD, do good to those who are good, whose hearts are in tune with You.

PSALM 125:4 NLT

Some years ago, musicians noted that errand boys in a certain part of London all whistled out of tune as they went about their work. It was talked about, and someone suggested that it was because the bells of Westminster were slightly out of tune. Something had gone wrong with the chimes, and they were discordant. The boys did not know there was anything wrong with the peals, and quite unconsciously they had copied their pitch.

We tend to copy the people with whom we associate; we borrow thoughts from the books we read and the programs to which we listen, almost without knowing it. God has given us His Word, which is the absolute pitch of life and living. If we learn to sing by it, we shall easily detect the false in all of the music of the world.

Being in tune with God and fellow believers is the most beautiful music you can make. When you find yourself out of tune, go back to the Word; and He will put a song in your heart.

GIANTS

Why will you discourage the heart of the children of Israel from going over into the land?
NUMBERS 32:7

In the Book of Numbers, the twelve spies returned from searching out Canaan. Two of them were upbeat, saying that with the Lord's help they could take the land. But the other ten discouraged the Israelites, planting seeds of doubt and pessimism. They worried about the giants in the land and about the fortified cities. As a result, the people's morale collapsed.

One of the problems with being discouraged is that we also become discouraging. When we fail to trust the Lord with our giants, we're telegraphing a message to others: "The Lord can't help you with your giants either." Discouragement becomes as contagious as smallpox.

Discouragement was one of Paul's concerns when he was persecuted. He was afraid his imprisonment would discourage his converts. Writing to the Thessalonians, he said, "We didn't want any of you to be discouraged by all these troubles. You knew we would have to suffer, because when we were with you, we told you this would happen" (1 Thessalonians 3:3–4 CEV).

If you're facing a difficulty now, may the Lord help you respond to it so that others will be encouraged to trust Him too.

NO DAY LIKE TODAY

Behold, now is the accepted time; behold, now is the day of salvation.

2 CORINTHIANS 6:2

On December 28, 1908, a devastating earthquake struck Messina, Italy, killing eighty-four thousand people. Just hours before the earthquake, local authorities passed a number of ordinances reflecting their ungodly character. In fact, the Christmas Day issue of the local paper had contained a parody actually daring God to make Himself known by sending an earthquake! And He obliged.

It is not wise to refuse the grace of God. Jesus gave such an opinion in a parable about some evil tenants (Matthew 21:33–41). They refused to give their landowner his rightful share of their harvest, even after he made numerous requests. They killed the landowner's messengers, even his own son, in their arrogant rejection of the landowner. So the landowner rejected them and gave the vineyard to others.

Many people have the mistaken notion that God is infinitely patient, that the rejection of His offers of salvation do not offend Him. But parables such as this warn us not to reject the grace of God when it is being offered. If you have heard the offer of God's salvation but have not responded, receive it while it is still being made.

Of all the days suitable for salvation, none is better than today.

VANGUARD OF VICTORY

Now when they began to sing and to praise, the LORD set ambushes against the people of Ammon.
2 CHRONICLES 20:22

When King Jehoshaphat faced the combined armies of Moab, Ammon, and Edom, he proclaimed a national fast and begged for God's help. "We have no power against this great multitude . . . " he prayed, "nor do we know what to do, but our eyes are upon You" (2 Chronicles 20:12). A prophet named Jahaziel gave this reply: "Do not be afraid nor dismayed because of this great multitude, for the battle is not yours, but God's" (v. 15).

It was then that Jehoshaphat realized he had a secret weapon. He appointed choirs to go before the armies of Judah. With all their hearts, these royal musicians sang and praised God for His assured victory. As this unlikely vanguard neared the battlefront, the Lord threw their enemies into confusion, and Judah won the battle—not with soldiers, but with songs.

How often we need to echo Jehoshaphat's prayer! Sometimes there are problems we can't solve. Sometimes our pressures are beyond us. "Oh Lord," you can pray, "I don't know what to do, but my eyes are on You."

Praise is the Christian's secret weapon. Satan is allergic to praise; he just can't remain where God is being glorified.

Rocky or Rock Solid?

Marriage should be honored by all.
Hebrews 13:4 NIV

Researchers at the University of Washington claim they can predict with 87 percent accuracy which newlyweds will divorce and which will stay together for a lifetime. Their predictions are based on how a couple talks to each other. Those expressing fondness and love to each other had marriages that tended to last. Those who were always rude and seemed unable to say good things often divorced.

At the dawn of history, God created a man named Adam and allowed him to experience loneliness, to feel incomplete and unfulfilled. The animals of the field and the birds of the air didn't satisfy Adam's physical and emotional needs. So the Lord created a woman—not a child, a son or daughter, or another man, but someone like Adam yet different. Bringing Adam and Eve together, the Lord established the ordinance of marriage with these words: "Therefore a man shall leave his father and mother and be joined to his wife, and they shall become one flesh" (Genesis 2:24).

When the writer of Hebrews later said that marriage should be "honored" by all, he used a word meaning to view as valuable, of great worth, priceless.

Your marriage is God designed and priceless. Take care of it.

SET FREE TO SERVE

But beware lest somehow this liberty of yours become a stumbling block to those who are weak.
1 CORINTHIANS 8:9

At the 1994 National Prayer Breakfast in Washington, D.C., Mother Teresa of Calcutta was the keynote speaker. Only four-and-a-half feet tall, she could barely see over the podium. But when she spoke, the president and other dignitaries heard a stinging rebuke: America had become a selfish nation, losing the meaning of love because of our practice of aborting unborn children.

America, the beacon of freedom for the rest of the world, has at times misapplied the meaning of the word. True freedom and liberty are experienced when we find the courage and power to serve the weak, the immature, the less fortunate than ourselves.

Like Mother Teresa, the apostle Paul had words of rebuke for Christians who cared more about their personal rights and freedoms than the spiritual needs of the less mature. Yes, Christians are free, not bound by rules and regulations. But if we use our freedom to offend another, we have become abusers, not servants. What freedoms have you set aside lately in order to serve someone who needed your strength?

The freest person in the world is the one who makes himself a voluntary servant of others.

Let's Roll!

And we know that all things work together for good to those who love God, to those who are the called according to His purpose.
Romans 8:28

In her book, *Let's Roll: Finding Hope in the Midst of Crisis,* Lisa Beamer writes about her feelings on the morning of September 11, 2001. "In that dark moment, my soul cried out to God, and He began to give me a sense of peace and a confidence that the children and I were going to be okay. But even that comfort didn't take away the wrenching pain or the awful sense of loss I felt."

Every person who lost a loved one in the 2001 terrorist attacks went through, and still lives with, heart-wrenching loss. But for the Christian, there is hope. Even Todd Beamer, one of the heroes of Flight 93, turned to God in the midst of his own trial. With a telephone operator, he prayed the Lord's Prayer and recited the Twenty-third Psalm, and was heard to whisper, "Help me, Jesus," several times before calling his fellow passengers to action: "Let's roll!"

Those with a sure confidence in God's purposes and plans are never frozen by fear. Todd Beamer was not. Lisa Beamer is not. And you will not be, through faith in the goodness of God.

The fact that God has a plan, not your knowledge of the plan, is the basis of your peace and hope.

WHERE TO FIND WISDOM

If any of you lacks wisdom, let him ask of God, who gives to all liberally and without reproach, and it will be given to him.
JAMES 1:5

F*orbes* magazine is one of the longest running and most respected business publications in the world. Its pages profile the wealthiest, most innovative, and most successful business leaders in the world. Yet in the midst of all its worldly wisdom, the magazine includes an acknowledgment of the true source of wisdom. The headline of the editorial page features a quote from Proverbs 4:7: "With all thy getting get understanding" (KJV).

The complete admonition from Solomon says, "Wisdom is the principal thing; therefore get wisdom. And in all your getting, get understanding." Why is this a good message for business leaders—and for every person? Because it's so easy to get caught up in getting what this world has to offer: power, position, and prestige. But wisdom and understanding do not flow from these things; they flow only from God. It's easy for the average Christian to think that powerful people need that lesson. But all of us are subject to the same temptation: to value man's wisdom over God's.

Remember: with all your getting, make sure you get—and keep—true wisdom from God.

The Whole Duty of Man

I devoted myself to study and to explore.
Ecclesiastes 1:13 NIV

What an enigma Solomon was—the wisest man on earth yet the most foolish. Scottish preacher Alexander Whyte said, "If ever ship set sail on a sunny morning, but all that was left of her was a board or two on the shore that night, that ship was Solomon."

In his Book of Ecclesiastes, Solomon applied his God-given wisdom to the pursuit of meaning in life. He explored every avenue, seeking satisfaction. He tried education, money, public works, fame, creative writing, sensual pleasure, and religion. But nothing satisfied.

Are you exploring, experimenting, and seeking satisfaction in similar things? Tennis star Boris Becker said, "I had won Wimbledon twice before, once as the youngest player. I was rich. I had all the material possessions I needed...It's the old song of movie stars and pop stars who commit suicide. They have everything, and yet they are so unhappy. I had no inner peace."

In Ecclesiastes 12:13, Solomon finally reached the conclusion of the whole matter: "Fear God and keep his commandments, for this is the whole duty of man" (NIV).

Only a life devoted to God through Jesus Christ satisfies the heart.

A FOUNDATION FOR GIVING

And all the tithe of the land, whether of the seed of the land or of the fruit of the tree, is the LORD's.
LEVITICUS 27:30

"Every good citizen . . . should be willing to devote a brief time . . . to the making up of a listing of his income for taxes . . . to contribute to his Government, not the scriptural tithe, but a small percentage of his net profits." So said U.S. Representative Cordell Hull in the House of Representatives on April 26, 1913.

Note that in 1913, the biblical tithe was well-enough understood in American culture to be used as a standard of comparison in public discourse. Note also that income taxes were suggested to be less than 10 percent! Today, however, a common reference to the "scriptural tithe" would bring blank stares from many in our culture.

Tithe is the English word meaning one-tenth, and it describes that portion of every Israelite's property and harvest that was set apart for the Lord. The tithe is not replaced in the New Testament but serves as a foundation upon which the overflow of giving by grace can continue.

Do you set aside for the Lord at least one-tenth of all you receive from Him? Doing so reflects an obedient and trusting heart.

What's in a Name?

No longer shall your name be called Abram, but your name shall be Abraham; for I have made you a father of many nations.
Genesis 17:5

A married couple named their new son "Foolish One." The name stuck; and by the time Fool was a grown man, he had lived up to his name. Once, he was befriended by a stranger but incurred the stranger's wrath when he failed to acknowledge his kindness. His wife, who was wise, did the right thing and settled Fool's debt—the shock of which caused Fool to have a stroke. A fool from birth, in ten days Nabal was dead.

That's right—Nabal of the Old Testament (1 Samuel 25) bore a name that, in Hebrew, means "fool." Why would parents burden a child with such a negative name? Naming is a powerful tool in the hand of a parent or any authority figure. When we name someone, we exercise a certain power over his or her life. That person believes us—why shouldn't he?—and thinks of himself in those terms. Just think: which would a Little League slugger rather hear from a parent in the stands: "Way to go, champ!" or "Way to go, chump!"?

Regardless of your legal name, if you're a believer in Christ, you have a new name: Christian, meaning "Christ one" or "little Christ." That's a name worthy of living up to.

Names are word pictures. Paint them ever so carefully.

PRAYERS TO BE RECKONED WITH

My . . . prayer to God . . . is that they may be saved.
ROMANS 10:1

By intercessory prayer," writes Oswald Chambers, "we can hold off Satan from other lives and give the Holy Ghost a chance with them."

A woman in Colorado told of a daughter who had been deeply ensnared in demonism, witchcraft, and the occult. "When she came back to the Lord," said the woman, "she credited my prayers and those of my friends. 'I didn't have a chance against your prayers, Mom,' she told me."

J. Sidlow Baxter points out that our loved ones may "spurn our appeals, reject our message, oppose our arguments, despise our persons, but they are helpless against our prayers."

Are you heavy-hearted because your child is away from the Lord? Your spouse? Your parents? Are you burdened for relatives or friends who don't know Christ? James said the prayer of a righteous person is "something powerful to be reckoned with" (James 5:16 MSG).

If you don't know what to pray, try turning the first verses of Psalm 40 into a prayer: "Lord, please pull my friend from the miry clay. Set his feet on a rock, and put a song of praise in his mouth." It may take a while, but keep on storming heaven. After all, someone once prayed like that for you.

LIVING OR DYING

For the wages of sin is death, but the gift of God is eternal life in Christ Jesus our Lord.
ROMANS 6:23

An aged Scotchman, while dying, was asked what he thought of death. He replied, "It matters little to me whether I live or die. If I die, I will be with Jesus, and if I live Jesus will be with me."

When you really consider life and death, is your attitude similar to the aged Scotchman? Sometimes it is easy to get caught up in the drudgery of everyday routines. But what makes life worth living is our hope in Jesus Christ. The Christian life is a commitment that always looks toward eternity.

Perhaps one of the greatest joys that comes with age is realizing that your relationship with God deepens and continues to reach new and amazing levels. Celebrate this joy by sharing the good news with younger generations. By being a living example of the hope you have in Christ, you are able to reach out to others with His amazing love.

Whether you die at the end of this day, or live—Jesus will be with you! Everyone must face death, but you can face it with Jesus by your side. Focus on the future of eternity with Jesus, so that every day you are alive is a reflection of Him.

Jesus Sees You

For the LORD your God . . . knows your trudging through this great wilderness. These forty years the LORD your God has been with you; you have lacked nothing.
Deuteronomy 2:7

What parent has not exhorted his teenager to behave properly "because God is watching"? From childhood, we are taught that God sees and knows everything—and so He does. But there's a flip side to that truth. While it's true He sees our failings, it is even truer that He sees our successes—and our struggles.

Family experts tell parents, "Instead of trying to catch your kids doing something wrong, catch them doing something right!" More often than not, when we are being faithful to obey the Lord and find it difficult, we think He is nowhere around. But that's not true. God is ever watchful, which means He sees our struggles when we're trying to serve Him faithfully. And He comes to us with aid in His time just like He did with the disciples when they were obediently rowing across the Sea of Galilee in a storm. Jesus was alone on a mountain praying, but "He saw them straining at rowing" and "He came to them" (Mark 6:48). If you are struggling in a storm, don't worry—Jesus sees you.

Knowing that Jesus is aware of our needs is a comfort beyond measure.

SAYING THANK YOU

For God so loved the world that He gave His only begotten Son, that whoever believes in Him should not perish but have everlasting life.
JOHN 3:16

A medieval monk announced he would be preaching next Sunday evening on the love of God. As the shadows fell and the light ceased to come in through the cathedral windows, the congregation gathered. In the darkness of the altar, the monk lit a candle and carried it to a statue of Christ on the cross. First of all, he illumined the crown of thorns; next, the two wounded hands; finally, the marks of the spear wound. In the hush that fell, the monk blew out the candle and left the chancel. There was nothing else to say.

The greatest example of God's love for us is that He gave His only Son so that we could have the chance to live with Him in eternity. How do you say thank you for the ultimate gift? By worshiping and honoring God in everything you do. Live like every action is a thank-you note to Him—while washing the dishes, driving your car, singing at church. Every moment you live is another opportunity to say thank you. By becoming involved in your local church and supporting other believers with your talents and offerings, you are opening up for God to work through you.

When you say thank you to God with your life, He will bless you.

Carry Them to Jesus

Do not cease to cry out to the LORD our God for us, that He may save us.

1 Samuel 7:8

Just as the four men in Mark 2 carried their sick friend on a bed to Jesus, we can carry our friends to Jesus on a stretcher of prayer. We bring them to Jesus as we intercede for them and as we plead for their salvation. He can heal them, He can forgive them, and He responds to our faith.

For many years, Cathy Crawford, missionary to France, prayed earnestly for her father's salvation. In time, she developed some health problems and was diagnosed with multiple sclerosis. She was able to continue her missionary work. While home on furlough, she had trouble traveling from church to church, so her retired father offered to drive her. As a result, he not only repeatedly heard her missionary testimony, but he heard biblical sermons almost every night of the week from the host pastors. By the end of the summer, he was won to Christ.

"I can be thankful for my illness," Cathy said, "for God used it to answer the greatest prayer in my heart, the one for my dad's salvation."

Do you have a friend or loved one for whom you're burdened? Don't cease to cry out for God to save that person, though the case is hard. Follow Jesus' advice: we "always ought to pray and not lose heart" (Luke 18:1).

DARE TO BE A DANIEL

Daniel purposed in his heart that he would not defile himself with the portion of the king's delicacies, nor with the wine which he drank.

DANIEL 1:8

A Roman emperor once said about the eloquent preacher John Chrysostom, "What in the world can you do with a man like that?" Chrysostom wouldn't be silenced. He disregarded threats and kept preaching whether imprisoned, banished, bound, or free.

How like Daniel. As Daniel functioned in his culture, we don't see him being a wild-eyed radical fundamentalist, as some call believers today. By outward appearances, he was as professional in that corporate culture as he could be. But inside, he was a radical subversive for the kingdom of God. His wisdom and integrity provoked envy and anger on the part of everyone around him.

Daniel performed his job with such excellence that he kept being promoted to the top. His critics followed him around, watching him everywhere he went, but they found no fault in him. Their only valid accusation was in his faithfulness to the law of his God.

Daniel's life glorified God, vindicated his faith, and changed history. Dare to be the same. The world just doesn't know what to do with people like that!

HERE'S HOW

The excellence of the knowledge of Christ Jesus my Lord . . .
PHILIPPIANS 3:8

How can we get to know the holy God? If He is so pure, so infinite, so high, and so lifted up, how can we approach Him, and how can we grow more intimately acquainted with Him?

First, we must come to Him by simple faith in Jesus Christ. Second, we must study our Bible and learn all we can about Him. Third, we must turn our knowledge about Him into knowledge of Him.

How can we do that? In his book *Knowing God*, J. I. Packer gives the formula. "The rule for doing this," writes Packer, "is demanding but simple. It is that we turn each truth that we learn about God into a matter of *meditation* before God, leading to prayer and praise to God."

Packer defines *meditation* as "the activity of calling to mind, and thinking over, and dwelling on, and applying to oneself, the various things that one knows about the works and ways and purposes and promises of God."

It is this activity of holy thought, this practice and pattern of letting our minds dwell on Him, that helps us become more deeply and intimately acquainted with the Holy One, who is our life.

SHOCKED BY THE BIBLE

All Scripture is given by inspiration of God, and is profitable for doctrine, for reproof, for correction, for instruction in righteousness.
2 TIMOTHY 3:16

A professor at a major university asked her class to write a short essay on the Sermon on the Mount (Matthew 5–7). At first, she was shocked at her students' responses: "a hoax…strict…no fun…perfectionism…extreme, stupid, unhuman." Then it dawned on her: this is how Jesus' original audience responded! The Bible is offensive. God's perspective on life is a wake-up call to those familiar only with the world's ways.

When Jesus says calling your brother a fool is as serious as murder and lusting is equal to adultery, do His statements seem narrow-minded? It's easy to get comfortable with the routines of Christianity—going to church and Sunday school, serving on a committee, giving of our money, helping a neighbor—without continuing to grow in a deep understanding of God's character through studying His Word.

If you are no longer "shocked" by what God expects and requires, it may be because you have stopped delving into the details. There is no substitute for reading the Bible when it comes to learning to think God's thoughts after Him.

To avoid shock when reading the Bible, read it more, not less!

THE GLORY OF FATHERHOOD

The glory of children is their father.
PROVERBS 17:6

Whatever happened to the idea that a father knows best? In a few short decades, we went from a television show called *Father Knows Best*, in which the father was a wise, strong, and loving head of his home, to the film *Father of the Bride*, in which comedian Steve Martin played a lovable doofus of a dad, always being corrected by his unflappable and all-together wife.

There seems to be little glory left in fatherhood in the modern world. Television shows (especially commercials) and movies have stereotyped fathers as either absent physically or absentminded. As usual, the culture has it all wrong. The term *father* is applied with honor to a host of biblical heroes: God Himself, prophets, priests, male parents, grandfathers, great-grandfathers, ancestors, and leaders such as Abraham and Paul. Those are big shoes for modern fathers to fill, but strong fathers are God's will.

Dads, don't succumb to the cultural demotion of fatherhood. Let your practice produce the honor that your position deserves.

Fortunately, every earthly father has a role model in God the Father. Being honored as a father begins with honoring your heavenly Father.

IMPERFECTIONS MADE PERFECT

And He said to me, "My grace is sufficient for you, for My strength is made perfect in weakness." Therefore most gladly I will rather boast in my infirmities, that the power of Christ may rest upon me.
2 CORINTHIANS 12:9

J. Stuart Holden tells of an old Scottish mansion close to where he had his little summer home. The walls of one room were filled with sketches made by distinguished artists. The practice began after a pitcher of soda water was accidentally spilled on a freshly decorated wall, leaving an unsightly stain. At the time, noted artist Lord Landseer was a guest in the house. One day when the family went out to the moors, Landseer stayed behind. With a few masterful strokes of a piece of charcoal, that ugly spot became the outline of a beautiful waterfall, bordered by trees and wildlife. He turned that disfigured wall into one of his most successful depictions of highland life.

Just as the artist turned a stain into a waterfall, so Jesus can turn your pain and problems into a beautiful picture of His all-knowing love. When you pray to God, ask to see the problems in your life in a new way. Romans 8:28 tells us, "And we know that all things work together for good to those who love God, to those who are the called according to His purpose."

When you meditate on this truth, you will begin to sense the Holy Spirit working on your attitude. With God, imperfections can be perfected.

KNOWING OUR PLACE

That none of you may be puffed up on behalf of one against the other.

1 CORINTHIANS 4:6

NBC news commentator Tim Russert described a meeting he had with Pope John Paul II. The pope put his arm around Russert and said, "You are from NBC. They tell me you're a very important man." Taken aback, Russert said, "Your Holiness, there are only two of us in this room, and I am certainly a distant second." The pope looked at him and said, "Right."

A degree of humility can keep us from stumbling in social settings. Humility is not only key in social settings but in spiritual service as well. As the writer of Proverbs said, "Pride goes before destruction" (16:18). Christians have been given the inestimable privilege of receiving gifts of grace from God—spiritual enablements that make it possible for us to serve Him in carrying out the ministry of Jesus.

And if that isn't enough, someday we'll be given rewards in heaven for using those gifts faithfully! God provides the gifts, the power to use them, and the rewards. Where is the room for pride in such a plan? Our place is to humbly receive and employ what God has graciously given.

The Christian who knows his place is the one whose place God will make known.

THE PURPOSE OF SUFFERING

It is good for me that I have been afflicted, that I may learn Your statutes.
PSALM 119:71

After spending thirty-five years in a wheelchair following a diving accident that left her paralyzed at age seventeen, Joni Eareckson Tada said, "I think that we all want to know Christ, that we want to know the power of His resurrection. But not many of us want to share in the fellowship of His sufferings, and nobody wants to become like Him in His death."

The apostle Paul said in Philippians 3:10 that "being conformed to [Christ's] death" is how we know "the power of His resurrection, and the fellowship of His sufferings." We are conformed to His death by dying to our old sinful nature. And that hurts!

God, motivated by His goal of having us become like Jesus (Romans 8:29), brings us face to face with that which is least like Christ. Maybe it's our impatience, our anger, our love of creature comforts, our fear of the future, our desire to do things our way. Dying to those things is the only way we will become like Christ, which is God's ultimate plan for us. If God is showing you, perhaps painfully, something that needs to go—let it go!

The power of Jesus and fellowship with Jesus are realized when we learn to embrace suffering like Jesus.

RESTORE SUCH A ONE

Brethren, if a man is overtaken in any trespass, you who are spiritual restore such a one in a spirit of gentleness.
GALATIANS 6:1

In his book *Returning to Your First Love*, pastor Tony Evans tells how his younger brother, after rebelling against their father's authority, was sent packing, suitcase in hand. Twenty minutes later, the banished one returned home, asking to be reinstated to the family. He had been put out in order to learn respect and was taken in when he learned it.

That's how church discipline works (1 Corinthians 5:1–13). But what happens when the one who has sinned repents? Paul says, "You should . . . forgive and comfort him, otherwise such a one might be overwhelmed by excessive sorrow" (2 Corinthians 2:7 NASB). How frustrating it would be for someone to say, "I'm sorry" only to find his cries landing on deaf ears!

Can you imagine God turning a deaf ear to a repentant sinner? As we are to forgive the same way God does, we are to restore and accept anyone who has accepted a measure of discipline for his sins (Ephesians 4:32). If there is anyone who has sinned against you, be sure you "restore such a one in a spirit of gentleness"—just as God restores you.

The surest sign of a person accepting his own forgiveness is the freedom with which he extends forgiveness to others.

THE RIGHT PATH

Be wise, and keep your heart on the right path.
PROVERBS 23:19 NIV

How does a worm get inside an apple? Perhaps you think the worm burrows in from the outside. No, scientists have discovered that the worm comes from inside. But how does he get in there? Simple! An insect lays an egg in the apple blossom. Sometime later, the worm hatches in the heart of the apple and then eats his way out.

Sin, like the worm, begins in the heart and works out through a person's thoughts, words, and actions. All humans have a sinful nature, and we are capable of self-serving, self-centered, sinful behavior. Romans 5:12 says, "Through one man sin entered the world, and death through sin, and thus death spread to all men, because all sinned." How you are inside will reflect out to the world through your actions.

If not for the mercy and grace of God, our entire lives would resemble the apple that might look good from the outside but is rotten and bruised on the inside. Guard your walk with the Lord. Stay in fellowship with Him in order to keep on the right path.

SPEAK, LORD

Do not be like the horse or like the mule, which have no understanding, which must be harnessed with bit and bridle, else they will not come near you.

PSALM 32:9

A certain harbor in Italy can be entered only through a narrow channel bounded by dangerous rocks and shoals. To keep ships in the center of the channel at night, three beacons stand on poles in the water. When all three lights are lined up perfectly so they appear as one, a ship's captain knows he is in the center of the channel. To enter when the lights don't shine as one is to risk certain calamity.

How foolish would a ship's captain have to be to enter that harbor while one of the lights was out of line with the other two—and especially if all three were visible? God has given the Christian three divine lights that, when aligned in one direction, give certainty concerning His will: a divine standard (the Bible), a divine witness (the Holy Spirit), and divine circumstances (the providence of God). He may, or may not, provide all three at once. But to ignore any, or all, of these guiding lights when they are given is to risk being outside of God's will.

God's guidance is seen most clearly by those who live in eager anticipation of receiving it.

October

FATHER ABRAHAM

Take now your son . . . whom you love, and . . . offer him.
GENESIS 22:2

Abraham is one of history's most famous fathers. Not only was he Isaac's father, but he was the father of the entire Jewish nation (Luke 1:73). Furthermore, Paul considered him the father of all who believe in Christ by virtue of his example of being justified by faith (Romans 4:11–12).

What was Abraham's greatest trait as a father? The quality of his fathering stemmed from his supreme love for God. In Genesis 22, God tested Abraham, commanding him to offer his beloved son, Isaac, as a burnt offering. This command implied the possibility that Abraham might have become more devoted to his earthly son than to his heavenly Father. Abraham passed the test. Despite his deep love for Isaac, the Lord came first.

Is it possible to love your children too much? No, but it is possible to love your Lord too little. Jesus warned, "He who loves father or mother more than Me is not worthy of Me. And he who loves son or daughter more than Me is not worthy of Me" (Matthew 10:37).

We'll love our children with a holier and healthier love if Christ comes before anything—or anyone—else in our hearts.

ACCOUNTABLE

You are a pleasure-crazy kingdom, living at ease and feeling secure, bragging as if you were the greatest in the world! You say, "I'm self-sufficient and not accountable to anyone!"
ISAIAH 47:8 NLT

Have you noticed how many business, professional, and leadership books have the word *accountable* in their titles? One best seller, for example, is *The Oz Principle: Getting Results Through Individual and Organizational Accountability*.

Accountability is important for the Christian too. Sinful habits can be pleasurable and desirable, and they can be hard to break. It's tough to do it on our own; we sometimes need to be accountable to others.

That's why the New Testament is so full of "one another" passages—pray for one another, encourage one another, confess your sins to one another, love one another, and admonish one another. If you're struggling with a sinful habit, covenant with a friend to be held accountable. Ask him or her to be your personal encourager and to monitor your progress.

Solomon said, "Two are better than one....For if they fall, one will lift up his companion. But woe to him who is alone when he falls, for he has no one to help him up" (Ecclesiastes 4:9–10).

CONSUME WITH CARE

Flee also youthful lusts; but pursue righteousness, faith, love, peace with those who call on the Lord out of a pure heart.
2 TIMOTHY 2:22

Shipwreck victims, adrift on the ocean without water, have died after consuming salt water in desperation. Because salt water contains seven times more salt than the human body can digest, the body begins to demand more water to flush out the salt. So the more salt water one drinks, the thirstier one gets. The body finally succumbs, consumed by its own desires.

Wise is the person who remembers the line from Samuel Taylor Coleridge's "The Rime of the Ancient Mariner": "Water, water everywhere, nor any drop to drink." And wise is the person making his way through this world who remembers the same thing with regard to the lusts and desires of the flesh. Just as the body has a natural desire for water, so the soul has natural desires as well: for intimacy, recognition, or achievement.

But any one of those legitimate desires can lead to spiritual death if too much of the wrong thing is consumed in pursuit of gratification. That's why Paul told Timothy to "flee also youthful lusts," and why he told the Roman Christians to "make no provision for the flesh, to fulfill its lusts" (Romans 13:14).

Meeting a legitimate need in an illegitimate way is a good way to be consumed by your own desires.

SEEING LIKE JESUS SEES

And He was moved with compassion for them, and healed their sick.
MATTHEW 14:14

Are you old enough to remember the 3-D craze of several decades ago? Using cardboard glasses with red and blue lenses, you could read comic books drawn and printed in a certain way and—*voilà!*—the flat, lifeless pages sprang to life in three dimensions. The 3-D glasses were even available for certain movies.

Wouldn't it be interesting to suddenly be able to look at the world through "Jesus-colored lenses"—that is, to be able to see the world as Jesus sees it? There must be a radical difference between what He sees and what we see simply because we don't always act like He did. For instance, what He saw evoked compassion on numerous occasions. Sick people, demonized people, lost people, hungry and homeless people . . . these were not just the froth on the wake of a fast-moving society. These were real people with real needs.

When Jesus looked at life, He always did the same thing—He gave. He gave of His time, His power, His wisdom . . . and ultimately, He gave His life. What do you see when you look at the world—and what do you do in response? The closer we get to Jesus, the more we'll see what He saw.

Seeing the world like Jesus means giving to the world like Jesus.

Reasons to Be Content

Do we have no right to take along a believing wife, as do also the other apostles?
1 Corinthians 9:5

If you need a new appliance, where do you start looking? You probably do an Internet search to find the best combination of value, price, and warranty. That same mindset has caused matchmaking and dating-service Web sites to be the fastest-growing segment of online business. Singles are shopping for mates the same way they'd shop for a toaster.

Marriage partners have become a commodity in our culture—something to be used up and discarded as tastes, desires, or circumstances dictate. The existing standard seems to be: if you're tired of being single, get married; if you're tired of being married, get single. The state most people seem to be most discontent with is the state they're in.

While it's true that God told Adam it was not good for him to be alone (Genesis 2:18), that statement was tied more to the procreative function of humans to fill the earth than to Adam's constitution as a single person. Every human being, single or married, should find his or her ultimate contentment in God.

Whether we are married or single should not determine our contentment in life. The way we live our lives is an expression of contentment with God.

ZACCHAEUS: A WALKING TESTIMONY

Let your light so shine before men, that they may see your good works and glorify your Father in heaven.
MATTHEW 5:16

The famous London preacher Charles Spurgeon and his wife would not give away the eggs their chickens laid but would sell them—even to close relatives. As a result, some labeled the Spurgeons stingy and greedy. But when Mrs. Spurgeon died, it was revealed that the egg money had been used for years to support two elderly widows. The Spurgeons endured the criticism in silence, knowing that time would validate their actions.

Another man's crafty financial dealings brought him far less praise when they were revealed. Zacchaeus was a Jewish tax collector in league with the Romans and hated by his fellow Jews. Tax collectors grew wealthy by charging citizens more than was due and pocketing the excess. But when Zacchaeus met Jesus, he immediately changed his ways. He confessed what he had done and purposed to pay back all he had stolen and more. Jesus validated Zacchaeus's change of heart: "Today salvation has come to this house" (Luke 19:9).

It's good to talk about your salvation, but it's even better to let your actions speak louder than your words. The world is waiting to meet Christians whose talk is drowned out by their walk.

Marks of a Servant

Nevertheless we . . . endure all things lest we hinder the gospel of Christ.
1 Corinthians 9:12

Philip Pillsbury had an international reputation as a connoisseur of fine foods. But to his employees, he was one of the troops. He bore the unmistakable mark of a journeyman grain miller—the tips of three of his fingers were missing. He would not allow his wealth and prestige to separate him from the workers he led, and he had the factory scars to prove it.

The term *servant leader* describes leaders who serve those whom they lead—leaders whose main task is to remove the obstacles that might keep their followers from succeeding. Jesus Christ was certainly a servant leader, as was the apostle Paul. In fact, Paul confessed that he would rather do anything than hinder the spread of the gospel. So he gave up his rights in order that none would be confused about his motives. He adapted himself to the lifestyle of those he sought to win to Christ. And he bore in his body the telltale marks of a follower of Jesus (Galatians 6:17).

What marks do we bear that reveal our willingness to serve those we are called to lead? Commitment to a cause is measured by the self-denial we're willing to endure to see it accomplished.

WILL YOU HEAR ME NOW?

My son, pay attention to my wisdom; lend your ear to my understanding.
PROVERBS 5:1

Does anyone really listen anymore? Are you frustrated by shallow conversation with the people you deal with from day to day? If so, you might want to check your newspaper. A woman once placed an ad in a suburban newspaper offering to listen to anyone talk for thirty minutes for five dollars. The next thing she knew, her phone was ringing off the hook! People were hungry to be heard, and they were more than willing to pay someone to listen to them. Listening intently with one's mouth firmly shut is an elusive grace.

Not being heard in relationships is equal to not being valued. We can't always offer a potential masterpiece in our relationship conversation, but we can always respond to others as though it were just that. When Jesus came to visit Mary and Martha, they responded in very different ways. Mary sat at the Lord's feet and listened to His words, while Martha busied herself in the kitchen.

There is a time and place for everything, but the highest priority with each other should be the willingness to listen. In Luke 10:41–42, Jesus responded to Martha, "You are worried and upset about many things, but only one thing is needed. Mary has chosen what is better" (NIV).

Choose what is better: choose to listen.

In the Arena

The things which happened to me have actually turned out for the furtherance of the gospel.
Philippians 1:12

Missionary Isobel Kuhn wrote a book entitled *In the Arena*, in which she described great difficulties she had faced, showing how each had become an arena in which her influence for Christ was magnified.

After they were thrown into the fiery furnace, the three Hebrews in Daniel 3 were promoted, and their reputation was enhanced. It was his imprisonment that allowed Paul to evangelize Rome's Praetorian Guard and that spurred the early church to action.

It was after Charles Colson had served time in a federal penitentiary for his role in the Watergate scandal that he became a prominent spokesman for the faith, establishing an effective ministry to men and women in prisons across America.

It was after his arm was amputated from cancer that the world began listening to the testimony of baseball player Dave Dravecky.

It was after months of uncertain captivity by the ruling Taliban in Afghanistan that Dayna Curry and Heather Mercer emerged to tell their stories and glorify God for His deliverance.

Are you in a season of suffering? God will use it to magnify your influence for Him. Trust Him, and be faithful.

A PRIDEFUL HEART

So they come to you as people do, they sit before you as My people, and they hear your words, but they do not do them; for with their mouth they show much love, but their hearts pursue their own gain.
EZEKIEL 33:31

In the summer of 1986, two ships collided in the Black Sea off the coast of Russia. Hundreds of passengers died as they were hurled into the icy waters below. News of the disaster was further darkened when an investigation revealed the cause of the accident. It wasn't a technology problem like radar malfunction—or even thick fog. The cause was human stubbornness.

Each captain was aware of the other ship's presence nearby. Both could have steered clear, but according to news reports, neither captain wanted to give way to the other. Each was too proud to yield first. By the time they came to their senses, it was too late.

Pride gets in the way of good intentions. The Bible calls believers to have a humble heart, to watch out for one another. In your life journey, are you aware of those around you?

Watch out for the other hearts that are cruising along the sea of life, and love the way you want to be loved. Practice humility.

SUITABLY SUBMISSIVE SPOUSES

Be filled with the Spirit . . . submitting to one another in the fear of God.
EPHESIANS 5:18, 21

After a church service in which the pastor preached a sermon on wives submitting to their husbands, a man told his wife, "From now on, things are going to be different around here. I'm going to call the shots. I'm the boss, and you're nothing!" "Big deal," his wife countered. "Boss over nothing!"

We might laugh in that case, but sadly neither the husband's rule nor the wife's response was commendable. We smile nonetheless because we know how prickly the subject of submission in marriage can be. Paul did indeed say that wives are to submit to their husbands (Ephesians 5:22). But that is not all he said about submission. In the preceding verse, he implied that submission to one another is an evidence of the filling of the Spirit.

In other words, submission is not primarily a wifely duty; it is a Christian duty. Further on, Paul pictures Christ as One who submitted Himself to suffering for the benefit of His bride, the church. True strength is seen in submitting rather than in forcing submission.

The strongest marriages are those built out of complementary stones held fast by the mortar of mutual submission.

God the Surgeon

For the wages of sin is death, but the gift of God is eternal life in Christ Jesus our Lord.
Romans 6:23

Dr. Evan O'Neil Kane was a pioneering physician who believed most surgeries should be performed with local, not general, anesthesia. To prove his point, he decided to operate using only local anesthesia. But where would he find a patient willing to be the test case for a new medical theory? Having performed nearly four thousand appendectomies, Dr. Kane applied a local anesthetic to himself and removed his own appendix—and made medical history.

Jesus said, "Greater love has no one than this, than to lay down one's life for his friends" (John 15:13). In a sense, God did for the human race what the good doctor did for his patients. God operated on Himself by sending Jesus Christ, the second person of the Godhead, to die for the sins of mankind. God assumed the risk and endured the pain when He placed the sins of the world upon the shoulders of His one and only Son. If the love of a doctor is seen by making himself a patient, how much more is the love of God seen by making Himself a sacrifice?

God performed the heart surgery that gave us new life.

In God We Trust

Some trust in chariots, and some in horses; but we will remember the name of the LORD our God.
Psalm 20:7

Before his 1971 fight with Joe Frazier, Muhammad Ali said, "There's not a man alive who can whup me." (He jabbed at the air with his blinding left.) "I'm too smart." (He tapped his head.) "I'm too pretty." (He showed the cameras his profile, like a bust on a pedestal.) "I am the greatest! I am the king! I should be on a postage stamp—that's the only way I'll get licked!" Then Ali lost to Frazier.

When confidence in one's abilities and resources changes to pride and then becomes arrogance, there's trouble ahead: "Pride goes before destruction, and a haughty spirit before a fall" (Proverbs 16:18). So how do we find the balance? Simply by remembering that every gift, ability, talent, and resource we have comes from God.

There's nothing sinful about recognizing and confessing what God has provided, but the difference between self-confidence and Christ-confidence is found in who gets the credit. A good way to keep this thought at the forefront of our life is to practice the art of thanksgiving. It's hard to be too self-confident when we acknowledge we are nothing without God.

Live confidently—as long as your confidence is in Christ.

When Faith Overlaps Faith

And teach [these things] to your children and your grandchildren.
Deuteronomy 4:9

Manasseh became king of Judah at age twelve and was a horribly wicked king until he came to know the Lord late in life. Manasseh's son Amon took over the throne at age twenty-two and was likewise wicked. But when Amon's son Josiah took the throne, he was one of Judah's most godly kings. How do you explain the change?

Josiah's righteousness was probably influenced by his first six years overlapping with his grandfather's last six years. When Amon was assassinated after only two years as king, Josiah took the throne at age eight. Therefore, his first six years were under the godly influence of his grandfather, Manasseh. In Hebrew culture, it was the responsibility of grandfathers to teach their children and grandchildren the righteous standards of God.

Every parent knows that children look at their grandparents as sources of wisdom and security. Linking the latter years of one with the early years of the other is a perfect way to pass on a love for the Word of God.

Grandparents are in a perfect position to build faith in young hearts by declaring the precious promises of God.

YOUR NEIGHBOR NEEDS YOU

You shall not take vengeance...but you shall love your neighbor as yourself.
LEVITICUS 19:18

During the American Revolution, a man named Michael Wittman was sentenced to die for treason. A pastor who had been an object of Wittman's hatred walked seventy miles to plead with General George Washington for Wittman's life. Washington refused until he discovered Wittman was the pastor's enemy, not his friend. Because the pastor had shown such love for an enemy, Wittman was released and became the pastor's fast friend.

One of Jesus' best-known parables was about two religious men, a priest and a Levite, who failed to show mercy and love to a dying man. Only when an enemy of the man, a Samaritan, came along was love revealed and the man saved (Luke 10:30–37). Jesus told this story to illustrate the true meaning of the command to "love your neighbor."

The willingness to love one's neighbor was first revealed by God when He sent Jesus to die for us, His enemies (Romans 5:8, 10). As Christ loved us, so we are to love others (1 John 4:11). The good Samaritan changed his world with love. Is there a neighbor in your world whose life could be changed by your love?

Who is your neighbor? Your neighbor is anyone who has a need that you have the ability to meet.

A Happy Marriage

That their hearts may be encouraged, being knit together in love, and attaining to all riches of the full assurance of understanding, to the knowledge of the mystery of God, both of the Father and of Christ.
Colossians 2:2

On her golden wedding anniversary, a grandmother revealed the secret of her long and happy marriage. "On my wedding day, I decided to choose ten of my husband's faults which, for the sake of our marriage, I would overlook," she explained. A guest asked her to name some of the faults. "To tell the truth," she replied, "I never did get around to listing them. But whenever my husband did something that made me hopping mad, I would say to myself, 'Lucky for him, that's one of the ten.'"

No one is perfect. So marriage is the union of two imperfect people, with their individual faults, bad habits, and undesirable qualities. As Christians, marriage should be a place to practice grace. When you can look past the faults of your spouse and concentrate on encouraging him or her, you will find satisfaction and peace. If you choose to turn his or her faults into the only things you can see about your spouse, you will find yourself in a lonely marriage.

A Christian marriage demonstrates love through grace and forgiveness, and it stands as an example for others to follow.

GET BACK TO WORK

[Peter] said to Him, "Yes, Lord; You know that I love You."
JOHN 21:15

Peter blundered a lot, but he passionately loved Christ; and in the end, that made the difference. Like Peter, we all have a set of personal regrets. All of us would do things differently if we could relive life, but we can't change the past. Instead, the Lord tells us to confess our sins, accept His forgiveness, and learn from our blunders.

There's a well-known story of an employee who made a mistake that cost his company a million dollars. His boss called him in, saying, "I'm not going to fire you, for I've just invested a million dollars in you. The secret of making a million dollars instead of losing a million dollars is making good decisions. And the secret to good decisions is learning from bad ones. Now get back to work!"

That was Jesus' approach to Peter—and to us as well. If you're suffering a load of regret, confess your sins to God. Trust His pardon to wash away the guilt, and depend on His providence to bring good out of bad. Like Peter, passionately love Christ and learn from your mistakes.

RIGHT OR RIGHTEOUS?

Woe to you, scribes and Pharisees, hypocrites! For you pay tithe of mint and anise and cummin, and have neglected the weightier matters of the law: justice and mercy and faith.
MATTHEW 23:23

Theologian Jack Deere writes about a period in his life when he was more concerned about being right than anything else. He was a scholarly professor at a well-known seminary, and he prided himself on knowledge and biblical correctness more than anything—until God did a work in his heart.

If anyone scored an A+ on being right in Jesus' day, it was the Pharisees. They knew the Law backward and forward. They tithed their herbs and made up laws about what was allowed on the Sabbath. And one of the things that was most certainly not allowed was the "work" of healing. So when Jesus healed a man born blind from birth, and did it on the Sabbath...well, that just wasn't right.

The Pharisees were too busy being right to rejoice with the man who could see for the first time in his life. They didn't have time for the righteousness, peace, and joy of the kingdom of God (Romans 14:17). Which is the greater priority in your life: rightness or righteousness?

Righteousness means being right in the eyes of God, not men.

The Golden Rule

And he who reaps receives wages, and gathers fruit for eternal life, that both he who sows and he who reaps may rejoice together.
John 4:36

When you hear phrases like "Land of a Thousand Lakes," "Sunshine State," "Famous Potatoes," "Big Sky Country," you'll probably think of license plates and state slogans. What about "Golden Rule State"?

In the spring of 2003, State Concurrent Resolution 1006 was passed, designating Arizona as the "Golden Rule State." In part, the resolution says, "Living and practicing the Golden Rule will have a powerfully positive effect on each individual and the society in which we all live."

Applying the golden rule to everyday life is contagious even in the secular world. But as Christians, we should treat others the way we want to be treated, not just because it's a decent creed to live by. Matthew 7:12 tells us to "treat people the same way you want them to treat you" (NASB). That's a tall order! But start out by taking it one day at a time—even one minute at a time.

Think about how you can affirm a loved one or a co-worker right now. If you would like to receive attention and encouragement, make sure you are giving them out.

The Job of an Evangelist

Bondservants, obey in all things your masters according to the flesh, not with eyeservice, as men-pleasers, but in sincerity of heart, fearing God.
Colossians 3:22

In 1990, following a televised Monday night game, eight players from the San Francisco 49ers and eight from the New York Giants knelt together at midfield to pray. The practice was criticized by *Sports Illustrated* magazine, and NFL officials indicated they might stop it—which they didn't. The practice continues today.

Being a witness for Christ means two things: making your faith a matter of public record and making sure your work style is consistent with the gospel. What would it do to the credibility of the gospel if an NFL player used abusive language, took cheap physical shots, and argued disrespectfully with referee rulings...and then knelt down to pray as a Christian after the game? Such a lifestyle in the workplace of a football player would significantly discredit the gospel.

The workplace can be a challenge to our spirituality. But Scripture says the way we work and honor our employer brings credit, or discredit, to Jesus Christ.

The job of an evangelist is to do his work so well that he is invited to explain what makes him different.

THE HARDEST QUESTION IN THE WORLD

Forgive us our debts, as we forgive our debtors.
MATTHEW 6:12

Greg Anderson learned that cancer would likely take his life in thirty days. Desperate for healing, he decided to forgive everyone against whom he held a grudge, including a man at work with whom he had developed a feud three months earlier—a man who was also diagnosed with cancer. Greg asked for and received the man's forgiveness. Years later, as a wellness crusader, Greg Anderson counts that act of seeking forgiveness as the turning point in his healing.

Doctors agree that bitterness and unforgiveness can lead to illness. With that kind of risk, it's amazing that anyone would hesitate to seek and offer forgiveness. Yet "Would you please forgive me?" has to be one of life's most difficult questions. And waiting for the answer may be a hard place to be—but it's a good place to be.

Saying, "I was wrong" or, "It was my fault" is a good start on the road to forgiveness, but it's not a good finish. If you've hurt another person, humble yourself and ask to be forgiven.

Why? Because "God resists the proud, but gives grace to the humble" (James 4:6). Which would you like Him to do to you?

If You're Happy and You Know It

For I wish that all men were even as I myself. But each one has his own gift from God, one in this manner and another in that.
1 Corinthians 7:7

When Margaret Achorn retrieved a large package from the post office one Christmas, she didn't recognize the sender's name. She became suspicious: what if it was a bomb? After the police bomb squad opened it, the only thing left in the debris was the warranty card for the new stereo. She never found out who sent such a nice gift, or why.

Sometimes Christians act suspicious about the gifts God has given them. While they may know the giver is God, they are hesitant to enjoy the gift, wondering what strings might be attached. A little-known reference to spiritual gifts in the New Testament is when Paul uses the Greek word *charisma* to refer to the inclination to be married or remain single (1 Corinthians 7:7).

Some unmarried Christians are fully content being single but get the idea from the world (and sometimes the church) that they shouldn't be—that marriage is always better. If you are single and content, stay that way, and use your gift for the glory of God.

Singles can build up the body of Christ with their gift only if the church recognizes the grace of God at work in their lives.

BE PREPARED

Then Hezekiah and all the people rejoiced that God had prepared the people, since the events took place so suddenly.
2 CHRONICLES 29:36

Golfing coach Bill Hartman insists that great golfers are made, not born. "I've seen great athletes play at all levels in a number of sports," he said, "and you know what separates the 'greats' from the 'good'? Their level of physical preparation."

The Lord is our heavenly Coach, preparing us for all the events of our lives as well as for the work He plans for us to do. He knows the future as well as He knows the past, and He is fully capable of preparing us for all that lies ahead. We mustn't disdain the preparation time.

Think of the eighty years He prepared Moses before sending him to liberate the children of Israel from Egypt. Think of David's years in the wilderness, running from King Saul and living as a fugitive. It was God's way of preparing him for the throne. Think of Jesus' hidden years in Nazareth and Paul's silent years in Arabia.

Ephesians 2:10 indicates that God is preparing us for the work that He is planning for us to do. The courage and confidence you'll have in the future will come from the preparation and practice you're experiencing right now.

Prayer That Never Stops

Pray without ceasing.
1 Thessalonians 5:17

If you have suffered from the flu, you know the symptoms: achiness, chills, fever, headaches, stuffy head—and that persistent, hacking cough that just won't stop. If you've had the flu—especially the cough—then you know what it means to be a spiritual warrior who prays without ceasing.

Paul wrote in 1 Thessalonians 5:17 that believers should "pray without ceasing." To make his point, he used *adialeiptos*, an adverb meaning "incessantly, constantly." It has been found in historical Greek documents to refer to a persistent, hacking cough—a flu-like cough, in modern terms. When you suffer from that kind of cough, you can't get rid of it; it's with you wherever you go and whatever you do. You're interrupted by it when you speak and you wake up with it in the night. You become one with your cough.

That's how prayer should be with the Christian—not the irritating, annoying part, but the persistent part. Praying without ceasing means to live in a continual state of God-consciousness, communicating with Him about everything. Stay well, and practice the presence of God wherever you go.

To lose one's consciousness of God's presence is to lose the ability to pray without ceasing.

Patience, Please

As for God, His way is perfect.
Psalm 18:30

Nothing is harder than praying and waiting. But God answers prayer and fulfills promises in His time, not in ours. Our times are in His hands. One man earnestly prayed for his child about a certain matter involving a phone call, but the Lord allowed the exact opposite of what he had requested. He was bewildered and angry, but that morning's Bible reading took him to Psalm 18, and God gave him verse 30: "As for God, His way is perfect." The Lord was working in His own way, on His own timetable.

Ruth Graham once said, "How often has God said no to my earnest prayers that He might answer my deepest longings, give me something more, something better."

The great church father Augustine came to the Lord after years of waywardness. His mother, Monica, prayed for him unceasingly, once begging God not to let Augustine go to Italy. Augustine went anyway—and there he was saved. Augustine later wrote, "Thou, taking Thy own secret counsel and noting the real point of her desire, didst not grant what she was then asking in order to grant to her the thing that she had always been asking."

Don't grow discouraged. Keep praying. Your times are in God's hands, and His ways are perfect.

RENOVATION

Therefore, if anyone is in Christ, he is a new creation; old things have passed away; behold, all things have become new.
2 CORINTHIANS 5:17

London businessman Lindsay Clegg told the story of a warehouse property he was selling. The building had been empty for months and needed repairs. Vandals had damaged the doors, smashed the windows, and strewn trash around the interior. As he showed a prospective buyer the property, Clegg took pains to say that he would replace the broken windows, bring in a crew to correct any structural damage, and clean out the garbage. "Forget about the repairs," the buyer said. "When I buy this place, I'm going to build something completely different. I don't want the building; I want the site."

Compared with the renovation God has in mind, our efforts to improve our own lives are as trivial as sweeping a warehouse slated for the wrecking ball. Ephesians 4:22–24 says, "You were taught, with regard to your former way of life, to put off your old self, which is being corrupted by its deceitful desires; to be made new in the attitude of your minds; and to put on the new self, created to be like God in true righteousness and holiness" (NIV).

When we become God's, the old life is over. He makes all things new. All He wants is the site and the permission to build.

Disconnect to Reconnect

So He Himself often withdrew into the wilderness and prayed.
Luke 5:16

Henri Nouwen, theologian and professor, once left his busy schedule to live for six months in a monastery. His life had become a paradox. As much as he felt burdened by the demands of his busy life, he lived in fear of the absence of activity. He had become dependent on the "compulsions and illusions" of his world and decided to seek out "the quiet stream underneath the fluctuating affirmations and rejections" that had become his security. That quiet stream, of course, was God Himself. But to find Him, Nouwen had to leave the noise and activity of his life behind and face the quietness and solitude of God alone.

In this age of wireless this and mobile that, we have become addicted to noise. By computer, cell phone, portable CD player, radio, or laptop, we have created umbilical cords that keep us tied to that which we believe affirms our existence. We are afraid to sit in silence, since silence suggests we are disconnected from affirmation.

Solitude is a periodic necessity—even for family members who are together 24/7. Find a time and a place to unplug and disconnect, so you can reconnect with God.

Being alone with God is to hear His voice above all others.

Lifted by Song

It is good to sing praises to our God.
Psalm 147:1

The Great Depression hit a man named J. C. Penney particularly hard, endangering his very health. Anxious and desperate because of huge financial losses, he felt he had nothing to live for. Even his family and friends shunned him. In the hospital one night, he grew so demoralized he expected to die before morning; but he heard singing coming from the little hospital chapel. The words of the song said, "Be not dismayed whate'er betide; God will take care of you."

Entering the chapel, Penney listened to the song and to the Scripture reading and prayer. He later wrote, "Suddenly—something happened. I can't explain it. I can only call it a miracle. I felt as if I had been instantly lifted out of the darkness of a dungeon into warm, brilliant sunlight." From that day, J. C. Penney was never plagued with worry, and he later called those moments in the chapel "the most dramatic and glorious twenty minutes of my life." When he died at age ninety-five, he left behind 1,660 department stores in his name.

Music is therapy for the soul. Today, lift up your heart in song; it is good to sing praises to our God!

Prayer Patrols

All kinds of prayers . . .
Ephesians 6:18 NIV

An urban church in Bristol, England, developed an interesting response to the high crime rate in its neighborhood. It developed "prayer patrols" that take place three times daily. Volunteers walk through the streets, knocking on doors, collecting prayer requests, and praying with the inhabitants. Police officials say that the number of robberies has been reduced by 51 percent, and burglaries are down by 21 percent. City officials say that prayer has broken the siege mentality that had gripped the neighborhood as a result of gang warfare.

There are many different ways and times to pray, and sometimes we get in a rut. Try walking through your neighborhood, praying for the families in the homes you pass. Try praying for the churches you pass on your drive to work. Try praying over your newspaper, interceding to God for the events of the day. Try praying out loud. Try writing out your prayers. Try composing a hymn of prayer to God.

The Bible says, "Pray in the Spirit on all occasions with all kinds of prayers and requests. With this in mind, be alert and always keep on praying for all the saints" (Ephesians 6:18 NIV).

Endless Possibilities

With men it is impossible, but not with God; for with God all things are possible.
Mark 10:27

Dr. Billy Graham is reported to have had a conversation with the former chancellor of West Germany, Konrad Adenauer. The chancellor asked Dr. Graham, "Do you believe Christ rose from the dead?" "Yes, I do," replied the evangelist. "Do you believe He is in heaven now?" "Yes, I do." "Do you believe He will return and reign over the earth?" "Yes, I do." "So do I," the chancellor concluded. "If He doesn't, there is no hope for this world."

The famous German leader had come to the same conclusion that millions throughout history have: the only one who can save the earth is God Himself. The world's problems continue to be addressed by many trying to help those who hurt. Others have resigned themselves to man's ultimate self-destruction and have insulated themselves from suffering with barriers of materialism and pleasure.

Both are right about one thing: man has created a world incapable of saving itself. And that is exactly the kind of world God is able to save—one in which man's possibilities are totally limited but God's are unlimited.

God can best demonstrate Himself when man has reached the limits of himself.

NEVER TOO OLD

Now also when I am old and grayheaded, O God, do not forsake me, until I declare Your strength to this generation, Your power to everyone who is to come.
PSALM 71:18

Sometimes an elderly Christian isn't sure what his or her role is at church. That wasn't true of two saints named Simeon and Anna. Simeon spent all his time at church involved in Bible study and prayer, and Anna, a godly widow in her eighties, worshiped, fasted, and prayed day and night. As it turns out, they were the first two people to pronounce blessings upon a baby boy named Jesus.

Somehow, Simeon and Anna missed the "retirement" message. Instead, they continued serving the Lord as they always had. As it worked out, their faithfulness was rewarded. They both recognized Jesus as the promised "Consolation of Israel," the Messiah, when His parents brought Him to the temple to be offered to the Lord as the firstborn son (Luke 2:25). Simeon and Anna declared His identity to all who were in the temple, and offered prayers and blessings over Him. Whatever your age today, plan on remaining faithful and active your entire life. If you're available, God will use you to bless someone.

The only aged saints who don't get used by God are those who have removed themselves from service.

November

CHANGE IS GOOD

I have been crucified with Christ; it is no longer I who live, but Christ lives in me; and the life which I now live in the flesh I live by faith in the Son of God, who loved me and gave Himself for me.
GALATIANS 2:20

John Wesley described his revelatory conversion to Christ this way: "In the evening I went very unwillingly to a society in Aldersgate Street where one was reading Luther's preface to the Epistle to the Romans...While he was describing the change which God works in the heart through faith in Christ, I felt my heart strangely warmed. I felt I did trust in Christ, Christ alone, for salvation."

Notice what caught Wesley's attention: the change that comes through genuine conversion. Wesley realized he had been devoutly religious but had never been changed. But after that night, John Wesley became a different person, changing his world through the power and person of Christ living in his heart.

Abraham and Sarah had to learn this lesson as well. They wanted to live in the past, walking by sight; but God wanted them to walk by faith. Have you experienced the changed life that only comes with knowing Christ? No one can meet Christ and stay the same; the old life is nothing like the new.

Conversion is one instance in which change is not only good; it's required.

FORGIVE WITH FEELING

And be kind to one another, tenderhearted, forgiving one another, even as God in Christ forgave you.
EPHESIANS 4:32

In 1982, John Hinckley Jr. attempted to take the life of President Ronald Reagan by shooting him with a handgun. Reagan's daughter, Patti Davis, later recounted what she learned from her father: "My father said he knew his physical healing was directly dependent on his ability to forgive John Hinckley. By showing me that forgiveness is the key to everything . . . he gave me an example of Christ-like thinking."

The Scriptures give Christians a clear standard concerning wrongs we experience. We are to forgive those who hurt us "even as God in Christ forgave [us]." Therefore, God's forgiveness is the model for how we are to forgive. Sometimes we dispense forgiveness like a soft drink from a vending machine—mechanically, with no feelings attached.

But Paul says two attitudes should accompany forgiveness: kindness and tenderheartedness. Why? Because that's the way God forgave us. Throughout Scripture, we find emotions such as kindness, gentleness, compassion, and tenderness—in word or by action—ascribed to God. Yes, He forgave, but He forgave with feeling. And we should do the same.

True forgiveness is as much an act of the heart as it is an act of the will.

SPIRITUAL SYNERGY

And they continued steadfastly in the apostles' doctrine and fellowship, in the breaking of bread, and in prayers.
ACTS 2:42

Euclid was a Greek mathematician who lived around 300 BC and is best known for his thirteen-volume treatise titled *Elements*. Two of Euclid's axioms of geometry have been revised to produce the modern saying, "The whole is greater than the sum of its parts." Another way of stating this principle is that something happens in a group that goes beyond the logic of math.

That something is called synergy, from the Greek word *sunergia*, meaning cooperation, or working together. Spiritual synergy can develop "where two or three are gathered together" in Christ's name for Bible study (Matthew 18:20). One person's insight brings a comment from another, which reminds a third of an illustration that really clicks in the mind of a fourth.

The Holy Spirit hasn't revealed everything to anyone. Therefore, Christians have to learn together to discover truth. It's God's way of encouraging the church to meet together and function interdependently. If you're not meeting regularly for Bible study with others, consider joining a group soon.

Wisdom is being willing to share what God has taught you and being willing to learn what He has taught others.

IN ALL THINGS, CHARITY

It seemed good to the Holy Spirit, and to us, to lay upon you no greater burden than these necessary things.
ACTS 15:28

There are dos and don'ts in the Bible, but we have a tendency to add to them—and to expect others to follow our lists. The church has invented lots of rules since the first century to define what it means to be a "good Christian." Over time, in our minds, these rules become traditions almost equal to Scripture. When the traditions of men become more important than God's people and God's law, they've gone too far.

Paul devoted Romans 14 and 15 to telling us that, while we must agree on the great central truths of Scripture (essential doctrines), there are many areas in which Christians may disagree (nonessential doctrines). "One person esteems one day above another; another esteems every day alike. Let each be fully convinced in his own mind" (Romans 14:5).

Have you been upset with someone who didn't agree with you on some nonessential point of doctrine? Have you been critical of someone whose opinion differed from yours? Perhaps in insisting on your list, you've forgotten the most important item on God's list: that we exhibit His love.

November 5

Who's Your Teacher?

But the Helper, the Holy Spirit, whom the Father will send in My name, He will teach you all things.
John 14:26

A graduate engineer worked in his field for a number of years and then served in a ministry vocation for nearly a decade. Returning to his previous career as an electrical engineer with a leading electronics company, he found himself woefully behind the technical curve.

Because of his absence, he felt like he was starting over as an engineer. It would have been nice for him to have a tutor accompany him throughout his absence from the engineering arena, teaching him and keeping him up-to-date. Nice, but impractical.

Having such a tutor is not impractical for the Christian. God has given us a full-time teacher to live with us twenty-four hours a day, keeping us up-to-date on "the things which God has prepared for those who love Him" (1 Corinthians 2:9).

That teacher is, of course, the Holy Spirit, sent by God to open the spiritual eyes and ears of every believer, to educate us about the kingdom of God, and to give us the mind of Christ. No believer should ever lack the wisdom and knowledge of God.

The Teacher is always ready. The question is whether we have taken our seat and opened our Book.

WHAT'S YOUR PERSPECTIVE?

As each one has received a gift, minister it to one another, as good stewards of the manifold grace of God.
1 PETER 4:10

As the last couple arrives for the potluck dinner, their hot casserole dish slides off its tray and crashes to the floor in the entryway. The sound of a crash and the accompanying groans bring the rest of the guests running to see what happened. And they instinctively take different courses of action.

A person with the gift of mercy wades through the stroganoff to hug the tearful wife who dropped the dish. A person with the gift of leadership starts assigning various clean-up tasks. A person with the gift of teaching bites his tongue just before saying that a plastic dish with a sealed lid might have prevented the disaster. A person with the gift of giving volunteers to drive to a nearby deli and pick up more food. And a person with the gift of prophecy starts explaining the spiritual lesson inherent in the mess—but then stops when he gets "the look" from his wife!

God has so gifted the members of the body of Christ that each has a unique perspective and contribution to make. Whatever your spiritual gift from God is, the body suffers to the degree you don't use it.

A gift given but unused is the same as a gift never given.

Praying Parents

Simon, Simon! Indeed, Satan has asked for you, that he may sift you as wheat. But I have prayed for you, that your faith should not fail.
Luke 22:31

It's a tough job to raise children today, but one of the secrets is to put God first and to pray for our youngsters. Find a spot at the kitchen table, by your bedside, or in a spare room, and spend time every day interceding for your kids. Some parents keep a journal with a picture of a child on each page, followed by various needs and prayer requests.

Don't know what to pray? Writer Lovelace Howard says, "Jesus' prayer for His disciples and St. Paul's prayers for his converts are ones we can always use with confidence in praying for our children. When, at any age, our children face temptation and danger, we can pray for them as Jesus did for Peter, that their faith may not fail and that their Heavenly Father will keep them from the evil one."

Or adapt Paul's prayer in Philippians 1:9–10: "Lord, I pray that my children's love may abound more and more in knowledge and all discernment, that they may approve the things that are excellent."

No child is more fortunate than one with a praying parent or grandparent.

Growing to Maturity

Do not labor for the food which perishes, but for the food which endures to everlasting life, which the Son of Man will give you, because God the Father has set His seal on Him.
John 6:27

One day following the end of World War I, General Louis Lyautey asked his gardener to plant a particular type of tree on his estate. The gardener objected that the tree, being unusually slow to grow, would take nearly a century to reach maturity. "In that case," the marshal replied, "there is no time to lose. Plant it this afternoon!"

Maturing is a long and sometimes slow process. You don't need to rely on church for your spiritual food. Rather, take in portions throughout the week—do a personal Bible study, attend a group Bible study, listen to Bible teaching on the radio or watch teaching on TV, be focused on your prayer life. As a child grows into a man, he is ready for solid foods. In the same way, when Christians mature spiritually, they crave deeper satisfaction.

It takes a lifetime of growth to become spiritually mature, but it's a beautiful and worthwhile process, just as waiting for a tree to blossom. Be patient as you work toward maturity in Christ.

ETERNITY-COLORED GLASSES

For now we see in a mirror, dimly, but then face to face.
1 CORINTHIANS 13:12

Author and evangelist Josh McDowell tells how he once wanted to purchase a new car. He had the car picked out and had settled on all the details. He knew he should pray about it first, so he began to pray. Every day, as he continued to pray, he began to sense that God was not giving him freedom to get the car. The more he prayed about it, the less important the car became until he finally prayed it right out of his life!

What happened to Josh and his new car will happen anytime we look at the things of this life through eternity-colored glasses. Imagine what the object of your concern would look like if you could transport it to heaven and set it down in the midst of the glory of eternity.

When we take our illness, our unemployment, our financial problems, our strained relationships, our fears and worries about the future—all the things that burden us in this life—and view them from God's eternal perspective, we will see them as they truly are. And we do that through worshipful prayer.

Take the things that concern you most into the presence of God. Through worship, you'll see them in a whole new light.

OPERATION ANDREW

Andrew . . . first found his own brother Simon, and said to him, "We have found the Messiah." . . . And he brought him to Jesus.
JOHN 1:40–42

Early in his ministry, Billy Graham wanted to mobilize local Christians to bring unsaved friends and relatives to his meetings. The Graham team devised "Operation Andrew," a simple plan whereby church members listed unsaved friends, prayed for them, and invited them to hear the gospel.

Why the name? Because every time we see Andrew in John's Gospel, he's bringing someone to Christ. He began with his brother, Peter. In John 6, he brought a lad to the Savior; and in John 12, he led a group of Greeks to Christ.

We can do the same. Years ago, a new Christian named Albert McMakin, age twenty-four, loaded his pickup truck with friends and took them each night to an evangelistic campaign in his city. You may never have heard McMakin's name; but you've heard the name of one of his passengers, a young man who was converted that week—Billy Graham.

Do you have room for someone in your "pickup"? When you walk in the footsteps of the Savior, you're walking the path of evangelism—and you never know whose life may be changed.

NOVEMBER 11

DETERMINED FAITH

And after my skin is destroyed, this I know, that in my flesh I shall see God.
JOB 19:26

The story of a famous man reads like this: chapter 1, he's wealthy and prosperous; chapter 2, he loses everything (even his children and his health); chapter 42, he is more prosperous than in chapter 1. Wouldn't you like to know what happened from chapters 3 through 41?

If so, you should read the story of Job, that prosperous patriarch of the Old Testament who had it all, lost it all, and got it all back in the end—doubled. You'll be blessed by reading his story in Scripture; but here's the word that summarizes Job's return to prosperity: *determination*. When Job lost everything, everyone around him tried to convince him to give up on God and give up on himself.

But Job had a determined faith—he knew God was just and fair. He wasn't about to give up on God or throw in the towel on his own faith just because he was stuck in a place he didn't understand. In the end, God met with Job, explained as much as he needed to know, and restored his health, family, and fortune.

If you're stuck in a place you don't understand right now, don't give up—on God or yourself. Faith that throws in the towel today won't have one to wave in victory tomorrow.

Jesus with Us

Then Peter said to them, "Repent, and let every one of you be baptized in the name of Jesus Christ for the remission of sins; and you shall receive the gift of the Holy Spirit.
Acts 2:38

Roald Amundsen was a Norwegian explorer who was the first to discover the magnetic meridian of the North Pole and to discover the South Pole. On one of his trips to the top of the world, Amundsen took a cage containing a homing pigeon—and released it near the North Pole. When his wife saw the pigeon circling their home, she knew her husband was alive!

That is a perfect picture of how God demonstrated His love for believers in Christ—by sending the Holy Spirit. First He sent the Holy Spirit, in the form of a dove, to indicate His anointing of Jesus (Luke 3:22). Then He sent the Spirit as a gift to the church at Pentecost (Acts 2:1–4). Jesus called the Holy Spirit the *paraklete* ("one called alongside"), sometimes translated as "Helper" (John 14:16). Just as Jesus loved and encouraged His disciples by being with them, so the Holy Spirit loves and encourages Jesus' disciples by being in them.

Jesus may be absent from us physically, but His presence is within us spiritually by the power of the Holy Spirit.

IF MY PEOPLE

If My people who are called by My name will humble themselves, and pray and seek My face, and turn from their wicked ways, then I will hear from heaven, and will forgive their sin and heal their land.
2 CHRONICLES 7:14

Just before his inauguration, Dwight Eisenhower invited Billy Graham to the Commodore Hotel in New York. "I'd like to quote one or two passages from the Bible in my inaugural speech," he said. Eisenhower felt one of the reasons he was elected was to help set the moral climate of America. Graham suggested 2 Chronicles 7:14.

Eisenhower prepared a speech that, to everyone's surprise, opened with what he called "a little prayer of my own." After his prayer, Ike's speech spoke repeatedly of spiritual things. "In the swift rush of great events," he said, "we find ourselves groping to know the full meaning of these times in which we live. In our quest for understanding, we beseech God's guidance." He was sworn into office with his hand resting on two Bibles, both opened to 2 Chronicles 7:14.

Take this verse as a personal mandate today—to humble yourself and pray that America might turn from any wicked way.

WHO'S THE BOSS?

. . . knowing that whatever good anyone does, he will receive the same from the Lord, whether he is a slave or free.
EPHESIANS 6:8

A group of men gathered one Saturday morning to help paint a friend's large two-story home. Toward the end of the day when the job was almost complete, a small bit of trim, which could not be seen from the ground, remained unpainted. One of the men said, "Since nobody can see that piece of trim, I guess we don't need to paint it." "Not true," said another of the crew as he went for a ladder. "God sees it."

The difference in the two approaches is the difference between working man's way and working God's way, working in light of the end of the day versus working in light of the end of life, and working for immediate rewards versus working for ultimate rewards. It's easy to get confused about whom we really work for in this life.

We go to work and interact with a human boss who makes the rules and signs the checks. We may face him at the end of the day; but at the end of the age, we will come face to face with the ultimate Boss, God Himself. What we got away with on the job will be made known, and what went unrewarded will be paid in full.

The best way to get high marks on our final "employee review" is to picture God as our employer each day.

Empathy

I sat where they sat, and remained there astonished among them seven days.
Ezekiel 3:15

In his book *Seven Habits of Highly Effective People*, Stephen Covey describes an experience on a subway in New York. A man and his children boarded the train, and the children were so loud and rambunctious they disrupted the entire car. The man sat down beside Covey, oblivious to the situation. Covey finally said, "Sir, your children are really disturbing a lot of people. I wonder if you couldn't control them a little more."

The man looked startled, then said, "Oh, you're right. I guess I should do something about it. We just came from the hospital, where their mother died about an hour ago. I don't know what to think, and I guess they don't know how to handle it either."

Covey's attitude instantly changed, and he later admitted that he learned a valuable lesson: seek to understand before seeking to be understood.

Sometimes people irritate or hurt us because they themselves are in pain. If they lash out at us, perhaps it's just the burst dam of personal frustration. Let's look beyond their words and see their hearts. Let's seek to understand before seeking to be understood.

The Choice Is Yours

Therefore choose life, that both you and your descendants may live.
Deuteronomy 30:19

When most people think of America, they think of democracy—and they're partly correct. In its purest form, a democracy means "the majority rules." America's Founding Fathers, knowing that the majority is not always right, wisely established America's government as a republic so that governing officials, elected by the people, serve as a buffer between pure "majority rule" and policy.

Besides government, there is another realm in which the majority is not always right: spiritual discernment. Jesus made it clear that life consists of two roads leading to two gates: a wide road leading to a broad gate that leads to destruction, and a difficult road leading to a narrow gate that leads to life (Matthew 7:13–14). The majority travels on the wide road leading to destruction, and the minority passes through the narrow gate leading to life.

People are like sheep—they tend to move blindly in herds without a lot of choice regarding danger. Which road are you on? Which gate have you chosen? Which destiny is yours?

The larger the crowd, the greater the cause for caution—especially when it comes to eternal choices.

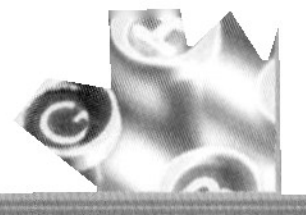

TIMELY FAITH

Yet who knows whether you have come to the kingdom for such a time as this?
ESTHER 4:14

Just before Charles Colson was to preach to three hundred inmates at San Quentin Prison, a lockdown confined the prisoners to their cells. To the few allowed to attend, he decided to go ahead and give the complete message he had prepared. Later, when he expressed disappointment that the three hundred were unable to attend, he was told, "We videotaped your message and will be showing it numerous times to all twenty-two hundred prisoners."

What if Colson had, as he first considered, just given a short devotional to the several Christians who were allowed to attend instead of the full evangelistic message he had prepared? More than two thousand needy souls would not have heard the gospel.

Being faithful in unlikely circumstances is what Esther is remembered for. As the newly appointed queen of Persia, she gained the ear of the king to plead for the safety of the Jews, who were about to be massacred. The king responded, and the Jewish people were saved.

An occasion may arise when you are the only person available to speak for God. Will you be faithful in such a moment as that? You are the most important person in the world to God when you are the one He has called to do something for Him.

Find the Way Home

For our citizenship is in heaven, from which we also eagerly wait for the Savior, the Lord Jesus Christ.
Philippians 3:20

Every year, Pacific salmon, having lived five to six years in the ocean, suddenly get the urge to return to the headwaters of their birth river. Battling fishermen, bears, and giant hydroelectric dams, the fish fight their way upstream, determined to reach their home.

Scientists don't know how the salmon make their way back to the exact river in which they were born after being in the ocean for several years. Some think they can taste or smell the fresh water from their river. Others think they may use the stars to navigate. However they do it, we know they don't use charts and compasses; their journey is intuitive. They have a longing for a particular river that isn't satisfied until they find it.

And that's exactly how it is with us. God created us for heaven, and nothing in this earthly life can satisfy our longing (Ecclesiastes 3:11). We should be like salmon—being in the ocean but not being of the ocean, not being at rest until we find our way home to heaven.

If fish know when they're home and when they're not, how much more intense is that knowledge in those who bear God's image?

Active versus Passive Parenting

And you, fathers, . . . bring [your children] up in the training and admonition of the Lord.
Ephesians 6:4

If you are a gardener, you know that planting a seed is only the first of a season's worth of steps. There's watering, fertilizing, weeding, and protecting the struggling plant from pests and diseases. Many flowers and vegetables require stakes, cages, or other supports to help them stand tall and bear their fruit. The gardener who does nothing but sow a seed shouldn't be surprised if plants never reach maturity.

Almost all living things in God's creation reproduce by sowing a seed: human beings, plants, birds, fish, and animals. When a plant seed is buried out of sight in the ground, there's little we can do to impact its growth. But when a new plant—and especially a new baby—enters the world, that's where the results of real husbandry and parenting can be seen.

Parents can have children, but only loving mothers and fathers actively nurture them to maturity. Feeding your child's mind, body, and spirit must be actively pursued. Passive parenting is letting a child grow on his or her own, while active parenting is bringing up a child "in the way he should go" (Proverbs 22:6).

It's true that we reap what we sow, but we also harvest fruit from what we carefully cultivate and nourish.

THE ENEMY OF GOD

Put on the whole armor of God, that you may be able to stand against the wiles of the devil.
EPHESIANS 6:11

A wealthy and godly farmer in the Middle East loses his home, his crops and livestock, his children, and his health. An Old Testament prophet prays to God for three weeks without hearing an answer to his prayers. A New Testament apostle suffers for years with a certain malady and finds no relief. These three individuals, though separated by time, were united by the common source of their problems: Satan.

In the cases of Job, Daniel, and Paul, Satan was allowed by God to enter their lives and bring pain, doubt, and discomfort. It is important for Christians to recognize that Satan is not an invention of Hollywood—he is a real being, intent on opposing God and His people at every turn.

But the Bible also clearly teaches that Satan is a troubler on a leash. He can go only as far as God allows and accomplish only that which fits and suits God's plans and purposes. While Paul explains in detail the spiritual armor of the believer against Satan's attacks, James summarizes it in just a single sentence: "Submit to God" (4:7).

The conscious choice to be under Christ's lordship is the surest defense against the devil's attacks.

THE NATURE OF LOVE

You shall not take vengeance, nor bear any grudge against the children of your people, but you shall love your neighbor as yourself: I am the LORD.
LEVITICUS 19:18

A holy man, sitting by a stream, noticed a large scorpion struggling to get out of the swirling waters. The holy man used a stick to try to push the insect ashore, but it only struck at the stick with its poisonous tail. A friend passed by and said, "Don't you know it's the nature of a scorpion to attack?" "Yes," said the holy man, "but it is my nature to save. Why should I change my nature just because the scorpion won't change his?"

That's a good question—one every Christian should consider. If ever we strike back at someone who has attacked us, we deny the very nature of Christ, who lives in us. The apostle Paul said, "It is no longer I who live, but Christ lives in me; and the life which I now live in the flesh I live by faith in the Son of God, who loved me and gave Himself for me" (Galatians 2:20). Did Jesus retaliate and strike back at those who mistreated Him? We know He did not (1 Peter 2:21–23). If Christ lives in us, we should not retaliate either.

Nothing can quench the fires of hatred like the healing waters of love.

BRING AN OFFERING

Give to the LORD the glory due His name; bring an offering, and come into His courts.

PSALM 96:8

In writing of her years in China, missionary Bertha Smith tells of a time when Dr. Wiley Glass, missionary educator, was kneeling during a prayer service at a large church. Mr. Wang, the church treasurer, was kneeling nearby. Suddenly Mr. Wang cried out, "Lord, have mercy on me! I've stolen! I'm a thief! I have stolen from God!" In astonishment, Dr. Glass thought, *Not you, Brother Wang; surely not you! All these years you have been such a trustworthy, devoted deacon, faithful trustee of the seminary, and upright Christian gentleman. You just could not have taken money from the church treasury!*

After a while, Brother Wang managed to explain, "I've not paid my tithe to the Lord! According to His Word, I've stolen it from Him!" The Chinese keep accurate records. Brother Wang calculated his tithe from the time he became a Christian, more than twenty years before, subtracted from it the total amount contributed to the church, and sold some land in order to pay what he felt he owed. From then on, he was aflame for Christ.

Do we love our Lord? How else can we express it except by giving? After all, God so loved us that He gave . . .

Choosing to Give Thanks

At midnight I will rise to give thanks to You.
Psalm 119:62

If you are in America on the fourth Thursday of November, there's a good chance you'll eat a big meal before the day is over. What began in 1621 as a conscious decision to give thanks to God was made a national day of thanksgiving in 1863 by President Abraham Lincoln. Today, Thanksgiving is a commercial and cultural institution in America.

Acts that are spontaneous and creative in the beginning often become formal and ritualistic. And that may be true of Thanksgiving in America. But it can also be true of thanksgiving in our personal lives. A quick way to determine whether your thanksgiving to God is creative and conscious, or rote and repetitious, is to examine when and where you give thanks to God. Is it only in church? Only during formal prayers? Only before you eat a meal? Or, are there instances when you stop and give thanks to God at unplanned times?

Maybe we don't rise at midnight to give thanks like the psalmist (119:62). But we should find ourselves giving thanks to God all during the day as events unfold (Ephesians 5:20).

The fourth Thursday in November is a great day to give thanks to God—just as are the other 364 days of the year!

Thanking and Speaking

She gave thanks to the Lord, and spoke of Him.
Luke 2:38

Like it or not, the holiday season is here, with all its frenzy and fun. Now is a good time to decide to be an Anna. This older saint is one of the original characters in the Christmas story—a prophetess, a widow of many years who virtually lived at the temple, awaiting the arrival of the Redeemer. She "served God with fastings and prayers night and day" (Luke 2:37).

Imagine her rapture when Joseph and Mary entered the temple, bearing in their arms the long-awaited Christ child. Somehow God assured her that this was the Messiah. Anna's reaction gives us a clue about our own attitude during the upcoming holidays: "She gave thanks to the Lord, and spoke of Him to all those who looked for redemption in Jerusalem" (v. 38).

Those are our two great obligations as we enjoy the seasons of Thanksgiving and Christmas: to thank God for Christ, and to speak of Him to others.

When was the last time you devoted more than a few seconds to thanking God for the Lord Jesus? Take some time today, and thank Him for Christ's life, His death, His resurrection, His ascension, His present intercessory ministry, and His soon return. Then speak of Him to someone else.

NOW THANK WE ALL OUR GOD

We give thanks to You, O God, we give thanks!
PSALM 75:1

Martin Rinkart pastored in Eilenberg, Saxony, during the Thirty Years War. The Swedish army surrounded the gates; and inside the walls, there was nothing but plague, famine, and fear. Hundreds of homes were destroyed, and people began dying in large numbers. There was a tremendous strain on the pastors, who expended all their strength preaching the gospel, caring for the sick, and burying the dead. One after another, the pastors themselves perished until at last only Martin was left. Some days he conducted as many as fifty funerals.

When the Swedes demanded a huge ransom, Martin left the safety of the city walls to negotiate, and there was soon a conclusion of hostilities. Knowing there is no healing without thanksgiving, Martin composed a hymn for the survivors of Eilenberg:

> Now thank we all our God, with heart and hands and voices,
> Who wondrous things hath done, in whom His world rejoices. . . .

It's been sung around the world ever since and is one of our greatest thanksgiving hymns. This is a time to focus our attention on God, who is the giver of all good things, and to thank Him for what is left, not what is lost.

Today, thank your God with heart and hands and voice.

Power of Persuasion

For Christ did not send me to baptize, but to preach the gospel, not with wisdom of words, lest the cross of Christ should be made of no effect.

1 Corinthians 1:17

The late Fred Rogers of television's *Mister Rogers* once attended church with friends while in seminary. During the sermon, he made a mental list of all the mistakes he felt the elderly preacher was making. When the service was over, he was caught short by the tears running down his friend's face. "He said exactly what I needed to hear," she said.

Sometimes what seems like poor preaching from a human perspective can be greatly used by God. What makes the difference? The Holy Spirit. Scripture and tradition give us reason to believe that the apostle Paul was not a very dynamic person, humanly speaking. Yet who can deny the impact of his words? No one, apart from Christ Himself, has accomplished more by his speaking.

Paul said it was good that his words were not "persuasive words of human wisdom" (1 Corinthians 2:4), lest people look to him instead of to God as the true source of power. We would do well to examine ourselves the same way—to see whom we rely on for power in our lives: the Holy Spirit or ourselves.

It's fine to use the natural gifts God has given us—as long as they don't replace His supernatural gift of the Spirit.

The Changed Centurion

So when the centurion . . . saw that He cried out like this and breathed His last, he said, "Truly this Man was the Son of God!"
Mark 15:39

An African woman became a Christian, which enraged her husband. He decided to get rid of her by accusing her of thievery—of stealing his keys. He threw his key ring in a river and planned to accuse her of taking it. Later that day, his wife bought a large fish for their supper and discovered her husband's keys in its stomach! When her husband came home later that night demanding to know where his keys were, she calmly handed them to him—and he was instantly converted to Christ!

While Christians are warned against walking by sight, sometimes it's true that seeing is believing. At some point, it becomes difficult to deny the evidence of the power and presence of a miracle-working God. A Roman centurion who watched Jesus suffer on Calvary—and then felt the earth shake when an earthquake accompanied His death—concluded that Jesus was truly the Son of God. Was he converted? The Bible doesn't say, but we know he was changed.

Think about how your life has changed since seeing Jesus. Seeing Jesus for who He really is always precedes seeing ourselves for who we really are.

No Accidents

Now to the King eternal, immortal, invisible, to God who alone is wise, be honor and glory forever and ever. Amen.
1 Timothy 1:17

"I have lived a long time," Benjamin Franklin, age eighty-one, told the Constitutional Convention, "and the longer I live, the more convincing proofs I see of this truth—that God governs in the affairs of men. And if a sparrow cannot fall to the ground without His notice, is it probable that an empire can rise without His aid?"

Nations rise and fall; leaders come and go. But there is only one King of kings and Lord of lords, and He who ordains the flow of history and guides the sparrow's flight also carefully attends to the needs of His children. A. W. Tozer wrote, "To the child of God, there is no such thing as accident. He travels an appointed way....Accidents may indeed appear to befall him and misfortune stalk his way; but these evils will be so in appearance only and will seem evil only because we cannot read the secret script of God's hidden providence."

God is eternal, so His perspective is broad. He is immortal, having no fear of death. He is invisible and always present. He is all-wise, always knowing just what to do. Trust Him—and give Him honor and glory forever and ever. Amen.

SHAPING THE FUTURE

Keep this forever in the...heart of Your people...and give my son Solomon a loyal heart to keep Your commandments and Your testimonies and Your statutes.

1 CHRONICLES 29:18–19

A retired French lawyer struck a deal with a ninety-year-old widow. For a payment of $500 per month to her until she died, he bought the rights to take over the lease on her fashionable apartment. At her age, it looked like a shrewd investment. In 1995, thirty years and $180,000 later, he was still paying—when she turned 120!

The future rarely turns out the way we think it will, so our best efforts to predict it ought to be held lightly. But there is one perspective on the future that is a sure thing: God's perspective.

Consider King David, for example. The days of his kingship over Israel were coming to a close. The nation was preparing to build a great temple for God, and Solomon, David's young son, was ascending to the throne. Instead of predicting or worrying about the future, David did the right thing: he prayed about it. He prayed for the people and he prayed for his son, that God would bless them and keep them faithful.

Shape your future, and your family's future, by committing everything to God in prayer. The only future that is a sure thing is the one to which God has said yes.

LEADERS IN GIVING

Be an example to the believers in word, in conduct, in love, in spirit, in faith, in purity.
1 TIMOTHY 4:12

William Wallace won the respect of his army of Scottish commoners by being on the front line of every battle they fought. The same commoners despised the fur-clad Scottish lords because they sat in the rear on horseback, never staining themselves with the soil or blood of battle.

In war or in peace—or in the life of the church—sacrifice is the admission price to the ranks of leadership. Leadership in giving must be no less sacrificial. If church leaders want members to give, they must set the example, as must parents who want their children to learn to give.

King David followed this pattern when raising money to build Israel's first temple. He gave generously from his own personal wealth; then the leaders of families, tribes, and other officials followed his example and gave. Their examples caused the Israelite people to rejoice in their own giving.

Everyone leads someone. What kind of an example of giving are you providing for those you lead? Are those you lead faithful in giving?

Before examining their habits, make sure you have examined your own. From the pattern comes the product.

DECEMBER

ALL IT TAKES

For the eyes of the LORD run to and fro throughout the whole earth, to show Himself strong on behalf of those whose heart is loyal to Him.
2 CHRONICLES 16:9

Dwight L. Moody preached the gospel to more people in the nineteenth century than anyone else in the world. He left home at age seventeen with the equivalent of a fifth-grade education. He was won to Christ as a teenager, and in 1873, a friend in England challenged him with the following statement: "The world has yet to see what God can do with a man fully consecrated to him." Moody's reply was, "With God's help, I aim to be that man."

That challenge certainly motivated Moody, but it wasn't altogether accurate. For the world had already seen what God would do with a man fully committed to Him. Daniel, taken from Jerusalem to Babylon by Nebuchadnezzar, immediately impressed his pagan captors. His physical appearance, his wisdom, and his unswerving commitment to his God elevated him to a place of influence—all without compromising his beliefs. Noah, Joseph, Daniel, Paul—all were ordinary people whom God used to do extraordinary things.

Will today's world see extraordinary things done for God? All it takes is a person like Daniel or Dwight L. Moody—that is, a person like you—fully consecrated to God.

KEEPING CHRIST IN CHRISTMAS

And the Word became flesh and dwelt among us, and we beheld His glory, the glory as of the only begotten of the Father, full of grace and truth.

JOHN 1:14

A survey of five thousand households, conducted in August 2003 by the Conference Board's Consumer Research Center, showed that consumers planned to spend more for Christmas that year than the previous one—in spite of continuing national economic woes. One-third of the families surveyed planned to spend $500 or more on presents in 2003.

No one knows exactly when it happened, but Christmas in America has become more about money than the manger. Certainly gift giving is a meaningful part of the Christmas celebration. After all, our gifts to one another and to God remind us of His greater gift of His own Son, Jesus Christ (Romans 6:23). But it's easy to let material gifts overshadow the greatest Gift, to think more about what we want than Whom we need, and to let money replace ministry in our attitudes toward others.

Why not begin this Christmas season, either alone or with family or friends, refocusing on the Reason for the season. Give to Christ the only gift He really wants, this and every year—the gift of your loving heart.

All the Christmas presents in the world mean nothing without the presence of Christ.

EVEN IN THE NIGHT

Yet I will rejoice.
HABAKKUK 3:18

John Newton, who penned the words to "Amazing Grace," was an eighteenth-century pastor in London who was devoted to his wife, Mary. Their relationship was one of the most tender in Christian history, and they sometimes worried that their love for each other was almost idolatrous. One day, she broke the news that a famous surgeon had diagnosed her with cancer. Newton's anguish was terrible. He said he felt like a bull caught in a net. When she died fifteen months later, friends worried because he seemed inconsolable.

But then, strengthened in faith, John preached her funeral, choosing as his text Habakkuk 3:17–18: "Though the fig tree may not blossom, nor fruit be on the vines; though the labor of the olive may fail, and the fields yield no food . . . yet I will rejoice in the LORD, I will joy in the God of my salvation."

We can still focus on God in worship even when we don't understand His decisions and directions in our lives. We're caught in time and trapped in transience. God, who transcends all, is eternal and infinite. We don't always understand, but He knows. He cares.

God works things together for good. He is worthy to be praised, even in the night. We can yet rejoice in Him.

CHRISTMAS CHEER

"Love the Lord your God with all your heart and with all your soul and with all your strength and with all your mind"; and, "Love your neighbor as yourself."
LUKE 10:27 NIV

Mamie Adams always went to a specific branch post office in her town because the postal employees were friendly. On a busy afternoon, just a few days before Christmas, she stopped by to purchase a few stamps. While waiting in the long line, a man pointed out that there was no need to wait; a stamp machine was in the lobby. "I know," said Mamie, "but the machine won't ask me about my arthritis."

The art of kindness has not been lost, but sometimes it gets tucked away, especially during the holidays. There are so many errands to run, goodies to bake, and gifts to wrap that we forget the spirit of Christmas, sharing the good news of Jesus' birth with others by showing our love and generosity.

When you take the time to encourage someone, it might be the small act that changes his or her entire life! Go the extra mile for someone in need—become involved in your community. The art of kindness is in you.

KNOWING AND DOING

For if anyone is a hearer of the word and not a doer, he is like a man observing his natural face in a mirror.
JAMES 1:23

A well-known seminary professor spent a summer studying in Jerusalem. In his apartment building lived an orthodox Jewish rabbi, with whom he studied Hebrew throughout the summer. One day, the professor sat and listened to his Jewish friend recite the entire Book of Psalms, in Hebrew, without missing so much as a jot or a tittle.

The lesson he brought back was the same lesson Jesus taught in Matthew 7:24–27: It is not the hearers and "knowers" of God's Word who will be blessed, but the doers. The knowledge of God's Word is important—without it, God's people have been known to suffer (Hosea 4:6). But great knowledge can also water the root of pride in the sinful human heart (1 Corinthians 8:1).

One man said that to consume the Bible without putting it into practice is the equivalent of going into a fine restaurant and eating the menu while ignoring the meal. Which are you more focused on in your Christian life: knowing the Word for the sake of knowing it, or knowing it in order to put it into practice?

Knowing the Bible should lead to living the Bible, which leads to honoring the Author of the Bible.

God Knows the Future

Behold the maidservant of the Lord! Let it be to me according to your word.
Luke 1:38

A marble slab in a New Hampshire cemetery holds an unbelievable epitaph: "Murdered by the Baptist Ministry and Churches." Apparently the deceased was accused of lying in a church meeting. She was expelled and reduced to poverty, and the church refused to allow any outside investigation. The assassination of her character led to an early death.

It takes great faith to stand under the weight of false accusation and shame. When a teenager named Mary was approached by the angel Gabriel and told she was to be the mother of Jesus, imagine what raced through her mind: *I am not married. If I become pregnant, people will think at worst that I am immoral or at best that my husband-to-be, Joseph, and I have had relations—neither of which is true!* But then she must have thought, *Surely God knows these possibilities. If He knows what could happen and still wants me to serve Him, then I will do it.*

The next time that obeying the Lord puts you at risk for being misunderstood, remember that God knows all the possibilities—and He has planned accordingly.

Saying yes to God means believing that He knows where that response will lead.

THE GIFT OF PRAYER

But the mercy of the LORD is from everlasting to everlasting on those who fear Him, and His righteousness to children's children.
PSALM 103:17

One of our favorite Christmas poems says: "Over the river and through the woods, to Grandmother's house we go. The horse knows the way to carry the sleigh through the white and drifted snow." Those words convey the joy of grandparents and grandchildren spending the holidays together.

But what if the grandchildren aren't coming? Many grandparents are sad this month because they can't be with their grandchildren. Are you among them?

Why not give your grandkids a special gift of prayer? Devote extra time every day to praying for your dear ones by name. Search the Scriptures for verses to pray into their lives. When Christmas Eve or Christmas Day arrives, set aside a "sweet hour of prayer" on their behalf.

One of the things grandparents can do better than anyone else is to pray for their grandchildren. How many of us had grandparents who were prayer warriors? Who can tell how much our lives were shaped and protected by their strong and ceaseless intercession?

If you can't spend this Christmas *with* your grandchildren, spend it *for* your grandchildren. Spend it on your knees.

IT'S ALL GOOD

[Barnabas] was a good man, full of the Holy Spirit and of faith.
ACTS 11:24

In his book *Wind and Fire*, Bruce Larson notes characteristics of sandhill cranes, which fly great distances across continents. In flight, no bird leads all the time, and only birds that can handle wind turbulence get to lead the flock. But most important, all the time the leader is breaking the wind resistance for the others, the entire flock pours forth a constant stream of affirming honks.

Whether given in the form of honks or hugs, encouragement probably has the highest cost-to-benefit ratio of any human act. Barnabas is the prototype of an encourager; we may have the Gospel of Mark today because of him.

Once, when Paul and Barnabas went on a ministry trip, they took young Mark with them—but he deserted them before the end of their trip (Acts 13:13). Later, Paul wouldn't take Mark on a second trip, so Barnabas took Mark under his wing (Acts 15:36–40). Barnabas's forgiving and encouraging attitude toward the young leader probably saved Mark's ministerial life. Look around—do you see someone with potential whose world you could change with a little encouragement?

Whether honks, hugs, hollers, or hallelujahs—encouragement is all good.

December 9

The Message of Holly

In Him we have redemption through His blood, the forgiveness of sins, according to the riches of His grace.
Ephesians 1:7

Millions of people this Christmas will go to their local garden center in search of the traditional *Ilex opaca*. Or they might even inquire about the fancier English *Ilex aquifolium*. If you can't remember the fancy Latin names, no problem. Just ask for Christmas holly, and you'll come home with the spiny green leaves and the bright red berries that have adorned wreathes and fireplaces for generations.

Over the centuries, red and green have been used as the two primary colors of Christmas. The shiny red holly berries and the bright green holly leaves are the perfect combination of the two most traditional colors. The small holly berries are thought to have originally reminded Christians of the drops of Christ's blood caused by the crown of thorns He wore on Calvary. The bright green leaves and all the evergreens used at Christmas speak of the never-ending life that the shedding of Christ's blood secured for all who believe in Him.

Even the sharp spines on the holly leaves remind us of what Jesus suffered on our behalf.

NEVER-ENDING UNION

And truly our fellowship is with the Father and with His Son Jesus Christ.
1 JOHN 1:3

From the early days of Irish Christianity, the Celtic cross has had a circle surrounding the intersection of the vertical and horizontal axes of the cross. Some believe the design originated with St. Patrick, who, upon seeing a round symbol of the moon goddess, drew a Christian cross over it, changing a Druid symbol into a new symbol for Irish Christianity.

In the same way that St. Patrick adopted a pagan circle and gave it new meaning, so other Christians adopted another circle and gave it new meaning to celebrate Christ's birth. When early Christians changed the Roman winter solstice celebration of the rebirth of the sun (originally on December 21) to a celebration of the birth of the "Son of Righteousness," the evergreen wreath was adopted as well—but given new meaning.

Instead of being simply a garland, the round Christmas wreath speaks of the never-ending unity and fellowship we have with God through Christ. It is a picture of what C. S. Lewis wrote: "Once a man is united to God, how could he not live forever?"

When you hang a wreath on your door or over your fireplace this Christmas, don't fail to notice that the wreath has no end. Likewise, there is no end to our union with God.

THE CHRISTMAS SPIRIT

Bearing with one another, and forgiving one another.
COLOSSIANS 3:13

In their book, *None of These Diseases*, S. I. McMillen and David Stern describe the damage we inflict on ourselves when we dislike someone or refuse to forgive him or her. "The moment I begin to hate a man, I become his slave. He controls my thoughts. He controls my feelings. He even controls my dreams. Stress hormones constantly surge through my bloodstream and wear down my body. . . . The one I hate hounds me wherever I go."

As your family gathers this holiday, perhaps there's a member you don't like or haven't forgiven. Perhaps a father-in-law or a stepchild. Maybe a brother or sister who hurt you years ago.

Remember that Christmas is all about God's love and forgiveness. Jesus left the infinite riches of the heavenly palace to sleep in an animal's food trough, choosing to live among unlovely people. He came to forgive and redeem. He can flush all the hatred from your heart if you'll only let Him.

If you're not looking forward to seeing someone in your family this Christmas, offer this prayer: "Lord, I confess that I don't like ______________, and I am dreading being with him (or her). Forgive me, and help me to forgive and forbear. May the love of the Christmas Christ be funneled through me this season."

LIFE THAT NEVER FADES

The cypress, the pine, and the box tree together, to beautify the place of My sanctuary.
ISAIAH 60:13

If you selected a Christmas tree blindfolded, your chances of choosing the right kind are good. There are only two kinds of trees in the world: deciduous (those whose leaves die annually) and evergreens (those whose leaves stay green). Still, you're better off peeking when you choose. Bringing home a six-foot oak with bare limbs might get you lumps of coal in your stocking.

Evergreen. The word itself brings up images of Christmas trees in December—cedars, spruces, and firs. And the scents! Evergreen garlands cascading down banisters and flowing over mantels fill the house with an aroma we wish would last forever. The evergreen tree is certainly the most traditional of Christmas decorations—though electric lights weren't used on them until 1882. But for centuries, evergreens have represented the most everlasting aspect of the first Christmas in Bethlehem—our eternal life with Jesus Christ. Our Christmas trees, once cut, won't last forever. But what they picture will: life in heaven forever.

When you put up your Christmas tree this year, remind family and friends that, though the green of the tree will ultimately fade, the greatness of our eternal life in Christ will not.

HOW GOD TREATS US

All things work together for good.
ROMANS 8:28

Anger is a universal emotion. Even babies lose their temper if they don't get their way. Few of us make it through a week without fuming or fussing about something. Occasionally our anger is justified, but often we harbor an unhealthy, unforgiving spirit.

Sometimes we're just angry at life. Grace Saxe, for example, a dedicated Bible teacher of an earlier generation, had hoped to become a missionary. After her acceptance by a mission's board, she packed her bags, bade her friends farewell, and prepared to sail off; but the night before her departure, her father was seized by a life-threatening illness. She was unable to leave, and the ship sailed without her. In a day or two, her father recovered.

"Why would God treat me like this?" Grace wondered. For several days, she was angry and depressed. At the end of the week, a report came that the ship was lost at sea and everyone aboard had perished. Grace's resentment melted into understanding, then into thankfulness.

Are you resentful at life's circumstances? Is your Christmas being marred by a bitter spirit? Give it to the Lord and let Him have His way. Trust Him, for He knows just what He is doing.

Christmas Gifts

When they saw the star, they rejoiced with exceeding great joy.
Matthew 2:10 KJV

The holiday season is one of the busiest times of the year. Who has time to take a break? But when we do slow down, we see why people are speeding around. If you visit any shopping center in the middle of December, read the newspaper advertisements, or look under the tree on Christmas Day—you will see that gifts have become the focus of this holiday.

As Christians, we know the deeper meaning of Christmas and gift giving. When we present a gift to someone, we say in a tangible way how much we appreciate him, respect him, and have concern for him. But most of all, we say how much we love him. Remember how Jesus' birth was celebrated with gifts: "And when they had come into the house, they saw the young Child with Mary His mother, and fell down and worshiped Him. And when they had opened their treasures, they presented gifts to Him: gold, frankincense, and myrrh" (Matthew 2:11).

The tradition of gift giving today is a powerful testimony to the deeper meaning of the season. Giving at this time of year is a rich and exciting experience, reflecting God's gift to us.

GIVING THE GIFT OF CHRIST

And remember the words of the Lord Jesus, that He said, "It is more blessed to give than to receive."
ACTS 20:35

The most endearing people associated with the first Christmas in Bethlehem in addition to the Christ child and His parents are the wise men. Their gifts of "gold, frankincense, and myrrh" suggest there were three. But their number is as much speculation as their identity, homeland, and vocation. "Magi" suggests wisdom, while "the east" suggests Arabia.

This we do know about the magi: They went to considerable effort and expense to do something for others. Their goal was to give something to Jesus, not to receive something for themselves. In doing so, they unknowingly embodied what ought to be the spirit of Christmas for every Christian.

Studies show that Christmas can be one of the most discouraging times of the year for many people. Widows and widowers, shut-ins, singles, the elderly, those with no family nearby . . . the list goes on of people who are often lonely and forgotten in the Christmas rush. This year, spread some Christmas cheer and the love of Christ to someone who may be in need of both. It might make this your best Christmas ever—and theirs.

This Christmas, remind yourself of why it is more blessed to give than to receive.

WHAT CAN YOU DO?

She has done a good work for Me. . . . She has done what she could.
MARK 14:6, 8

D. James Kennedy tells of a Christian peasant woman living in Africa more than fifty years ago. People were bringing gifts as offerings to the Lord, but she had nothing to bring. When she appeared with a dollar to place on the altar, the missionary was suspicious of its origin, given her poverty. He inquired and discovered she had sold herself as a slave for life to a nearby plantation—for a dollar.

What this woman did for Christ shocks our modern sensibilities—and makes us squirm with shame. But it was the woman's attitude, not her act, which should be our example. The apostle Paul said there is a lack of wisdom in making carnal comparisons (2 Corinthians 10:12). We should not try to be like others in our giving. Instead, we should ask the Lord, "What can I do? What can I bring?" The magi brought expensive gifts to Jesus because they could.

The poor woman in Africa could not copy the wealthy magi in actions, but she could in attitude—she brought what she could. Look around and consider what God has given to you that you could give back to Him (and don't make the mistake of looking only for money).

Our goal is not to bring what God has given another but what God has given us.

COME AND COMING

Blessed is he who waits.
DANIEL 12:12

The prophet Daniel never put up a Christmas tree, never lit an Advent wreath, and never sang a holiday carol. But he celebrated Christmas anyway. He anticipated the coming of the Messiah, and his whole life was lived against the backdrop of Christ's appearance. It gave him daily encouragement. In Daniel 7:13, he said: "I was watching in the night visions, and behold, One like the Son of Man, [was] coming."

For us, too, the promise of His coming imparts optimism. Our attitude is that of Revelation 1:7: "Behold, He is coming with clouds, and every eye will see Him."

Imagine how excited you'd be if your loved one were returning after a tour of duty in a war zone. You'd be almost giddy with excitement, straightening the house, planning a menu, calling friends, and preparing for the long-awaited reunion.

How wonderful that Jesus came, clothed in humanity, born of a virgin, laid in a manger. How wonderful that He is coming again, clothed in triumph, descending with angels, crowned with glory.

Celebrate Christmas this year with both a backward glance and a forward look. Rejoice! Our King is coming.

OBEYING THE COACH

Then Joseph, being aroused from sleep, did as the angel of the Lord commanded him and took to him his wife.
MATTHEW 1:24

Earl Weaver, former manager of the Baltimore Orioles, had a rule: no base stealing without a sign from him. The great Reggie Jackson decided to steal second without a sign from Weaver. Though Jackson was successful, Weaver took him aside after the game and explained two negative ways in which Jackson's "successful" steal impacted the game. Jackson saw only his desire, while Weaver was watching the whole game.

Sometimes those in authority over us ask us to do things we don't understand. Along with our children, we ask the "Why?" question as often as not. The maturing Christian learns that God explains reasons sometimes, but other times He does not (Deuteronomy 29:29). Knowing that God sees everything provides a solid foundation for our obedience.

Think about Joseph when he learned that his betrothed, Mary, was pregnant before their wedding. As practically hard and publicly humiliating as it might have been, Joseph obeyed God's instructions to stay engaged to Mary.

When you're tempted to steal away in your own direction, remember—God is watching the whole game.

FROM WHY TO WHO

We are more than conquerors through Him who . . .
ROMANS 8:37

The word *why* occurs twenty-four times in the Book of Job, as the afflicted patriarch grapples with multiplied problems. "Why did I not die at birth?" he wondered (3:11). "Why have you made me your target?" he asked God (7:20 NIV).

At one time or another, many of our Bible heroes asked the question, "Why?" Trace the word through a concordance, and you'll be amazed at how frequently it's found. Even our Lord Jesus cried, "My God, My God, why have You forsaken Me?" (Matthew 27:46).

But at some point we've got to move from "Why?" to "Who?", as in, "Who loves us?" It is possible to worship God even when we don't have all the answers. We live by promises, after all, not by explanations. Sometimes we're in green pastures and beside still waters; other times we're in the valley of the shadow of death. In both cases, our Shepherd is before us, and goodness and mercy are following.

Faith is keeping our eyes on Jesus regardless of the storms and shadows. It is being fully persuaded that God has the power to do what He has promised. It's lifting our voices in praise even when our spirits are low.

Do you have unanswered questions in your life today? Trust God with your whys and focus on the Who.

A CHRISTLIKE CHRISTMAS

Though He was rich . . . He became poor.
2 CORINTHIANS 8:9

Poor, distraught Johnny. It was Christmas morning, and he had opened the last of his eleven presents. There wasn't a twelfth one, and he felt as deflated as a leaky hot water bottle. How strange that our culture has turned Christmas inside out, making it a frenzy of materialism, greed, indebtedness, and exhaustion.

Christmas, to Jesus, meant selflessness. Though "in the form of God, [He] did not consider it robbery to be equal with God, but made Himself of no reputation, taking the form of a bondservant" (Philippians 2:6–7).

Christmas, to Jesus, meant service. He came not to be catered to but to minister to others (Mark 10:45). He wasn't as interested in being given to, as in giving. He gave Himself, and in giving Himself, He gave His all.

Christmas, to Jesus, meant submission. In claiming to be "sent" from heaven, He implied His obedience to the Sender—His Father. And Christmas, to Jesus, meant sacrifice. His birth set the stage for Calvary.

God's people must reverse the trends of our culture and begin seeing our Lord's birth as He saw it. Can you think of a way in which you can be a selfless, submissive, sacrificing servant today?

If so, you've got a divine corner on Christmas.

THE PURE IN HEART

Rejoice, highly favored one, the Lord is with you; blessed are you among women!
LUKE 1:28

Elizabeth I, queen of England from 1558 to 1603, set out to implement a full Protestant reformation in Roman Catholic England. That movement became known as Puritanism because of its emphasis on personal regeneration and purity, household prayer, and strict morality. Those who embraced this movement were called Puritans because they wanted to purify the church of all ceremonies, vestments, and customs inherited from the medieval church.

In today's world of loose morality and liberal theology, the term *puritanical* is used negatively to refer to those who are out of step with modern thinking and progressive ways. And it is usually an accurate description, since those who desire to live as the pure in heart do find themselves in the minority.

A teenage girl in the town of Nazareth, more than two millennia ago, could be called a Puritan for all the right reasons. She had a heart that was set upon knowing and serving God, and she lived in such a way that she found favor in God's sight. Mary, the mother of Jesus, wasn't perfect or sinless, but it was her desire to serve God that attracted His attention.

Puritanical in the world's eyes may equal pure in heart in God's eyes.

CHRISTMAS OPPORTUNITIES

Make the most of every opportunity for doing good in these evil days.
EPHESIANS 5:16 NLT

Christmas gives us opportunities to do things for people we might otherwise neglect, and we must take advantage of each opportunity. As long as we're on earth, God has work for us to do. When He's finished with us here, He'll take us home.

Seventeenth-century preacher Thomas Fuller said, "God's children are immortal while their Father hath anything for them to do on earth." Missionary David Livingstone said similarly, "Men are immortal until their work is done."

The British preacher Charles Spurgeon said, "Whatever occurs around us, we need not be alarmed. We are immortal until our work is done. And amidst infectious or contagious diseases, if we are called to go there, we may sit as easily as though in balmy air. It is not ours to preserve our life by neglecting our duty. It is better to die in service than live in idleness—better to glorify God and depart, than rot above ground in neglecting what He would have us to do. Unto God belong the issues from death. We may, therefore, go without temerity into any danger where duty calls us."

There is a child, a bag lady, a prisoner, a soldier whom God wants you to touch this Christmas season. Make the most of every opportunity.

BE AN ANGEL

Glory to God in the highest, and on earth peace, goodwill toward men!
LUKE 2:14

By the fourth century AD, a psalm was in use in Christian churches, and it is still in use today, called *Gloria in Excelsis Deo*. Its title comes from the Latin Bible's translation of the words proclaimed by the angels as they announced the birth of Jesus to the shepherds: "Glory to God in the highest . . . we praise thee, we bless thee, we worship thee, we glorify thee, we give thanks to thee for thy great glory."

If angels do anything, they worship God. In Scripture, we find them doing many things on earth—delivering messages, guarding and coming to the aid of the saints, doing battle. But in the heavenly places, the heavenly host seems to have one primary agenda—to proclaim the glory of God forever and ever.

It is not surprising that at the birth of Jesus, the glory of God was the first thing on the angels' lips. They were not unaware, after all, of the cosmic struggle going on between Satan and man. When the Father's own Son was dispatched to earth to defeat the enemy, angels accompanied the announcement by proclaiming God's glory. Is His glory and praise the first thing on our lips this Christmas season?

Imitate the angels this Christmas by declaring the glory of God to someone who has not beheld it.

HIS NAME SHALL BE CALLED . . .

But who do you say that I am?
LUKE 9:20

Strange how many people feel depressed on Christmas. It's called the "Christmas blues," or seasonal affective disorder. Whatever it is, if you're down in the dumps today, stop thinking about Christmas. Think instead about Christ.

He is our Prophet, Priest, and King. He is the Master, the Bridegroom, the Good Shepherd, the Holy One of God. His name is Emmanuel—God with us. His name was called Jesus. John introduced Him as "the Lamb of God who takes away the sin of the world" (John 1:29). The wise men recognized Him as the "King of the Jews," and even the demons called Him "the Holy One of God" (Matthew 2:2; Mark 1:24, respectively).

"Is this not the carpenter?" asked the people of Nazareth in Mark 6:3. "Could this be the Christ?" asked the woman by the well in John 4:29. Thomas called Him, "My Lord and my God" (John 20:28).

Today isn't about Christmas but about Christ. It isn't about presents but about His presence. You may or may not have family nearby, but your Father is close at hand, and your faith is more important than your feelings. He sets us free from chains we can never remove ourselves. He is our hope.

Don't worry about celebrating Christmas. Just celebrate Jesus!

THE JOY OF CHRISTMAS

Where were you when . . . the angels shouted for joy?
JOB 38:4, 7 NIV

From 27 BC to AD 180, the Mediterranean world enjoyed what history calls *Pax Romana*—the Roman peace. It was a period of unprecedented peace and prosperity brought about by the dominant presence of the Roman Empire. Roads and aqueducts were built, cities were modernized, the rule of law brought stability, and religions were tolerated. Into *Pax Romana* the Prince of Peace was born.

Some might ask, "What need was there for a prince of peace when there was Roman peace throughout the land?" The peace of man is very different from the peace of God—the *Pax Romana* lasted only two hundred years. No wonder the angel who appeared to the shepherds said he was bringing "good tidings of great joy . . . to all people" (Luke 2:10).

The angels had been overjoyed once before when the Son of God, through whom all things were created, laid the foundations of the earth (Job 38:1–7). But now the same Son was coming to dwell upon the earth He created! The joy only the angels had known would now be a joy spread throughout the earth to all people. Have you experienced the peace of which the angel spoke?

While the peace of Rome has passed away, the peace of God endures forever.

GIVING THE VERY BEST

And when they had opened their treasures, they presented gifts to Him: gold, frankincense, and myrrh.
MATTHEW 2:11

O'Henry's famous short story "The Gift of the Magi" tells the story of Jim and Della, each of whom wanted nothing more for Christmas than to give a gift to their beloved. Della sold her beautiful hair to a wig maker to buy Jim a gold chain for his watch, while Jim sold his watch to buy Della beautiful combs for her hair. The sacrifice of their most treasured possessions showed the depth of their love.

Wanting to give the greatest of gifts to one's spouse is understandable. With each passing year of a relationship, love should deepen and gifts become more precious. But when a small group of astrologers journeyed from their distant land to bring expensive gifts to the infant Jesus, it was a remarkable act of worshipful recognition. He was just a young child, born to poor parents in the most humble of circumstances. Yet somehow they knew He deserved the best they had—and they gave it.

The magi present to us a thoughtful question: if they who knew Jesus not at all gave to Him their best, how much more should we who know Him give?

Make a New Year's resolution to give Jesus the gift that keeps on giving—the gift of your love.

THE PROMISE OF FELLOWSHIP

But if we walk in the light as He is in the light, we have fellowship with one another.
1 JOHN 1:7

The festive spirit of Christmas is captured perfectly in the beloved carol, "Deck the Halls": "'Tis the season to be jolly . . . strike the harp and join the chorus . . . sing we joyous all together. . . ." It's not hard to picture friends and family together enjoying fellowship while they "deck the halls with boughs of holly."

The evergreen garlands that line stairs, mantels, doors, and windows at Christmas create a festive venue that speaks of gathering together with friends at Christmas—and year-round as well. The pine and cedar boughs we use to "deck the halls" today are just another way of saying to guests that they've entered a setting of warmth and celebration. The smell of evergreen, mixed with enticing aromas from the Christmas kitchen, communicates Christmas love to those who gather in your home this Christmas season. Christmas is a perfect time to show our love for Christ by opening our homes to those who share that love.

Why not have some friends in for a post-Christmas time of sharing—while the garlands are still fresh and the cider and cookies still plentiful? Christmas fellowship is a great way to prepare for living close to those you love for the rest of the year.

IF CHRIST HAD NOT COME

The Lord Jesus Christ, our hope.
1 TIMOTHY 1:1

Christmas isn't just an optional holiday on the calendar, but a foundational event that undergirds all we are and believe. We shudder when we realize that if Christ had not come, our Bibles would be untrue, for the story of the Incarnation fills both the Old and New Testaments.

If Christ had not come, our God would be unknown, for Christ is the image of the invisible God, the Word made flesh. He is Immanuel—God with us.

If Christ had not come, our sins would be unforgiven. The chief purpose for Christ's being born in Bethlehem was to save us from our sins. His very name—Jesus—means "Jehovah saves!" John the Baptist called Him "the Lamb of God who takes away the sin of the world" (John 1:29).

If Christ had not come, our prayers would be unanswered. Hebrews 4:15–16 says that since we do have a High Priest—namely, Jesus—we can approach the throne of grace with boldness.

If Christ had not come, our hope would be unfounded. We'd have no future, no life, no heaven, and no eternity. No reunions with our loved ones. Nothing beyond the grave.

But now, we praise God! Christmas is real, and Jesus Christ is our hope of glory.

GLORY AND JOY IN THE NEW YEAR

Therefore, whether you eat or drink, or whatever you do, do all to the glory of God.

1 CORINTHIANS 10:31

In 1642, the English parliament abolished the episcopal system of church government in the Church of England. An assembly of 120 ministers and thirty laypersons was called to Westminster Cathedral in London to rebuild the English church. The documents coming out of the six-year Westminster Assembly are some of the most famous in church history.

The first question in the Westminster Shorter Catechism reads, "What is the chief end of man?" Answer: "Man's chief end is to glorify God, and to enjoy him forever." The implications of that question and answer, profound in their simplicity, are that to glorify God is to enjoy God, and to accomplish both is to fulfill man's ultimate purpose in life. It is a rewording of Paul's famous words: "Whatever you do, do all to the glory of God."

What are you going to do in the coming year? Are there areas of your life that are not glorifying to God, and you are therefore not enjoying? Purpose to do two things well in the new year: glorify God and enjoy Him all year long in every area of your life!

The same words that rebuilt a national church can also rebuild a personal life.

LOVING AND KEEPING

If you love Me, keep My commandments.
JOHN 14:15

When Eddie Taubensee of the Cleveland Indians was sidelined by a recent injury, he saw a divine plan behind it. "I'm not in the spotlight anymore, which is okay," he said. "I can handle that. In one sense, I'm free to do anything I want. But I'm going to make myself a slave to everybody—to my teammates, to whoever I come in contact with—to win as many as possible for Christ."

When Jesus said, "If you love Me, keep My commandments," He meant for us to make every occasion in life, good or bad, an opportunity for obedience. As we celebrate God's Christmas gift to us, why not ask yourself, "What gift of obedience can I give to Him today?"

Perhaps you need to bring your temper under Christ's control. Perhaps you need to change your vocabulary. Maybe God is nudging you to forgive an offense or overlook an insult. Do you need to express your love more freely to your wife? Are you presenting yourself modestly in your wardrobe (1 Timothy 2:9)?

As this year slips away, it's a good time to leave behind some old habits. Confess your sins to God and determine to give Him not idle words but obedient deeds as the new year dawns.

PASSION

I press on, that I may lay hold of that for which Christ Jesus has also laid hold of me.
PHILIPPIANS 3:12

Josh Davis, winner of three gold medals during the 1996 Olympics, is a Christian who credits Christ with his success. One of the keys to his intensity, he told an interviewer, is Colossians 3:23: "And whatever you do, do it heartily, as to the Lord and not to men."

This verse has its Old Testament parallel in Ecclesiastes 9:10: "Whatever your hand finds to do, do it with your might."

As we prepare to begin a new year, let's determine to start it with passion, to press on with a desire to lay hold of what God wants us to do—and to do it with all our might.

In 1938, the great writer and preacher A. W. Tozer wrote a New Year's editorial in his magazine, saying in part: "If you ask God to give you a special message for the opening year, one that will be made seasonable and real in every exigency of the unknown future, you will be surprised how faithfully He will fulfill His Word, and how fittingly the Holy Spirit will speak to you of things to come, and anticipate the real needs and exigencies of your life."

Ask God to show you His plan for the New Year, and then live it out to the fullest . . . until He comes.

To *all* the Turning Point

Circle of Friends family

who surround us *with* their love,

strengthen us by their prayers,

and encourage us *with* their

faithful financial support.